*Nell Brinkley and the New Woman
in the Early 20th Century*

Nell Brinkley and the New Woman in the Early 20th Century

TRINA ROBBINS

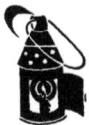

McFarland & Company, Inc., Publishers
Jefferson, North Carolina, and London

Library of Congress Cataloguing-in-Publication Data

Robbins, Trina.
　　Nell Brinkley and the new woman in the early 20th century / Trina Robbins.
　　　　p.　　cm.
　　Includes bibliographical references and index.

　　ISBN-13: 978-0-7864-1151-1
　　(softcover : 55# alkaline paper) ∞

　　1. Brinkley, Nell, 1886–1944.　2. Illustrators—United States—Biography.　3. Feminism and art—United States.　4. Women—United States—Social conditions—20th century.
NC1429.B8237R63　　2001
741'.092—dc21　　　　　　　　　　　　　　　　　　　　　　2001030716
[B]

British Library cataloguing data are available

©2001 Trina Robbins. All rights reserved

No part of this book may be reproduced or transmitted in any form or by any means, electronic or mechanical, including photocopying or recording, or by any information storage and retrieval system, without permission in writing from the publisher.

Manufactured in the United States of America

Cover caption: *Kathleen and the Great Secret,* 1920.

McFarland & Company, Inc., Publishers
　Box 611, Jefferson, North Carolina 28640
　www.mcfarlandpub.com

This book is gratefully dedicated to
Althea Lechtaler (1919–1990),
whom I never met, but whose lifelong love
of Nell Brinkley made this all possible.

Table of Contents

Preface 1

Chapter One: 1908   7
Chapter Two: Edgewater   25
Chapter Three: Before Nell   31
Chapter Four: The Teens   41
Chapter Five: The Great War   65
Chapter Six: The Twenties   79
Chapter Seven: The Thirties   113

Afterword 139
Bibliography 141
Index 143

Preface

It seems that no one, including me, ever noticed the most important thing about Nell Brinkley. I was introduced to her work in 1970 by Bill Blackbeard, curator of the San Francisco Academy of Comic Art, who kindly gave me two color pages from her Betty and Billy series. This was the worst possible introduction to Brinkley's work. It was impossible for me to miss the enchanting beauty of her delicate pen lines and the innocent sexuality of her Brinkley girls, but the Betty and Billy series, no matter how gorgeous, showcases Nell at her most sugary and sentimental. At the time I thought sumptuous art and exquisite women were all there was to Brinkley, and I didn't bother looking for more. Indeed, her lush illustrations were enough for me, as they have been for her small cult group of fans and collectors for years.

I included paragraphs on Brinkley in both of my books on women cartoonists,[1] and through the years I added more as the information presented itself. Unfortunately, because of the paucity of research material, my entries on Brinkley in both books are riddled with misinformation. She has been briefly and inaccurately mentioned in entries in the *World Encyclopedia of Cartoons*[2] and the *American Illustrators Research Group*.[3] In fact, Brinkley's own write-up in the latter misinforms the reader about her age, her marital status, and even her hair color! It could, of course, be worse: in her otherwise excellent 1987 book on John Held, Jr., writer Shelley Armitage refers to "Neil Brinkley" and uses the pronoun *his*.

The files of the New Rochelle Public Library contain several letters, written as recently as the 1980s, from interested people who at one time or another considered writing about Brinkley. Article and letter writers all seem to have been seduced, as I was, by the splendor of her art, but seem to have missed the words beneath the pictures, so that Bill Blackbeard's entry in the *World Encyclopedia of Cartoons* describes her work as having "emphasized the sprightlier sides of young romance, superbly limned in Brinkley's intricate webs of line work," neglecting to mention anything that Brinkley may have had to *say*.

Enter the goddess of lost women cartoonists, on the wings of cyberspace. In 1997 a friend in New York forwarded me an e-mail from a woman named Gail Heggelund. Heggelund's mother, Althea Lechtaler, had passed away and left her lifelong collection of Nell Brinkley newspaper pages, the post said. Now she wanted to pass her mother's prized collection on to someone who knew and cared about the artist. The internet spans the world; Gail Heggelund—and her mother's collection—could have been anywhere on this planet. That they turned out to be not more than 45 minutes away from my home in San Francisco proves, at least to me, that there was a goddess involved.

Gail and her husband brought over Althea Lechtaler's collection, a two-foot-high pile of newspaper pages and clippings neatly filed away in the plastic sheets of spiral-bound scrapbooks. I was in hog heaven, but I was also writing another book, and had to put Althea's collection away after just a glance at the luxuriant pages. Not until I had finished my book did I have the time to take the scrapbooks out again and carefully go through them, page by page.

That was when I had my epiphany. What I had before me was a richly illustrated record of the foibles and progress, the dreams and victories of early 20th century women! Nell Brinkley was not just an exquisite artist—although that would have been plenty—she was a chronicler, a feminist, a blood-and-thunder storyteller. Sure, she drew and wrote enough romance and sentiment to wet all the hankies in the United States of America, but she also drew beautiful women (and men) of all races, taking pains to say that no one race had the patent on beauty. She sympathized again and again with working women at a time when most people still thought a woman's place was in the home. And she gloried in women's accomplishments, from her *Day of the Girl* series, drawn before there ever was a Women's History month, to her enthusiastic renditions of Amelia Earhart and Eleanor Roosevelt.

Brinkley's empathy with working women brought me to another realization. In comparing Nell to Charles Dana Gibson and John Held, Jr.

(both at different times her contemporaries, both known for drawing women), I realized that both Gibson and Held drew *rich* girls. The Gibson girls attend the opera and soirées, and glide passively down the aisle as their fathers marry them off to impoverished European nobility. Held's flappers are more independent and active as they feverishly Charleston through life, but they're co-eds attending expensive colleges, the tuition paid in full by their rich daddies. Brinkley never went to college; in fact, she was a high-school dropout. Her panels appeared in the publications of William Randolph Hearst, the inventor of yellow journalism, who hardly went out of his way to attract readers from the upper classes. His newspapers, with their lurid five-inch headlines, catered to the middle and working classes, and it was the women of these classes who read and loved Brinkley's panels, and whom she drew.

In a typically Brinkleyesque 1910 panel, she draws a beautiful young couple at a rooftop garden performance. While dancing girls pirouette on the stage behind them, the pair have eyes for only one another. The title is "What I Did Yesterday—On my Saturday Afternoon Off." These young lovers are working-class people who get only a half day off on Saturdays. When Brinkley does depict rich women, it is often to contrast them with their maids or with other working women, and the rich girls usually come out as losers.

Sitting on the floor, surrounded by yellowing newsprint, I knew that I had found the Nell Brinkley that even her small handful of collectors didn't know. The world needed to know about this amazing and talented woman.

Someone had to write the book, and so I did.

Newspapers in the early 20th century were longer and wider than they are today, and it is simply impossible to reproduce well Brinkley's full-page art, or even most of her half-page panels, in a normal-sized book, and have them resemble anything but microscopic gray lines. To do justice to the delicate linework, I've chosen instead to excerpt details from her larger works. I apologize for this necessity, and hope that someday the art can be printed full-size.

In continuing my research from the starting point of Althea Lechtaler's collection, I've been fortunate to run across many helpful people, without any of whom this would be less of a book. Elayne Riggs started it all by forwarding the fateful e-mail to me; Gail Heggelund continued it with her invaluable gift of her mother's collection. Connie Fox, president of the Edgewater Historical Society, provided me with priceless photographs and information about Brinkley's home town that was invaluable to this tenderfoot who had been led to believe that Nell came from Denver. Brinkley's

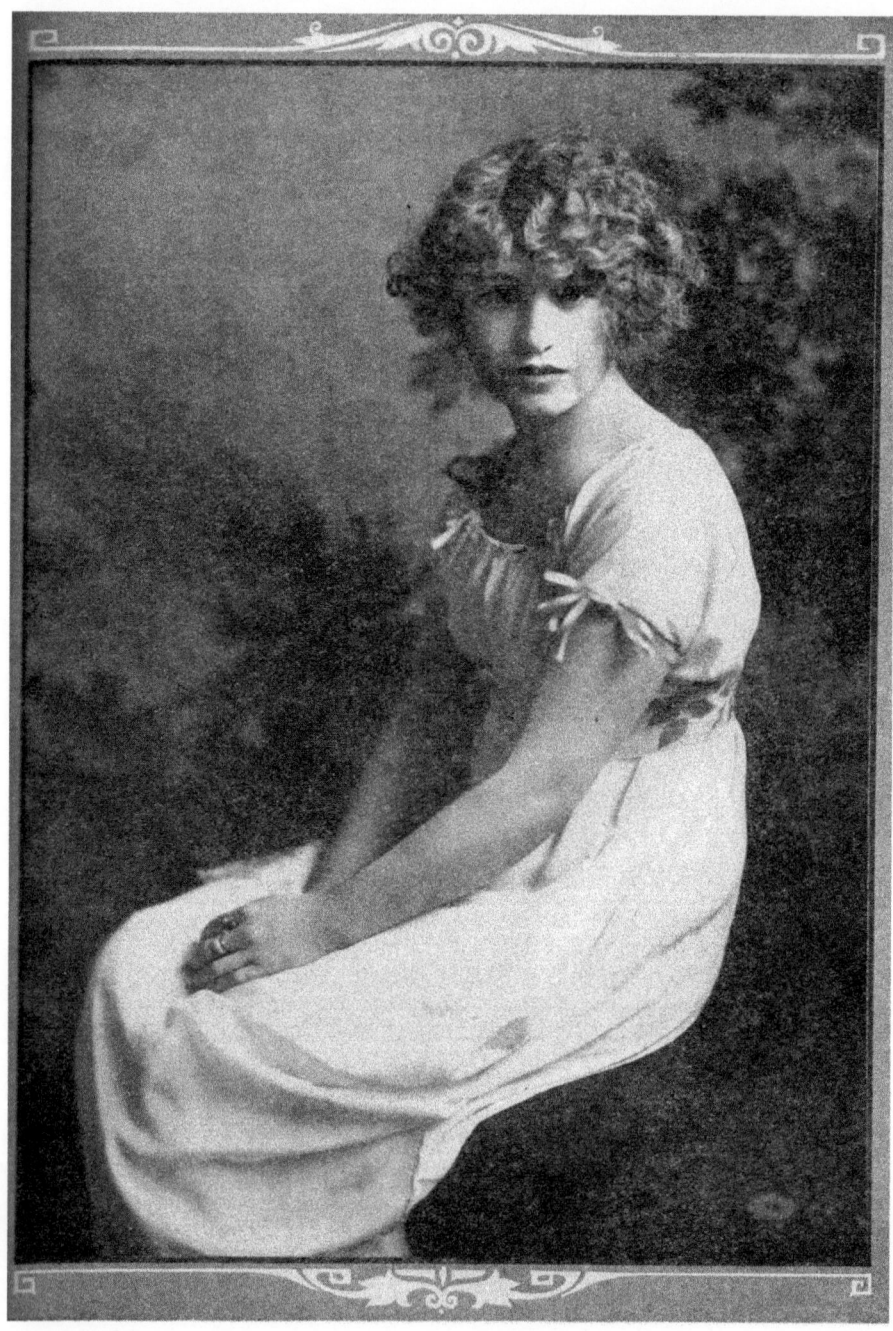

Nell Brinkley, 1917.

granddaughter, Anne Macrae Clarke, provided me with memories of her late father and of *his* memories—as close as I could come to the artist herself—and still more priceless photographs. Chris Nolan, one of a handful of people who actually collect Brinkley's work, lent me important pages from *Girls Who Work for Uncle Sam* and *Golden-Eyes and Her Hero, Bill*, enabling me to piece together the entire saga. Steve Thompson, president of the Pogo fan club, just happened to find copies of *The Cartoonist* magazine from 1917, with Nell in them, and had a feeling that I might be interested. Thanks to Michael Kurland, who read my manuscript, supplied excellent suggestions and, being the writer that he is, advised me to get a better title; and to Steve Leialoha, photoshop master extraordinaire. Thanks also to Al, the helpful gatekeeper of Beechmont cemetery; to Jeremy, who went that extra mile for me at the New York City Library of the Performing Arts; and to the nameless good Samaritan and his daughter, who gave me a lift from the New Rochelle Public Library to the house on Pryor Terrace, which I had naively believed was within walking distance. The lyrics that start each chapter come from the website of the remarkable and erudite Don Ferguson: <http://www.bright.net/~mrbanjo/>. Finally, I am especially grateful to the Thanks Be To Grandmother Winifred Foundation, whose grant helped make my research possible, and to the John Anson Kitteridge Fund, whose grant enabled me to attend the Feminist Forerunners conference in Manchester, England, and exchange information on the New Woman in early 20th century journalism.

When I first started writing this book, I referred to Nell Brinkley in the correct scholarly manner, by her last name. As I became increasingly immersed in her work and her life, I realized that I had to call her by her first name. It's an old fashioned name—no one is named Nell anymore—and it speaks of ruffles and curls and golden twilight streaming through a lead-paneled window to rest on an old spinet. She had a nickname—she gave everyone nicknames, including herself—but to me she is Nell.

In June 2000, Nell Brinkley was finally inducted into the Society of Illustrators Hall of Fame.

Notes

1. *Women and the Comics*, 1985, and *A Century of Women Cartoonists*, 1993.
2. Edited by Maurice Horn, Chelsea House, 1980.
3. This was a small group of amateur researchers, centered in Southern California, who self-published short papers on illustrators.

CHAPTER ONE

1908

*She's only a bird in a gilded cage, a beautiful sight to see,
You may think she's happy and free from care, she's not, though she seems to be.*
—"A Bird in a Gilded Cage," Arthur J. Lamb and Harry Von Tilzer, 1900

The year was 1908 and, though the first Model T's gave Americans a shiny icon for the age of mass production, the country seemed stuck in the previous century. Men wore top hats, and women were heavily corseted from their armpits to their hips to give them the fashionable hourglass figure of the Gibson Girl, as drawn by artist Charles Dana Gibson. It was a time of stark contrasts, when magnates like the Rockefellers, the Astors and the Vanderbilts threw sumptuous parties at which they spent fortunes while the poor crowded their families into rotting slum tenements and slaved in sweatshops under unspeakable conditions.

The first *Ziegfeld Follies* had opened in New York a year before and would become an annual tradition, introducing performers like Will Rogers or Irene and Vernon Castle to the world. No one could stop humming "The Merry Widow Waltz," from Franz Lehár's 1905 operetta, *The Merry Widow*, which had opened in New York to rave reviews a year earlier. A more literal translation of its original Viennese title, *Die Lustige Witwe*—"The Lusty Widow"—would never have flown in 1908 America.

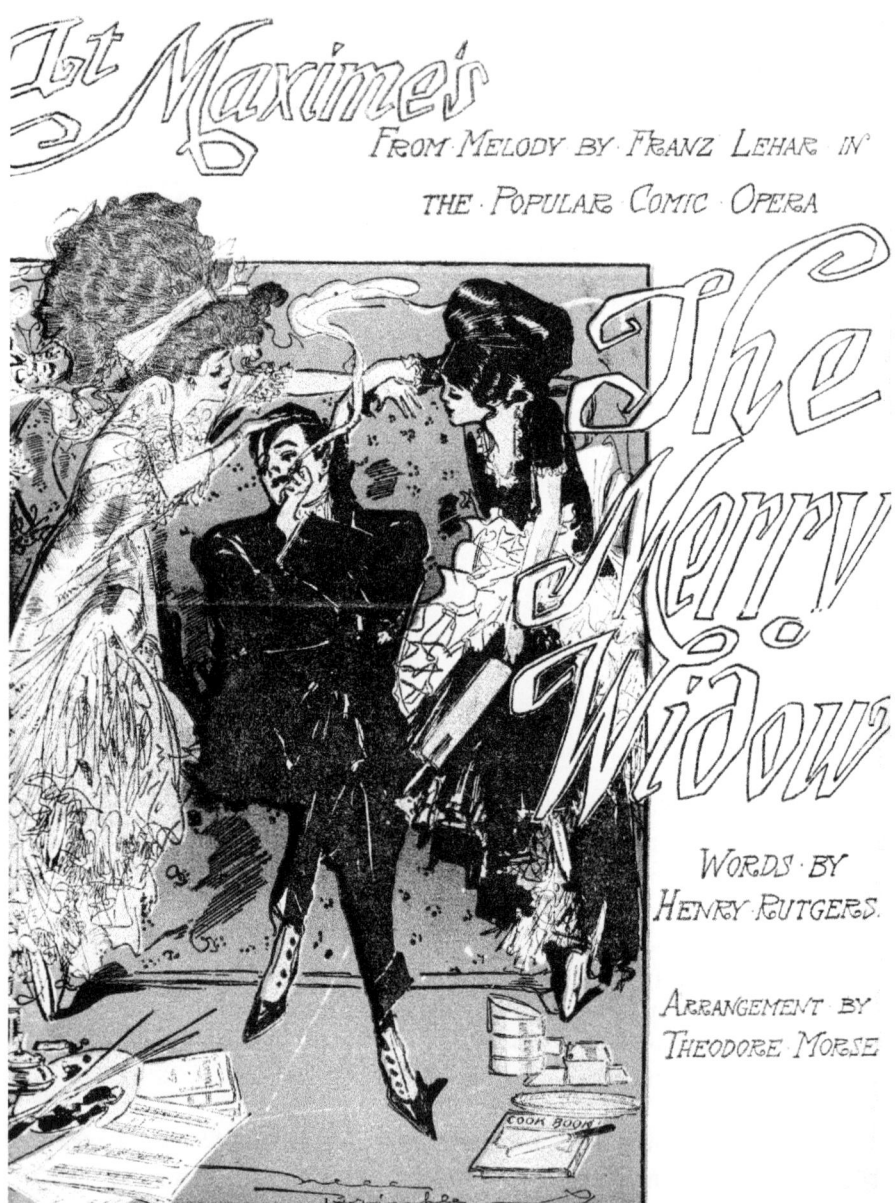

Sheet music cover, *The Merry Widow*, 1908.

One. 1908

In New York City, operettas like *The Merry Widow* and lavish productions like the *Ziegfeld Follies* were staged in rooftop gardens where the very rich ate, drank, and amused themselves from midnight until two in the morning. Working class people,[1] with far less time on their hands, contented themselves with taking in a Saturday matinee.

That year the names in the headlines of newspapers and on everyone's lips were Harry K. Thaw and Evelyn Nesbitt. There would be other trials during the next 82 years which would be called the Trial of the Century, such as the Lindbergh or the O.J. Simpson trial, but in 1908, the trial of Harry K. Thaw for the 1906 murder—at a rooftop garden—of famed architect Stanford White received unprecedented media coverage. It featured all the ingredients needed to cook up a delicious scandal—sex, money, murder, and a beautiful woman. Evelyn Nesbitt, Thaw's ex-model, ex–Floradora Girl wife,[2] had been White's lover when she was still a teenager. Thaw justified shooting White by claiming that the architect was a profligate who had drugged and raped his wife and hundreds of other girls and that by his act, Thaw was saving countless innocents from a fate worse than death.

Thaw's first trial had taken place in 1907 and ended in a hung jury. His second trial started in January 1908, to the accompaniment of five-inch-high newspaper headlines that ended in exclamation marks. Although it was Thaw who was on trial for murder, the newspapers concentrated on his beautiful wife, featuring drawings and photographs of her, and even reprinting some of her own drawings. On January 6, 21-year-old Nell Brinkley entered the courtroom along with Hearst newspapers' veteran woman journalist Dorothy Dix. Under a wide-brimmed picture hat that perched upon her upswept golden hair, Nell Brinkley was every bit as beautiful as the star of the show, Evelyn Nesbitt Thaw. With a big sketch pad tucked beneath her arm, she found a seat in the press row and set to work on a series of sketches of Nesbitt from every angle and in every mood. Her portraits would run in the *New York Evening Journal* for the duration of the trial.

Nell and Dorothy Dix were not alone. Nesbitt's role in the trial provided a juicy women's angle, making this the first trial covered by women journalists like Winifred Black, Ada Patterson and Nixola Greely-Smith, all of whom described the ex-showgirl sympathetically in passionately overwrought prose.[3] Although scores of male artists had already delineated Evelyn Nesbitt, Nell Brinkley was the only woman who drew her. (Harry Thaw, on trial for his life, drew surprisingly little interest from the artists.)

Nell had been on the staff of the *Journal* for a scant three months when the new trial started. She had come after two years on the *Denver Post*, bringing with her a talent for pretty-girl art that had not yet matured

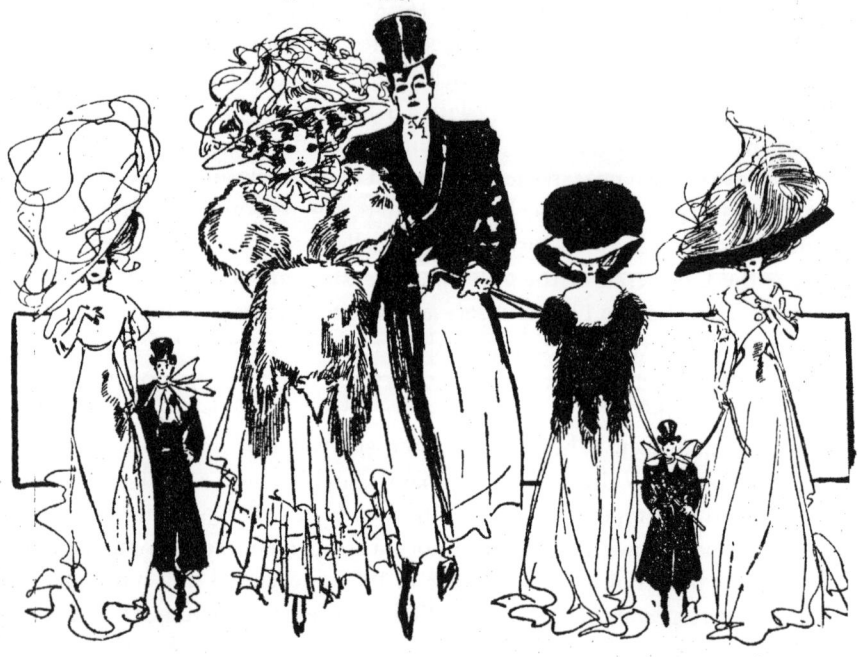

"Nell Brinkley Tells of Gowns and Women in 'Peacock Alley,'" November 28, 1907. It was Nell's third panel and commentary for the *Evening Journal*.

into the delicately fine-lined art-nouveau style for which she would become famous. She also brought with her a unique writing style, combining the then-popular overblown prose with her penchant for using baby-talk slang like "kiddie," for *child* or "pic" for *picture*. One favorite expression of hers in those days was "Ah, di mi," which at first sounds like it comes from Italian opera but was actually her little-girl way of exclaiming, "Ah dear me."[4] Nell christened all the pretty girls she drew "Betty," and called all the boys "Billy." The headline that accompanied her first published drawing of Evelyn Nesbitt read, "'She Is One of the Most Exquisite Things I Ever Saw,' Says Artist—Writer—'It Pays to Have a Pretty Betty When You've Killed a Man.'"[5]

At first *Journal* editor Arthur Brisbane seemed unsure of where to put his new artist. According to a 1908 article in the *Denver Post*, he wanted her to do a line of comics:

> "But that is not what I came here to do," this bit of a girl answered. "I expect not," the man of men in the newspaper game replied in a fatherly

way. "But that's what we want you to do, little girl, and you must do what we want." "But I won't make comics," she declared.... "I've got a good daddy back in Denver and I'll go back there to him." For quite a little bit the big man looked at her almost reverently. "It took me twenty-five years to reach a point where I could say 'I won't,'" he mused aloud.... Then smiling quaintly, he said to her: "You needn't go back to your daddy, little girl. You just stay here and draw any kind of pictures you want to make."

Nonetheless, Nell's November 26, 1907, debut was on the comics page, with an illustrated panel and article on actress Valeska Suratt, written in Nell's usual superlatives ("The Most Wonderful Woman I Ever Saw"), and her next day's subject was Ethel Barrymore. By November 28, Brisbane must have decided he would keep her, for he wrote this introduction to her offering, "Nell Brinkley Tells of Gowns and Women in 'Peacock Alley'":

> Nell Brinkley, who has the faculty of telling and picturing what she sees, is going hereafter to study human beings on and off the stage for Evening Journal readers. You have seen some of her work. Here is more of it.

Nell's art, however, hardly fit in with the broad humor of comic strips by W.K. McGill and T.E. Powers, and on November 29, her work was missing from the paper; Brisbane was trying to figure out what to do with it. The next day her by-line resurfaced on the home page, which she shared with Beatrix Fairfax's *Advice to the Lovelorn*, still more advice from Dorothy Dix ("Can a Man or a Woman Know the Other *Before* Marriage?"), popular poet Ella Wheeler Wilcox, and articles like "Mothers of Great Men." Nell was progressively given more space for her art and writing. She supplied her own advice, from the knowledgeable pen of a 21-year-old ("Woman Woos! Nell Brinkley Says So") and covered actresses like Nazimova and Mary Garden, describing their outfits in loving, if alarmingly awkward, detail:

> Her dress caught her under the arms and fell—and fell—away in crawling lengths. It was cool and sage green with a silver high light ... her hat was frothy with green feathers.

Nell's work or the readers' response to it must have pleased Brisbane, because on December 13, he took her off the women's page and gave her page two—her first break—supplying the women's angle on a six-day bicycle race: "Six-Day Race as a Woman Sees It," and on December 21, she reviewed *The Merry Widow*. By January, Nell was ready to cover the trial of the century.

Her first portrait of Evelyn Nesbitt, published on January 7, was

Ethel Barrymore Colt and Her Baby Lover   By Nell Brinkley

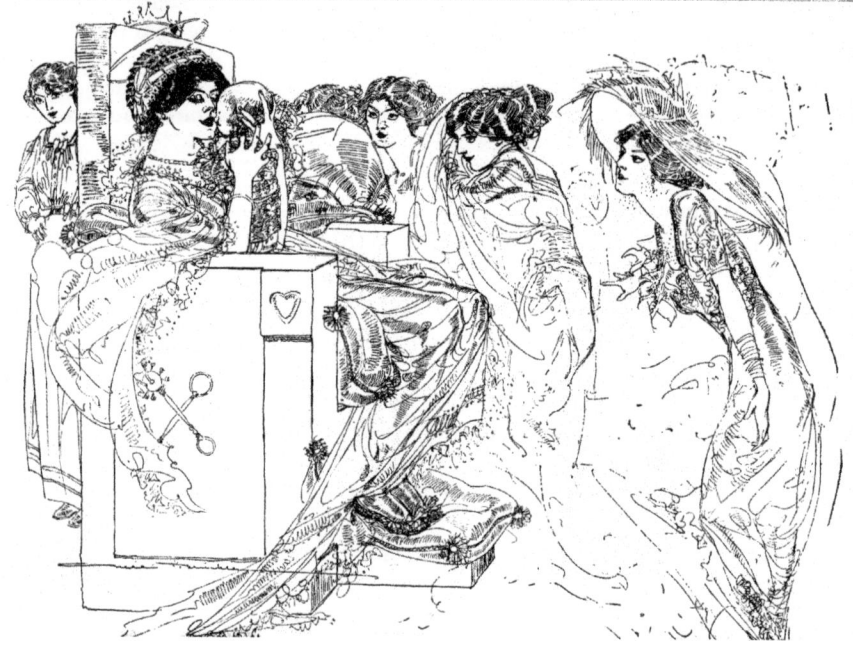

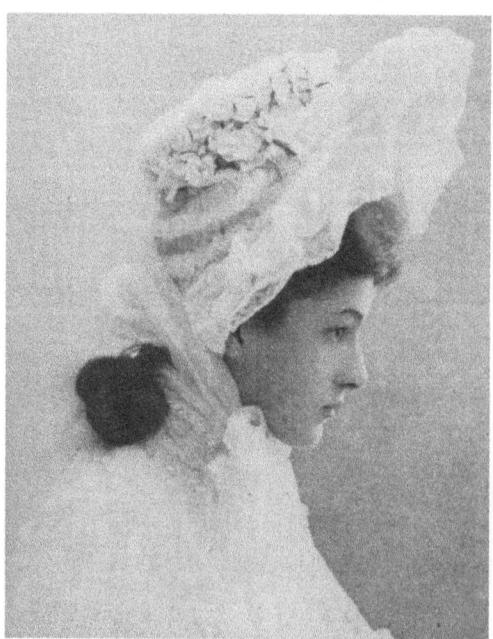

labored and over-rendered—the young artist was anxious and had fussed over it too much with charcoal or pencil—but it only took her a day to hone her skills, and the next day's portrait was clean and elegant. Her trial illustrations ran on page two of the *Journal*. They were of course in black and white, but Nell obviously wanted to work in color. Her commentary was filled with color references:

> Maybe it was the gray, rainy day, with its pearly light, but Evelyn

**Top: Ethel Barrymore, 1910.
Left: Evelyn Nesbitt, circa 1906.**

One. 1908

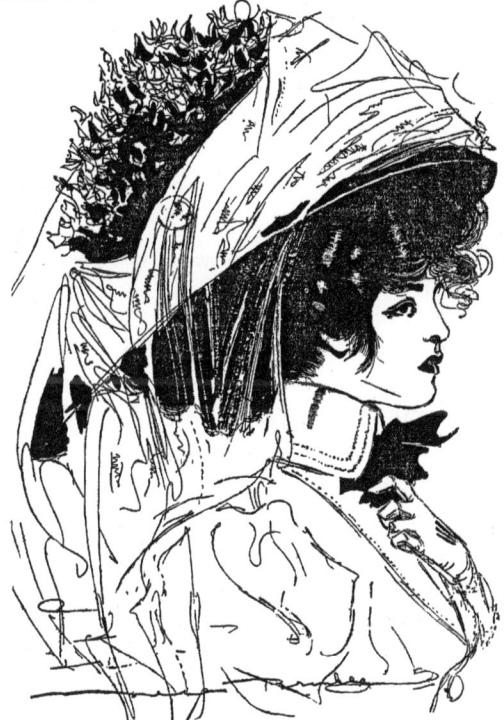

EVELYN THAW'S PROFILE.

Nell's second published drawing of Evelyn Nesbitt, January 8, 1908.

Thaw's face was paler hued yesterday. It was all gold on Monday, with no color in the cheeks, and this day it was paler, with a faint stain like violet wine.... Oh, but what a little, little child she is![6] You want to pet her.

Nell wrote in the pop culture style of the early 20th century. At the same time that authors like Jack London and Edna Ferber were creating great literature that survives today, writers of the day's best-sellers were, like Nell, producing breathless prose filled with run-on sentences and liberally sprinkled with dashes. Elinor Glyn was one of the most popular writers of the day, with a huge following that consisted mostly of women. Among her other accomplishments, she coined the term "It," to describe a certain kind of indefinable sex appeal, thus boosting the career of silent film star Clara Bow, who was crowned the "It Girl." Many of Madame Glyn's turgid romances were turned into silent films. Her 1907 novel *Three Weeks* was made into a film in 1924. This excerpt from *Three Weeks* reads like something Nell herself might have written:

> In front of the fire, stretched at full length, was his tiger(skin)—and on him—also at full length—reclined the lady, garbed in some strange clinging garment of heavy purple crepe, its hem embroidered with gold, one white arm resting on the beast's head, her back supported by a pile of the velvet cushions, and a heap of rarely bound books at her side, while between her lips was a rose not redder than they—an almost scarlet rose.

Thomas Aloysius Dorgan, the cartoonist who signed his work "Tad," was the *Journal*'s sports cartoonist. He was ten years older than Nell and had a hard-boiled sense of humor. He is credited with inventing such terms as *hot dog*, *twenty-three skidoo*, and *cat's meow*. Tad seems to have found the new artist and her flowery prose absolutely hysterical, no matter how stylish it may have been at the time. The day after Nell's piece about Evelyn Nesbitt, instead of commenting on the latest boxing match, his daily sports page cartoon was titled "Letty Lolita at the Bunk Trial, a Conglomeration of Colors, by Violet Pumpkin." Using his regular funny animal characters Silk Hat Harry and Bunk, he parodied Nell's illustrations and her writing style. She had written,

> All the artists make "pics" of just one face of her. Always the sad face of haunting eyes and down drooped mouth. They never make her when she is gay or glad. I tried to make her.... Always I needed color.... Orange and gold and sepia and green and amber and wine color—and violet and grape purple.

LETTY LOLITA AT THE BUNK TRIAL.—By TAD.

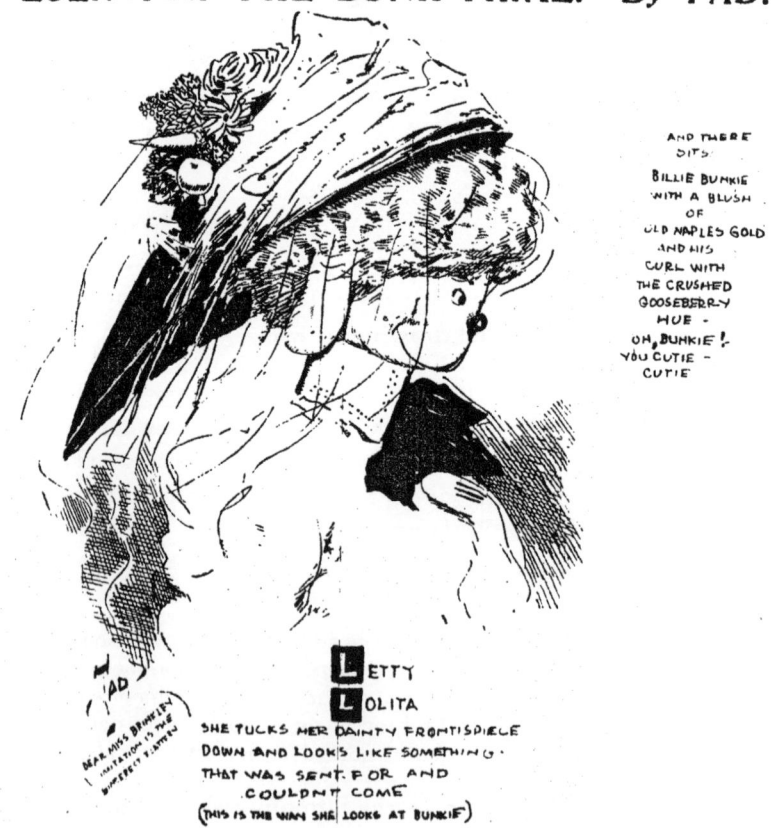

Tad parodies Nell "Letty Lolita at the Bunk Trial."

One. 1908

Tad's version:

> All the artists make "Pics" of her the same way. Why not as she is, with her ripe chianti purple lips ... that pucker and waver and change in color like the chameleon...?

He didn't have to work hard to parody Nell. She had written of Nesbitt, "She tucks her head down and looks wise as the ages." Beneath his cartoon animal version of Nesbitt, he wrote, "She tucks her dainty frontispiece down and looks like something that was sent for and couldn't come," and, "Silkie Hattie Harry with the coy look that almost makes you want to huggie himmie. Oh di mi." Beneath his signature, he added, "Dear Miss Brinkley, imitation is the sincerest flattery."

On January 14, Nell's illustration was titled "How I Sketched Evelyn Thaw—By Nell Brinkley," and, still infatuated by colors, she wrote,

> She is one of the most exquisite things that ever I saw in this world! She is gold and brown; her hair the color of warm sepia—not such wonderful hair, but beautifully colored. Her brows and eyes are the same moist, coffee color ... her skin is gold as pale bronze—and around her eyes and ears and neck where the hair grows it deepens to orange and brown.

And she drew herself painting four portraits of Nesbitt. How could Tad resist? The next day, his cartoon, titled "Bunkie, With Pilsner Gold Eyes—By Tad," read,

> Bunkie is hard to draw; he is so beautiful, so highly colored and so grand.... He has pilsner gold eyes, with a tiny thread of purple color running through it. His eyebrows are a bit darker plaster-house coffee colored. His little moufy down from his nose a pale slate and runs to madder lake.
> He is as white as a tablecloth on top of the head, but by the ears he is softened by a little misty bit of turquoise blue.... Oh, but it's softie and nice and richie in tonie. Under his chin he is mauve colored. The madder lake on the mouth and the mauve on the neck make a beautiful combie.

And he drew himself painting four portraits of Bunkie, but he gave himself long sausage curls and a sketch pad labeled "Sketchie Paddie."

Nell actually interviewed Evelyn Nesbitt for the January 25 *Journal*, and managed to say nothing at all of importance. Her article, headlined "'I Like Pies,' Evelyn Tells Nell Brinkley," gives the impression of two girls in their twenties who just want to have fun:

> I talked with Evelyn Thaw at the Tombs today. Once before I saw her there, but we only had a smile at each other and didn't talk but a bit....

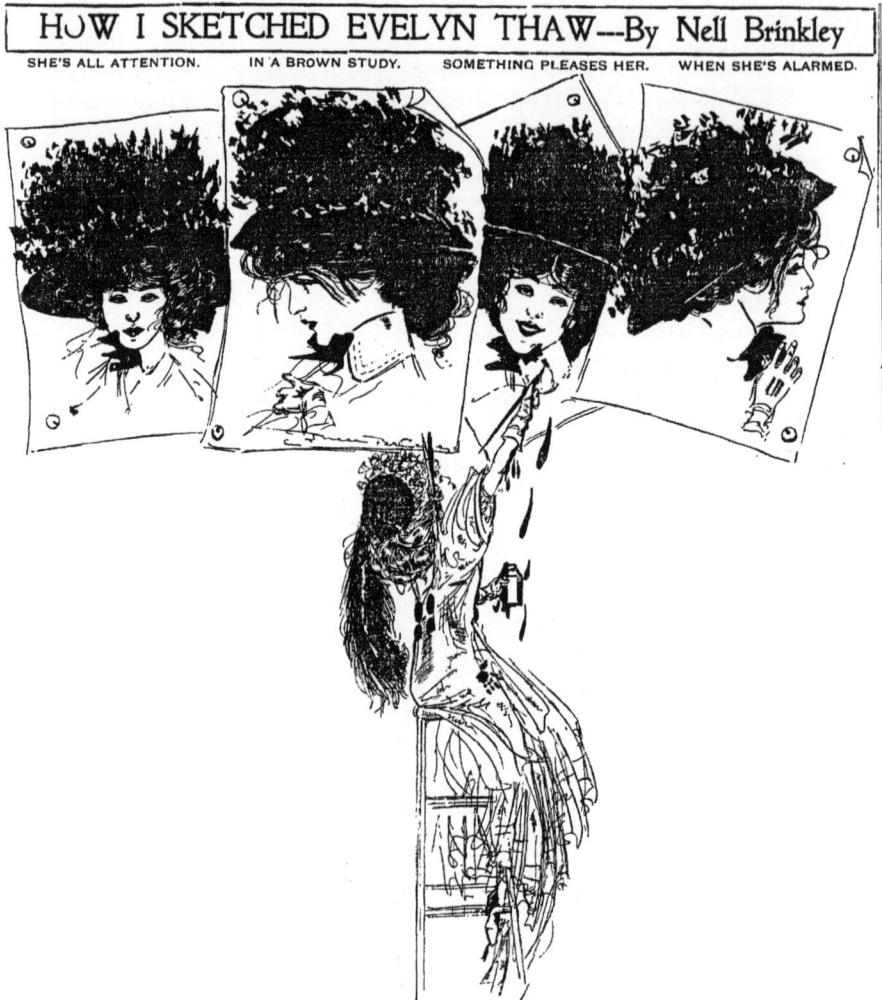

Evelyn Nesbitt, January 14, 1908.

It was as gray as some girls' eyes and the light that came in was cold and white. The other sunny day I forgot the bars at the windows, even with their shadows at my feet and this day they stood up black in my mind and I kept remembering them all the time.

Maybe it was because there was no sun, but her face was grayer and darker, and not so gold and brown. But she was gay and light on her feet when she came in.... I sat down on the edge of the long seat against the wall, and she hitched herself up on the table and swung her feet and we looked at each other and then a little laugh began to laugh and giggle away down in the bottom of her eyes and then we both laughed much.

One. 1908

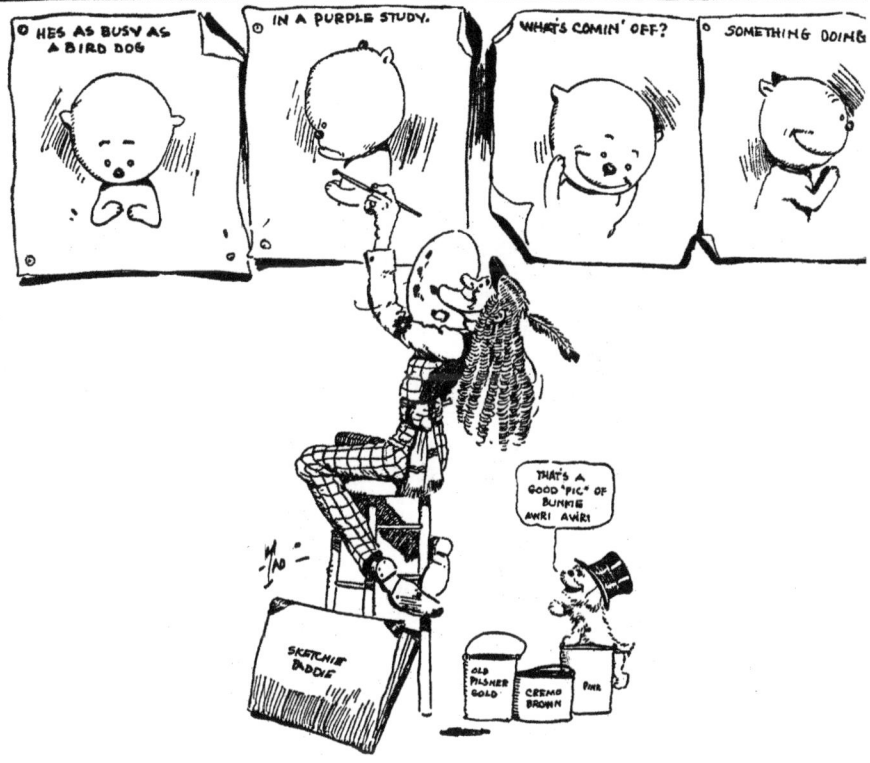

Tad's parody, January 15, 1908.

By January 28, when a drawing titled "Scene at the Thaw Trial, and Places Occupied by the Notable Figures" appeared on page 2 of the *Journal*, along with the judge, the attorneys, and Harry and Evelyn Thaw, artist John LaDor had placed Dorothy Dix and Nell Brinkley in the foreground. Nell was now a "notable figure." Of course, Tad just couldn't let this pass unparodied, and he drew "New York's Advanced Vaudeville—by Tad." His three-ring-circus scene had Evelyn Nesbitt, labeled "The Pallid Chee-ild," at center stage, and Thaw himself as a spear-carrier, off to the side, complaining, "I wish they'd give me a speaking part." A Floradora sextette, their bodies molded by corsets into the uncomfortable but fashionable s-shape stand in the background, singing, "For I've got a pain in my back/From being a Gibson Girl." Off to one side, a girl in a wide-brimmed picture hat, labeled "Nell," draws in a "sketchie paddie" and says, "Oh di mi it's hard to make a 'pic' of this."

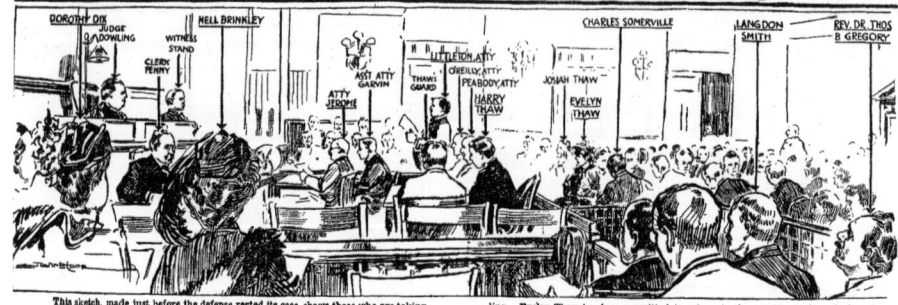

"Scene at the Thaw Trial," John LaDor, January 28, 1908.

The trial ended; Thaw was judged insane. In her January 15 column, headlined "Thaw's Pride Crushed, Says Dorothy Dix," Dix reported:

> Yesterday was the black day of Harry Thaw's life. All day long he sat amidst the dust and ashes of humiliation, his pride and vanity shattered to atoms about him. All day long he listened while his lawyer iterated and reiterated that he was mentally deficient, and proved by witness after witness that he had always been regarded as abnormal, irrational, imbecile, an object of pity to those about him.... His pallid skin turned to a gray white. His face twitched, and with all his efforts he could not stop the trembling of his long upper lip as he set it against its fellow. His restless hands that are never still for a single minute picked aimlessly at his coat, his hair, his papers upon the table. His dull, brooding eyes sank upon the floor as if he could never raise them again. Almost it seemed as if he would rather have died for his crime than to have purchased his freedom at such a price.

But a mental institution was preferable to the alternative, and by 1926 Thaw was out and had written a book about his experience, *The Traitor*. In a style every bit as lurid and purple as Elinor Glyn's, he recounted,

> The agony of Evelyn in the years of her girlhood formed the prelude to a long continuous drama of sorrow, the murk and gloom of which was never illuminated by a ray of sunshine until what occurred on the roof of Madison Square Garden and Stanford White fell dead.... After ten years during which a group of moneyed libertines made life almost as unsafe for virgins as did the Minotaur, a revolver made New York safer for other girls.

Even after Thaw was sent to the loony bin and Evelyn started divorce proceedings, the dueling cartoonists continued. Nell drew a little autobiog-

One. 1908

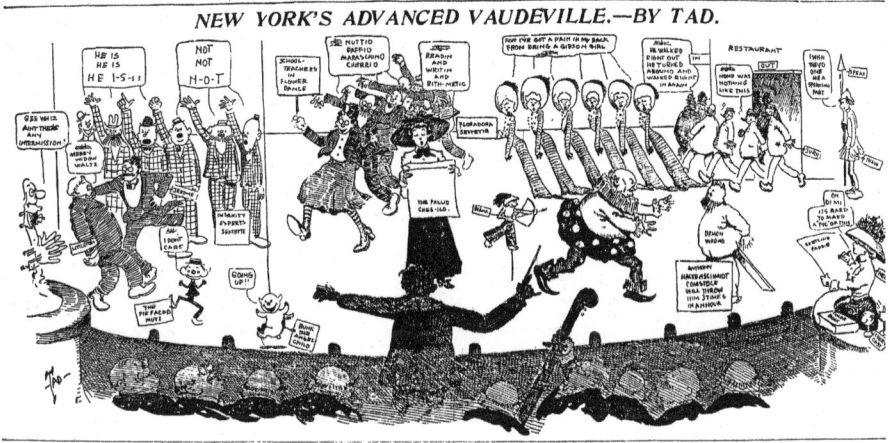

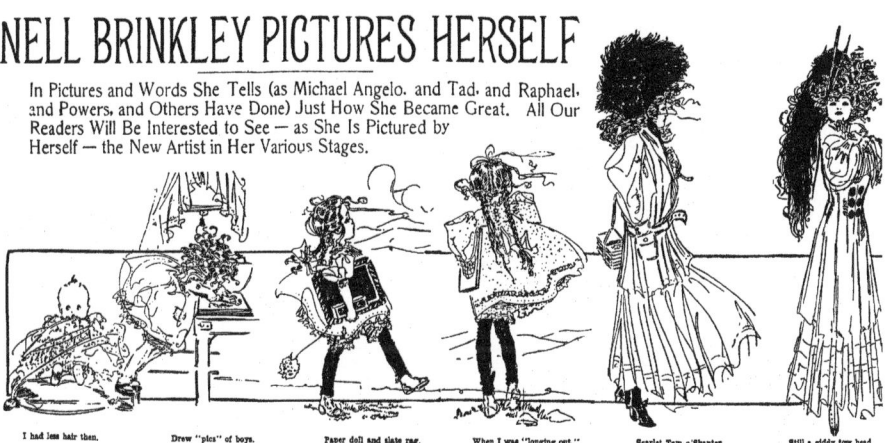

Top: "New York's Advanced Vaudeville," Tad, 1908. *Bottom:* "Nell Brinkley Pictures Herself," 1908.

raphy called "Nell Brinkley Pictures Herself," subtitled "In Pictures and Words She Tells (as Michael Angelo, and Tad, and Raphael, and Powers and Others Have Done[7]) Just How She Became Great." Powers was T.E. Powers, the cartoonist who sometimes shared the page with her. Tad responded with "Tad Pictures Himself. In Pictures and Words He Tells (as Clarence Closeclutch, and Harold Hangover, and H-a-double-r-i-g-a-n, and Boshter Bill, and Others Have Done) Just How He Became Great." Tad perfectly parodied Nell's drawings of herself as an infant, then a child, growing up to become an artist, finally drawing himself with corkscrew curls, his cute doggie character saying, "Make a 'pic' of me, will you?" and

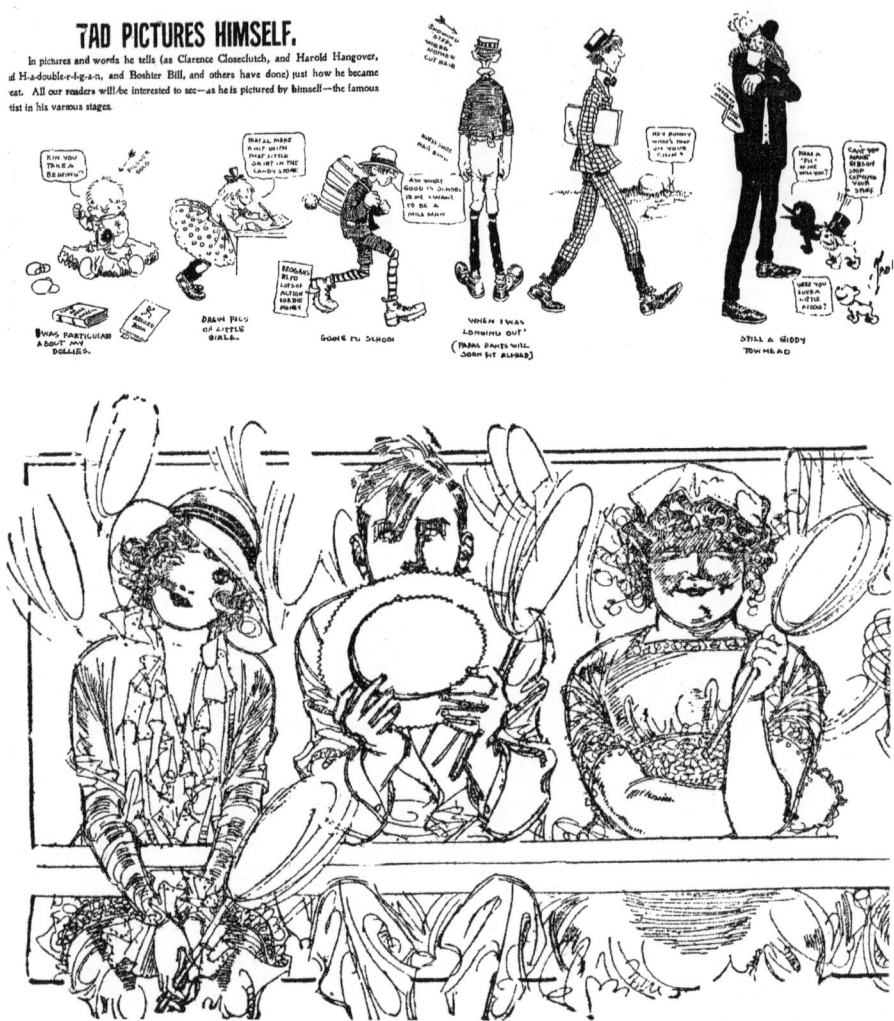

Top: "Tad Pictures Himself," 1908. *Bottom:* "Baseball Fannie," 1913.

as an injoke to Nell, whose Brinkley Girl was already supplanting the Gibson Girl[8]: "Can't you make Gibson stop copying your stuff."

Although she drew in black and white, Nell continued what would prove to be her life-long fascination with color. She began a series called *Just the Right Betty for Billy to Marry*, in which she assigned different colors to her Betties and Billys, and then matched them up by their color: "The Billy of Violet Dreams and the Betty of Scarlet," or "The Billy of Opal and

Change, and the Betty of Brown." In the latter, Billy is an artist, and practical brown Betty handles life's realities, like the accounting and housekeeping, so that he can be a great creator.[9] Tad, by now addicted to Nell Brinkley parodies, produced "Bunk Tells What Billies Are for Certain Betties," in which he paired up the Bottle Green Betty with the Lavender Billy, and the Heart-of-Lettuce-Green Billy with the Salmon Pink Betty.

Nell and Tad continued to poke friendly fun at each other throughout the following years. In 1913 he took her to a baseball game, and she drew them seated together, an embarrassed-looking Tad hiding his face with his hat while Nell looks wide-eyed and innocent. "This is me," she wrote, "and I'm with Tad. And didn't he have to answer a lot of foolish questions, oh!" In 1915, she drew a panel showing Brinkley girls tossing wedding and engagement rings over a cupid. She called it "An 'Indoor Sport.'" Tad, of course, was the sports cartoonist covering the event. She wrote, "Did Tad Ever Make This?"

After the Thaw trial, Nell returned to the women's page and made forays into the entertainment section with reviews of new plays and musicals. She met the famous actresses of her time, rendered them with hair-thin, swirling lines and wrote about them. On a trip back to Colorado by train that summer, she stopped in Cheyenne, Wyoming, to see the British actress Olga Nethersole play the lead role in *Sapho* and called her the "Wonder Woman of the Land of Make Believe."[10]

Nell's art was now featured in Hearst newspapers all over the country, and Americans were sitting up and taking notice of this new young artist. Readers of the *Los Angeles Examiner* responded to a feature on Nell by mailing in letters of appreciation, and even poetry. In his poem "The Twinkley, Brinkley Girl," W.L. Larned alluded to the widely accepted notion that Nell had replaced Gibson in the public eye. Larned added to the list of passé pretty-girl artists Howard Chandler Christy, Harrison Fisher, and *The Fluffy Ruffles Girl*, a newspaper cartoon by Wallace Morgan:

> The Gibson Girl has had her day, likewise the fluffy ruff:
> Of Wenzel-Christy-Fisher Girls we've surely had enough;
> The sheath-gown maiden, so petite, although of recent date,
> Must step aside along the avenue, content to wait.
> The smartest, tartest, artest Girl has surely come to pass.
> Give us the stunning, funning, punning pretty Brinkley lass.

Another fan, signing herself "a young woman who admires [Brinkley's] work," wrote,

> You're the daintiest and the dearest, the funniest and the queerest
> Of all the women writers that I know;

Your use of words is stunning, interspersed with "tricks so cunning,"
And your drawings, I assure you, on one grow.

It was not only fans who wrote lyrics about Nell. Later that year she attended the opening of the second Ziegfeld Follies. The Follies of 1908 introduced a new song, "Shine On, Harvest Moon," by Nora Bayes and Jack Norworth. Also new that year was a tableau called "Nell Brinkley Studies," in which five Betties and four Billys, all costumed in black and white, were arranged to look like one of Nell's drawings. To go with the tableau, there was another song, "The Nell Brinkley Girl," by Harry B. Smith and Maurice Levi. If the lyrics were not brilliant, the song was nonetheless portentous:

> I'm the latest craze on Broadway
> Sweet Nell Brinkley girl
> Ev'ry fellow sighs to kiss me
> Fair Nell Brinkley girl,
> If you ever found one like me
> You would have a pearl
> So if you'll be my Nell Brinkley boy
> I'll be your Nell Brinkley girl.

Nell was a star.

Notes

1. Six- and even seven-day work weeks were common in those days before labor unions. A sign that was often seen in the front rooms of factories read, "If you don't come in on Sunday, don't come in on Monday."

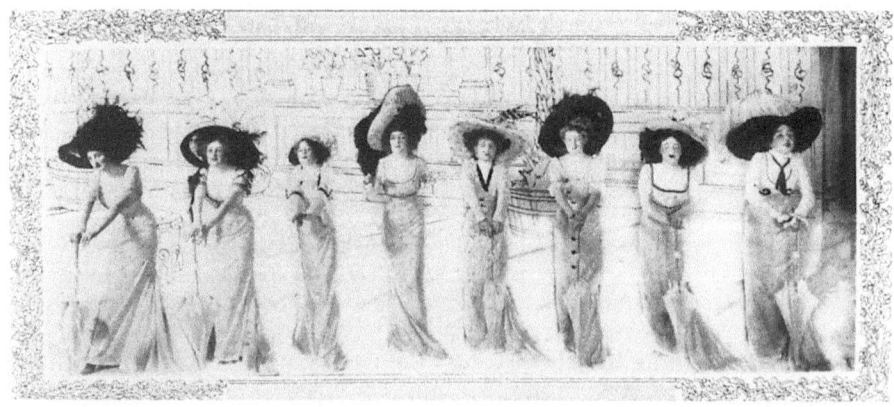

"Nell Brinkley Girls in 'Follies of 1908,'" from the Ziegfeld Follies of 1908.

One. 1908

2. The Floradora Sextette, early 20th-century chorus girls, was a synchonized group of tap dancers who performed on the Broadway stage.

3. Evelyn Nesbitt's testimony of her rape by White so unnerved the delicate Edwardian sensibilities of two lady journalists that they fled the courtroom. Irvin Cobb, one of the journalists at the Thaw trial, scornfully christened Dix, Black, Patterson and Greely-Smith "sob sisters" for their writing style. The name stuck and was long used for all girl reporters.

4. The use of baby talk seems to have been common among women in this period. Evelyn Nesbitt used it in her letters to Harry Thaw while he was in prison: "Him so nice & booful & much soothin to her when she has fits. See him tomorrow—dearestes—Love and tisses." (Harry K. Thaw, *The Traitor*, Dorrance and Company, 1926)

5. The name Betty, used as a generic term for girl, seems to have survived through the years, and pops up in names like Betty Boop or Betty of *Betty and Veronica*. Contemporary beach boy slang for surfer girls is *Surf Betty*, and a shop in San Francisco's Haight-Ashbury that specializes in a style of clothing calls itself *Back-Seat Betty*, a name that needs no explanation.

6. Evelyn Nesbitt was a year older than Nell.

7. This motley list was based on an editorial from the July 20, 1908, *Los Angeles Examiner*, defining the escapist properties of art: "Nell Brinkley, Raphael, Gibson, Michael Angelo, Tad, Boucher, Powers, Phidias and Swinnerton, all help us to get away from that which is natural."

8. In a July 12, 1908, article for the *Denver Post*, James R. Noland commented, "The prim staid Gibson girl has never aroused the enthusiasm the Brinkley girls have called forth."

9. This is what her mother, May, actually did for Nell all her life.

10. This opinion differed sharply from the one published by the *Journal* when the play first opened in New York in 1900:

> The Journal calls the attention of the police to the play *Sapho* given here last night at Wallack's Theater by Miss Olga Nethersole.... A great many improper plays have been given in New York recently. "Sapho" is the limit—it should not be performed again. If the police do not interfere no man or woman who values his or her good name should ever go to a performance.

Nethersole was actually arrested for "violating public decency," but it took a jury all of 15 minutes to acquit her. The reason *Sapho* was considered so improper? It was about a married woman having an affair with another man.

CHAPTER TWO

Edgewater

Nothing to do, Nellie darling, nothing to do you say,
Let's take a trip on memory's ship back to the by-gone days.
Sail to the old village schoolhouse, anchor outside the school door.
    —"School Days," Will D. Cobbs and Gus Edwards, 1906

When Nell Brinkley made her triumphant return visit to Colorado in 1908, the Denver newspapers were quick to claim her as one of their own with as much praise as possible. "Nell Brinkley is the graceful, blonde, fluffy little Denver girl who used to do art stunts on the News and Times," wrote Roy A. Giles in the *Rocky Mountain News*, "and whose work attracted so much attention that New York reached out for her with the long hand that it puts out for brains and talent." Frances Wayne of the *Denver Post* wrote,

> The same dear cuddly, honey-sweet, friendly-true voice that I heard nine months ago saying "goodby" through the phone said "good morning" today.... Nell Brinkley has come home, conqueror of a wondrous realm, but the same unspoiled true as steel, clear eyed, sane visioned, hopeful, loyal little genius of a Nell who went away to fame and fortune that cold November day.

Denver Post reporter James R. Noland had visited Nell in New York. His interview, timed for her Colorado visit, bore the long headline "Nell Brinkley, a

Denver Girl Who 'Made Good' in New York: James R. Noland Tells of His Visit to the Adopted Home of the Western Artist, Whose 'Betties' Have Taken the Place of the Gibson Girls."

> All hail the Brinkley girl! The Nell Brinkley girl of Denver if you please. The dainty, beruffled creation that has sent the Gibson girl to retirement and has captured the hearts of all New York....
> It was the first part of last November that Nell Brinkley came out of the glorious West, bent on conquering the critical East.... In less than a year she has gone to the front with such a burst of speed that these brainy people of the big town have stood aghast.

The truth was, Nell actually hailed from the tiny town of Edgewater, which in 1900 had a population of 311 and had only been incorporated for six years when she went east. Little Nell had slogged through muddy, unpaved streets to attend Ashland Grade school, where there was no electricity until the year she left.

Pioneers from all over America flocked to the Denver area in the 1880s in search of gold and silver, and they stayed to form towns and raise families. This was the Wild West, home of the legendary Buffalo Bill Cody, and some towns catered to a rough clientele with saloons, gambling and prostitution. In the late 19th century, Edgewater was one of those permissive towns. Nearby Denver already had strict liquor laws, but Denver men in search of a good time could visit half a dozen saloons in Edgewater, try their luck against the infamous gambler Soapy Smith or pass the time with Madame Silk and her perfumed butterflies. As for the "water" in the town's name, that had been the result of a man-made accident in 1860 when early settler Thomas M. Sloan drilled for water and got more than he bargained for. The underground spring he uncovered flooded two hundred acres of land and formed two lakes, Cooper's Lake and Sloan's Lake. Drinking water for the town was hauled from an irrigation ditch or a nearby spring, or purchased in barrels from a traveling water-seller.

There was another side to Edgewater, however, consisting of hard working middle class families. Nell's father, Robert Serrett Brinkley, and her mother, May French Brinkley, had come west from Illinois, and a year before Nell's birth on September 5, 1886, he was listed in the Denver city directory. By 1895 the Brinkleys had moved to Edgewater, and their address was listed in the directory as "Calhoun, bet. Emerald and Agate Avs, Edgewater." The town was simply too small for house numbers. Like the other husbands and fathers of the town, he commuted to Denver, working for the Hallack & Howard lumber company. Little Nell was probably kept blissfully unaware of the bawdier part of town. In a 1908 article, she waxes poetic about the move: "And then we moved out into the country and I lived in a white house with a gay little garden around it, above a blue lake, and I went to a school out where 'the mountains slip down into the prairie.'"[1]

Edgewater incorporated in 1901, and Robert Brinkley was a member of the board of trustees which went to work smoothing the rough edges of the frontier town. Public drinking on Sundays became illegal, and nightly closing times for the saloons were enforced. Ladies were banned from entering the bars, firearms were banned from public streets, and "An Ordinance to Suppress Bawdy and Disorderly Houses of Ill Fame or Assignation" was passed. Soapy Smith left town, as did Madame Silk and her ladies of easy virtue. Other ordinances were passed to "Prevent Quarreling or Fighting and Other Disorderly Conduct" and to "Prevent the Leaving of Dead Carcasses or Other Offensive Substances within the Town." The muddy streets were paved over with wooden boards, and telephone service was installed. By the time Nell was 17, Edgewater had been civilized and her father had become its second mayor. Then the mayor's 17-year-old daughter announced that she wanted to leave Edgewater High School a year before graduation, to draw for a living.

The mayor of a town of just over 300 people is not a rich man, and the town directory of that year still listed Robert S. Brinkley as working for Hallack & Howard. Robert was a practical man, and didn't hold with starving in a garret. Nell could leave school, he ruled, if she could actually earn real money from her art. Nell had begun to draw at an early age, and she indulged her appetite for creation whenever inspiration struck and with whatever "sketch pad" might be available—including her mother's oilcloth-covered cookbook and her father's starched white shirtfronts. She had already sold her first art, a set of decorated blotters for $5, at the age of 13.[2] She brought her lifetime collection of art to the *Denver Post*, and was hired for $7 a week. In 1903, that was a considerable wage.

For the *Post*, Nell drew editorial cartoons—not her forté—and was fired after only six months when she submitted a very bad drawing of the Pope.[3] But she had convinced her father of her ability to earn a living as an artist, and he paid for two years of art school for her.

Then, at 19, Nell took sought work at the *Denver Times*, whose editor, Mr. Paddock, was the same man who had hired her for the *Post* two years earlier. Apparently the art lessons had done their job. Mr. Paddock hired Nell for the *Times* and put her to work doing what she did best: romantic drawings of pretty girls.[4] By 1907, Nell had proudly gotten herself listed in the Edgewater directory as "Brinkley, Nell, Miss, artist *Times*," but she was already on her way to New York. One of her drawings in the *Times* had

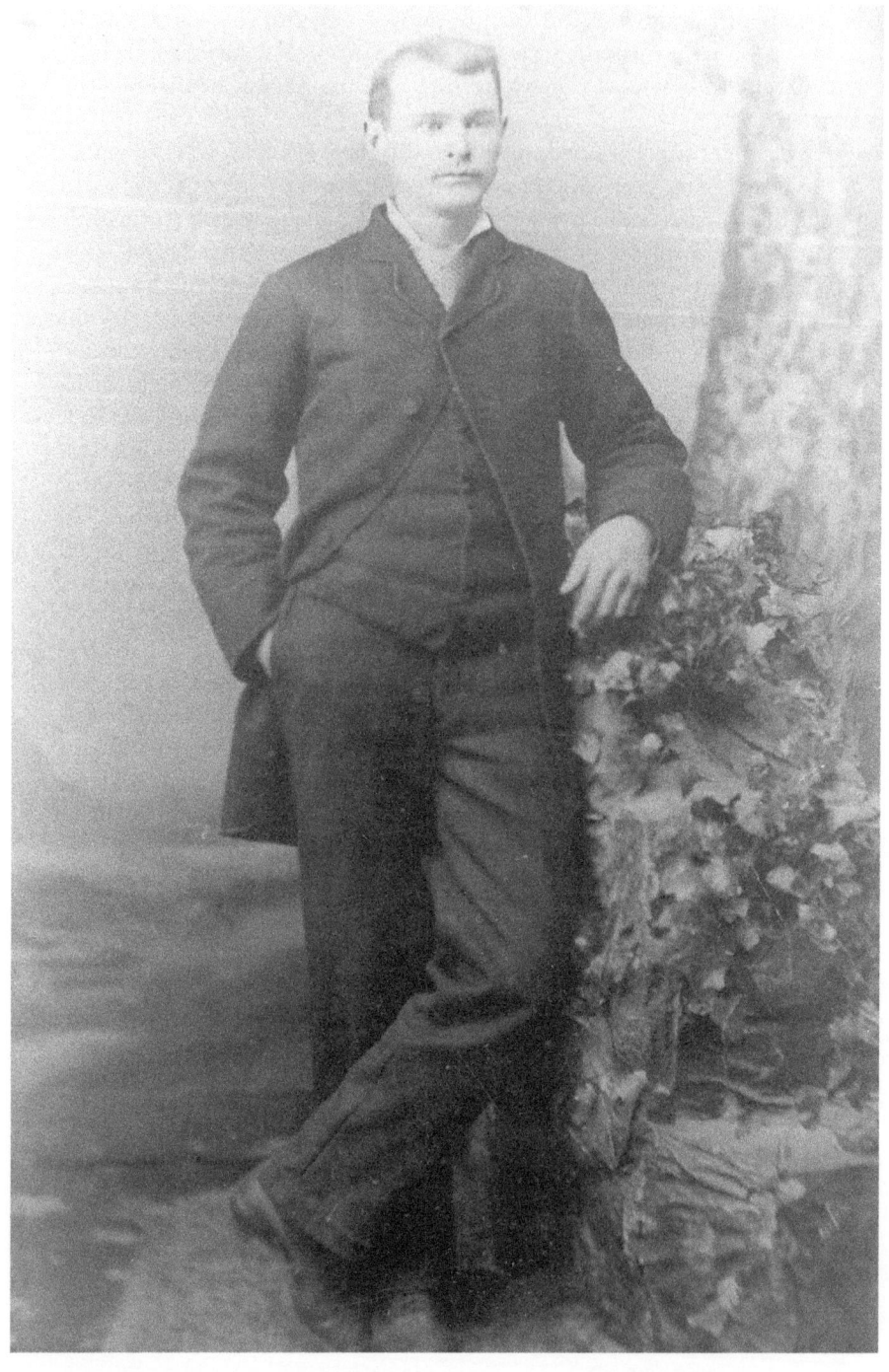

caught the eye of Arthur Brisbane, editor of the *New York Evening Journal*.

The family split up. Nell traveled east with her mother. Robert stayed behind and, in fact, never would live with his wife and daughter again. Freed from the necessity of supporting a family, he eventually left Hallack & Howard, and went into business for himself, opening a cigar store. The Denver city directory for 1911 lists him as, "Brinkley, Robert S., cigars."

Since divorce was so frowned upon at that time, it's possible that Nell's move to New York was a handy excuse for separation for a husband and wife who may not have been getting along. Whatever the reason, Nell missed her father. She wrote, "I'm homesick for the blazing blue and gold West and the dandiest, youngest-hearted, sportiest Dad that ever a girl had, that I left out there."

She missed Colorado. She would return often to her home state, developing her visits into subjects for her daily panels. In James Noland's *Denver Post* interview she said,

> Do I ever get homesick for Denver? Why sometimes when I think of that wonderful Colorado sky that comes down all around me like a great blue veil, I just feel like hiking right back home on the first train. Do I get homesick? Oh no, I just die for the sight of God's country.

Notes

1. "Nell Brinkley Pictures Herself," in the *New York Evening Journal*, February 1908.
2. She bought a zither with the money.
3. During this period at the *Post*, poor Nell earned the nickname of "Little Smearo."
4. An article in the August 20, 1910, issue of *The Fourth Estate* lists Nell's ages as 15 when she left school to work for the *Post* and 17 when she went to the *Times*, but Nell had already shaved two years off her age by the time the article was written.

Opposite: Robert Serrett Brinkley, early 1900s.

CHAPTER THREE

Before Nell

>   *They say the old-times things are the best...*
>   *But I'm going to let the old things be,*
>   *'Cause they are certainly not suited for me.*
>   —"There'll Be Some Changes Made," Billy Higgins
>   and W. Benton Overstreet, 1923

When Nell Brinkley walked into the courtroom in 1908 to cover the Harry K. Thaw trial, and to effectively start her career, she entered through a doorway of opportunity that had been opened for her by other women as early as the mid–19th century. Before the 19th century, women artists were rare. Political, legal, cultural and economic restrictions conspired to keep women in the home. Married while still in their teens, they almost immediately commenced a lifetime of childbearing. There was a high mortality rate, with many young mothers and their babies dying at childbirth. Surviving women spent their every waking moment taking care of their children, their husbands and their home. There was little or no time to be creative.

Among the more well-to-do, those with nurses for their children and servants for their homes, a form of creativity was encouraged, but such activities as embroidery, sewing, and even drawing and painting were meant solely to decorate the home. That an upper class woman would even consider using her artistic talents outside of her home to earn money was almost unthinkable. Any woman who, despite popular opinion, aspired to a career as an artist was out of luck unless, like 17th century artist Artemesia Gentileschi, she had an artist father to train her. Art academies of the 17th and 18th centuries did not accept women as students.

The situation started to improve by the 1850s. Women began marrying later in life and bearing fewer children. In 1862 the United States Post Office hired women for the first time. The Bell telephone system, founded in 1876, brought middle-class women into the workforce as switchboard operators. The introduction of the typewriter in 1873 brought women into offices, where they worked alongside men, almost as equals. The feminist movement, an outgrowth of the largely woman-centered mid-century abolition movement, suggested to women that they *could* be men's equals.

Education, too, opened the minds of young women. Mount Holyoke, the first American women's college, opened in the 1830s, followed, after the Civil War, by Vassar, Smith, Wellesley, Bryn Mawr and Radcliffe. And Oberlin admitted a few women students in 1837 despite criticism that education was harmful to women, whose delicate minds, unable to cope with the hard subjects, would develop brain fever.[1] By 1890, 2,500 American women had graduated from college. At last talented women were able to get training in art, in women's colleges like the Philadelphia School of Design for Women and in coed schools like the Art Students League in New York and the Pennsylvania Academy of the Fine Arts.

In 1900 the famous illustrator Howard Pyle, who had since 1894 been teaching art classes at Drexel Institute in Philadelphia, founded his own private art school in Wilmington, Delaware. Of his more than 100 students, a select group of young artists who had already proven to him their talents and abilities, roughly one third were women. Many of these female pupils went on to successful careers in the arts, especially in illustration. It's interesting to note that the largely self-taught Nell Brinkley studied and admired Pyle's work, and she is likely to have been influenced by it.

The years 1880 to 1914 were the golden age of illustration. Photoengraving, a revolutionary printing method utilizing photographic reproduction, replaced the old wood engraving process and made it possible to reproduce artwork directly from the original page. In 1896, new methods of color printing brought full color sections to the Sunday newspapers. Illustrated magazines filled the newsstands, and bookstores carried richly illustrated books. The illustrators themselves became celebrities, and there was work for any talented artist, male or female. Such students of Pyle as Elizabeth Shippen Green, Violet Oakley, and Jessie Wilcox Smith had more work than they could handle.

Illustration was in fact considered quite an acceptable occupation for

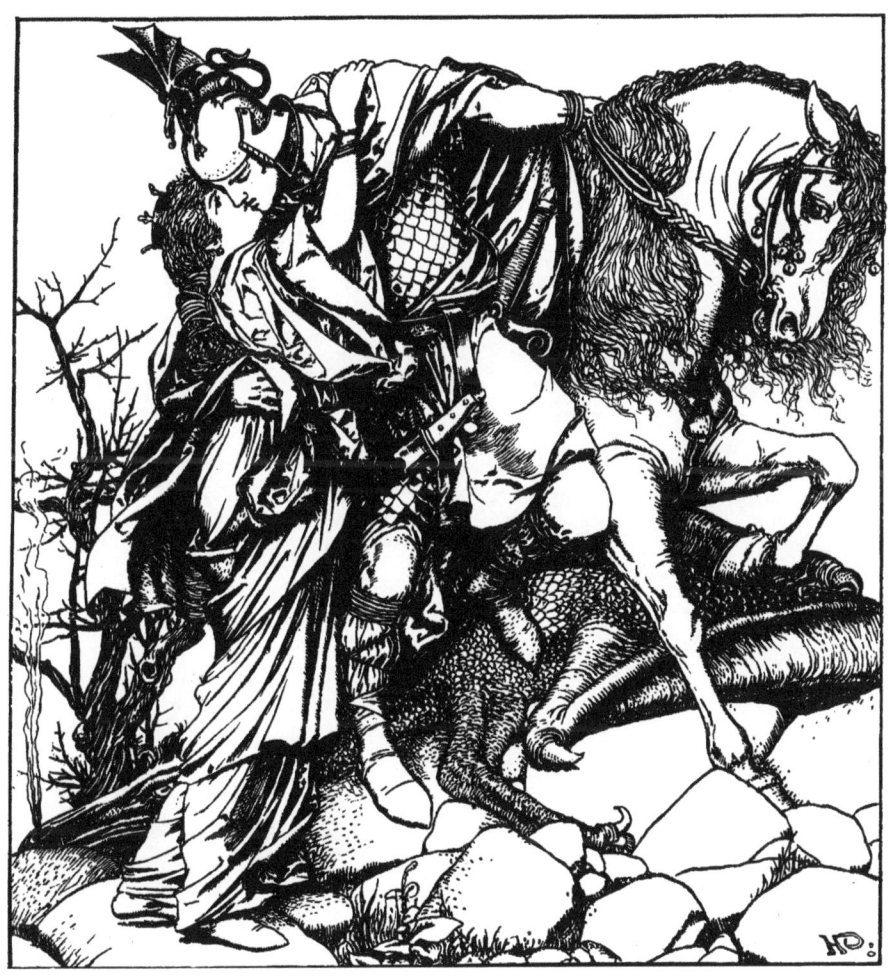

Howard Pyle, "The Wonder Clock," 1888.

women. Not regarded as "serious" art, it was considered a craft, not far removed from the embroidery and china painting with which upper-class women had been encouraged to amuse themselves a century earlier. Another factor that made women's illustration acceptable was their subject matter. Unlike male artists, who might draw ships, battle scenes, knights in armor, whatever they pleased, women, no matter how talented, for the most part confined themselves to renderings of domestic or romantic scenes drawn for children's books and women's magazines. Even Mary Cassatt, generally considered the best American woman fine artist of the last century, specialized in paintings of mothers and babies.

"Stolen Away!"

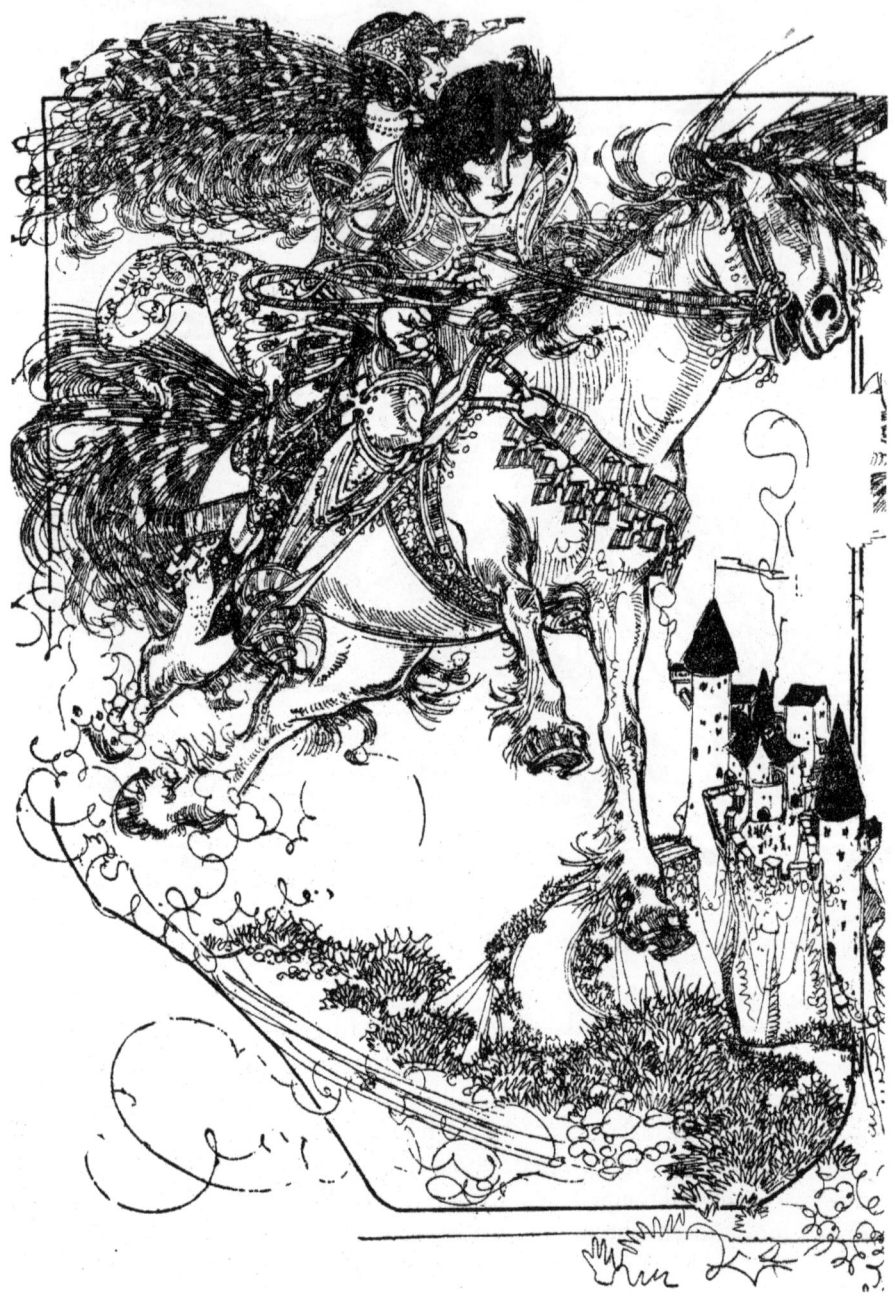

Three. Before Nell

Rose O'Neill illustrated books and magazines exquisitely but was most popular for her sentimental, babylike Kewpies. Excellent artists like Maude Humphrey and Frances Tipton Hunter were famous for their renditions of apple-cheeked babies. This early 20th-century baby art proved lucrative for their creators. Grace Drayton designed the Campbell Kids, and Maude Humphrey produced countless books, cards, and calendars of baby art. Her rendition of her seven-month-old son, the future film star Humphrey Bogart, became nationally known as the Maude Humphrey Baby.[2]

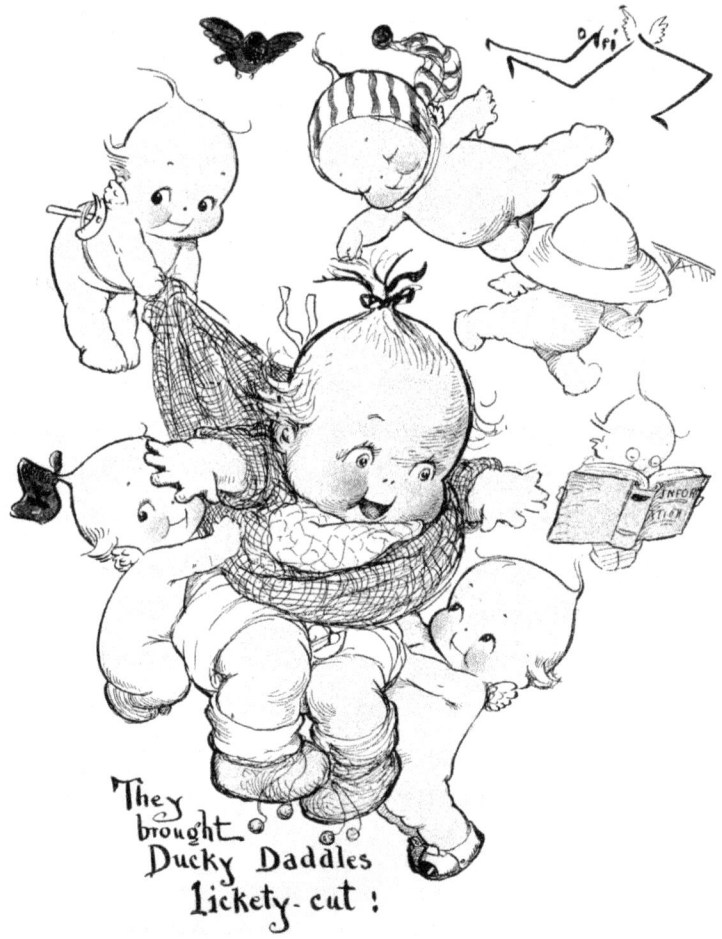

Rose O'Neill, "The Kewpies and Duckie Daddles," which ran in *Good Housekeeping* Magazine, May 1915.

Opposite: Nell Brinkley, "Stolen Away," 1914.

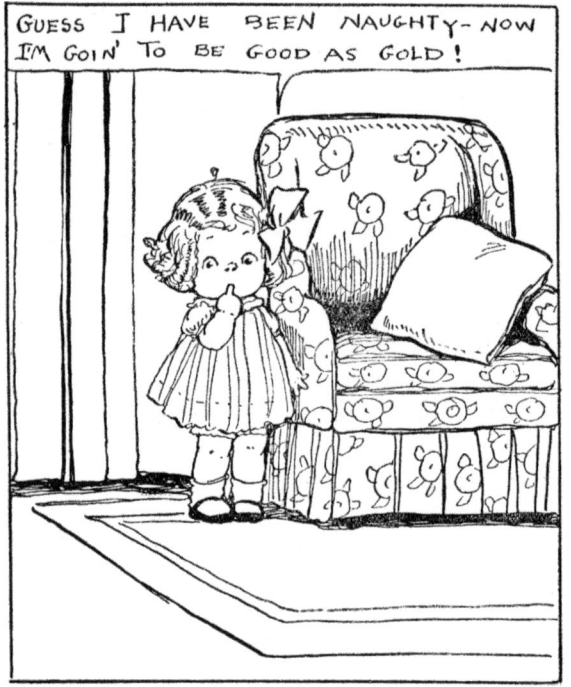

Grace Drayton, "Dimples, She Tries So Hard to Be Good," 1917.

Artist Thornton Oakley, a student of Howard Pyle, quotes his teacher as saying that "when a girl married, that was the end of her." Unfortunately, marriage and child rearing continued to put an end to the careers of many promising women. Some, like Fanny Y. Cory, married in 1902, returned to professional illustration after their children grew up. Ellen Thompson Pyle resumed her career after her husband's death. Some of the most successful women illustrators, like Violet Oakley and Jessie Wilcox Smith, never married.

Most of these women had preceded Nell in illustrating by at least ten years and were correspondingly older than her. Comics by women like Kate Carew, Jean Mohr, and Inez Townsend had already appeared in the pages of America's newspapers at least five years before Nell's daily panels started in the *Journal*. What they all, except for Nell, had in common was their subject matter: babies, toddlers, children. Any women depicted were usually mothers. Even Nell's two most famous contemporaries, Grace Drayton and Rose O'Neill, stuck with that acceptable subject. Grace Drayton, all of whose cherubic toddlers were clones of her Campbell Kids, produced an endless array of kid strips with saccharine names like *Dolly Dingle, Dollie Dimples, Dolly Drake,* and *Dottie Darling*. Rose O'Neill's Kewpies, while supposedly little winged elvish creatures, looked suspiciously like babies and interacted with children. Only Nell, while certainly also contributing her share of bouncing babies and enough pudgy cupids to fill several Renaissance paintings, specialized in women, usually single women.

Fay King was a contemporary whose career closely paralleled Nell's. King's art and commentary also appeared in the Hearst papers, and, like

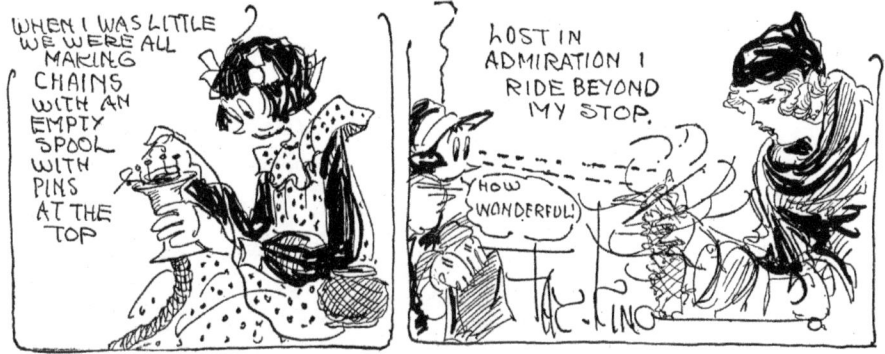

Fay King, "Flashing Crochet and Knitting Needles Fascinate Fay King," 1937.

Nell, she got her start at the *Denver Post*. King avoided the ubiquitous kiddie comic strip in favor of daily commentary, and although she had a bohemian reputation, her commentary, like Nell's, was not of the most world-shaking sort. In a series of comic strips from 1925, Fay King advised married women to stay as cheerful as they had during courtship, told women they looked better in dresses than in shorts and reminded them that the way to a man's heart was through his stomach. One strip, titled "Use Caution, Good Sense in Summer Flirtations, Fay King Says," warned against summer vacation romances with strangers. In the last panel, a distraught woman, hanging up her phone, exclaims, "Good gracious! He's wanted by the police, and they found my name in his address book!" Like Nell, Fay King also reviewed the latest Broadway plays in her daily strip. Her style, however, was as different from Nell's as they both were from the reams of sentimental baby art produced by their sister illustrators. King drew in a much broader cartoon style and usually put her self-portrait into her strips, portraying herself as a skinny, big-footed Olive Oyl look-alike.

Although they avoided the mother and child ghetto that most other women cartoonists and illustrators seemed to have inhabited, both artists were still ghettoized simply by drawing for women. A glance at the magazine page of the 1917 *Chicago Evening American*, featuring a half-page drawing and commentary by Nell, reveals the other contents—"Wartime Menus," "Advice to the Lovelorn" by Beatrice Fairfax, and two serialized romances called *Patsy Kildare, Outlaw* and *The Other Woman*—were holdovers from the women's page.

Of her contemporary male illustrators, Nell Brinkley was most frequently compared to Charles Dana Gibson, who preceded her by about twenty years and who also worked in a pen-and-ink style.[3] Gibson's name

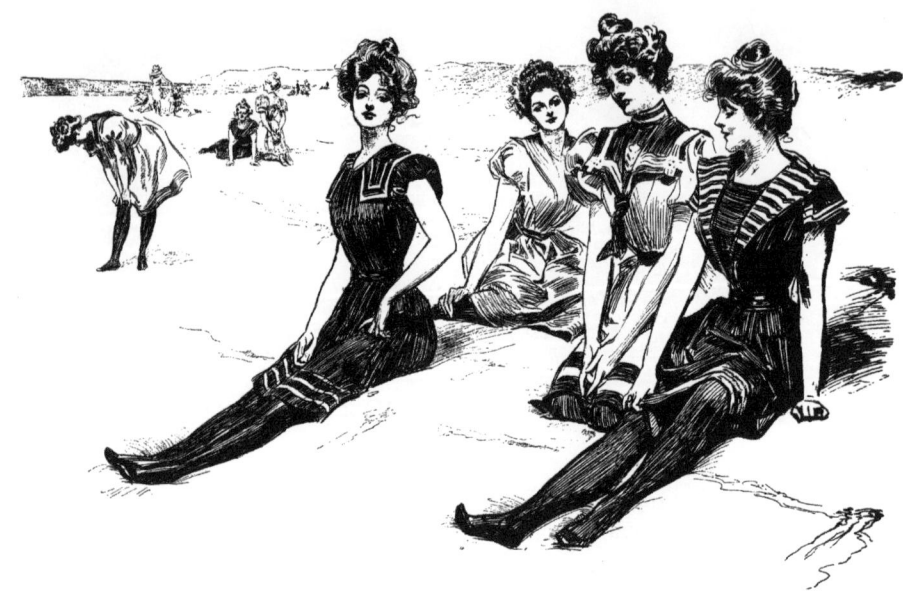

  By *NELL BRINKLEY*

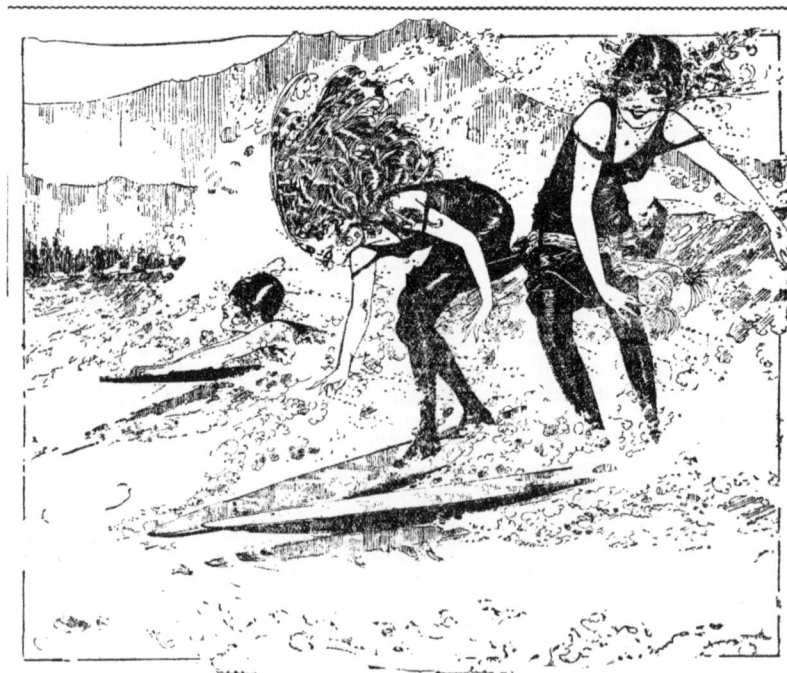

Three. Before Nell

was as much of a household word as Nell's would later be. When he was the subject of a battle between two magazines, *Life* and *Colliers*, each vying to be his exclusive publisher and each offering him more pay, the public eagerly followed the contest in the daily papers.

Gibson's women, still known today as Gibson girls, supposedly personified the American girl at the turn of the 20th century. They represented instead only upper-class young women. Despite the fact that the 1900 federal census had counted five million women in the workforce, Gibson did not draw poor or working-class women. Gibson's women are also passive: a common theme in his art was satirizing the then-popular custom of nouveau-riche American fathers marrying their daughters off to impoverished European nobility. In these cartoons, the daughters seem to placidly go along with the plans, no matter how unattractive the European duke or earl. Neither are the Gibson girls particularly active: they appear to glide rather than walk, or they sit passively and decoratively on the beach in their one piece bathing suits, eyes cast demurely down, smiling enigmatic Mona Lisa smiles.

In contrast, the Brinkley girl laughed out loud, with her mouth wide open, her wild hair streaming in the breeze. She leaped through the snow, splashed and swam in the water, ran through the grass. And she often held a job.

Lyrics to the 1909 song, "The Brinkley Bathing Girl," from the Ziegfeld Follies, describe how Nell's more modern creations were already supplanting Gibson's old fashioned girl:

> You know the Gibson bathing girl, so haughty and so tall;
> She rules just like a queen upon the beach.
> She captures ev'ry fellow's heart, she wins them one and all;
> The artists say that she's a perfect peach.
> Of late we've seen a bathing girl of rather dif'rent sort:
> Her cleverness and grace we can't ignore;
> And ev'ry chap who sees her thinks that swimming is a sport,
> And hails her as the Venus of the shore.
> Oh, the Brinkley bathing girl, of the ocean she's a pearl.
> She shows good form, your heart she'll storm
> And set your brain a-whirl.

Charles Dana Gibson's young women were holdovers from a Victorian era. Nell Brinkley brought the new woman into the twentieth century.

Opposite, top: **Gibson girls on the beach, 1900.** *Opposite, bottom:* **Nell Brinkley, "Coming and Going," 1914.**

Notes

1. Oberlin was also the first college to admit black students.
2. That Maude Humphrey created the Gerber Baby is no more than myth.
3. Coincidentally, Evelyn Nesbitt Thaw had been one of Gibson's models.

CHAPTER FOUR

The Teens

Hello, my baby! Hello, my honey! Hello, my ragtime gal!
Send me a kiss by wire, baby my heart's on fire!
—"Hello Ma Baby," Ida Emerson and Joe E. Howard, 1899

Nell was the subject of two popular songs in 1909. The second song, written by George M. Cohan, would today be at the least controversial, and probably considered racist. Its title was "The Brinkley Coon," and it was probably originally sung by a white woman in blackface:

> The Brinkley coon, the Brinkley coon,
> They call me the Brinkley coon.
> One really would think she was from pen and ink
> Of the popular paper cartoon.
> Her fluffs, her puffs of the Brinkley style,
> She's cultivated a Brinkley smile,
> The popular Brinkley, hair so kinky,
> Beautiful Brinkley coon.

However, a century ago, "coon songs"—songs sung in blackface by white performers—were not considered racist. In fact, they originated in the black community, written by black composers like Ernest Hogan and Scott Joplin, and were popularized by white entertainers along with the cakewalk, a dance that also originated in the black community.[1]

As for Nell, her art was never racist. She seemed constitutionally incapable of drawing women as other than pretty, no matter their race; in fact, her cartoons featured a number of women from different races and cultures—all beautiful in true Brinkley style—each regarding the other with amusement. These panels bore titles like "My, How Funny She Looks!" "My, But You're Funny!" "What Is Beauty?" and "What Is Beautiful?" Under the latter illustration, after describing a typical European beauty, she adds:

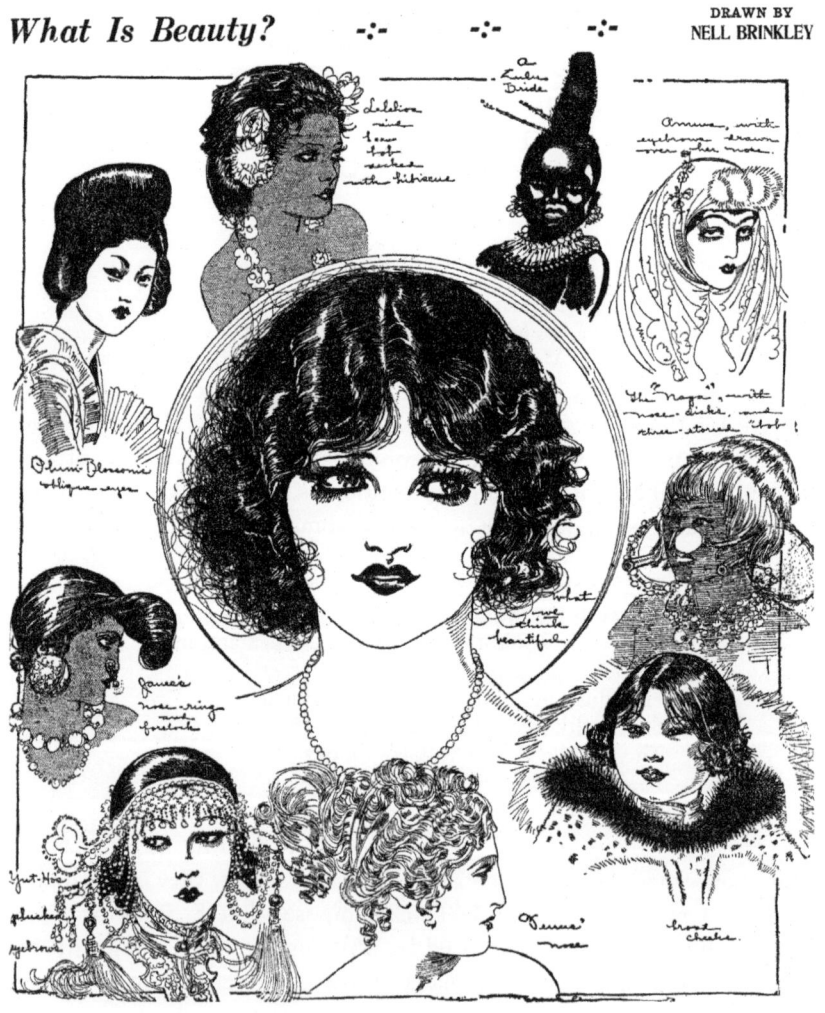

"What Is Beauty?" 1922.

What Is Beautiful?

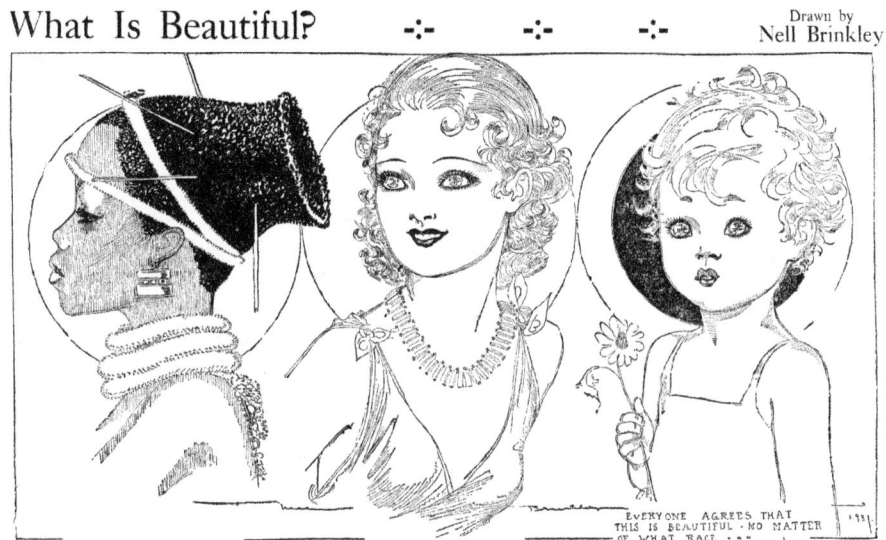

"What Is Beautiful?" 1931.

> The Zulu does not think *her* beautiful. She looks like buttermilk to him—a queer idea of a beautiful young woman ... faded. No richness of tone. For him the young woman on the left—brown-skinned, with the latest coiffure, bone beads, beads for a skirt, brass-studded collar, with a lovely flat nose...

Nell loved any excuse to draw interesting outfits, and she delighted in depicting the exotic costumes of her African, Chinese, and Inuit women. At a time when Jews were satirized and caricatured, Nell presented her version of Reba, the Jewish girlfriend of Abie the Agent, from a then-popular comic strip by Harry Hershfield. Hershfield, himself Jewish, found nothing wrong with rendering his characters in a way that would be considered offensive today, but Nell's Reba was a beautiful Semitic girl. She drew Harry and Reba together in the front seat of a convertible, and added a dark-haired, Semitic cupid between them.

In 1926, Nell even presented a male version of "What Is Beauty?" entitled "What Is a Good-Looking Man?" On either side of the American flapper and her two Billies, she drew a Native American, a Maori, an Inuit and a Korean—and they were all equally handsome.

Nell was earning top dollar. Upon arriving in New York, she had found herself a home in Bensonhurst, but by 1911, she and May, her mother, moved to New Rochelle, a toney artist's community about an hour away from Manhattan by train. Successful artists and illustrators like Norman

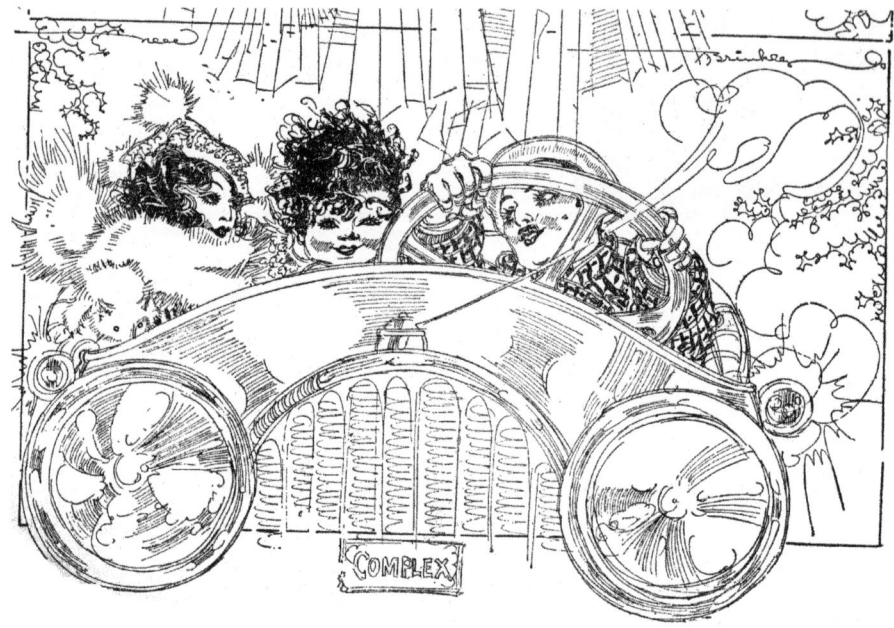

Reba, 1916.

Rockwell, J. C. Leyendecker and cartoonist Clare Briggs lived there. A residence in New Rochelle meant an artist had arrived.

And Nell had indeed arrived. Her work now appeared in newspapers all over the country, and she was newsworthy. Her 1915 visit to San Francisco made the front page of the *San Francisco Call*,[2] and in return Nell produced a flattering panel titled "The San Francisco Girl." The April 1917 issue of *Cartoons Magazine* printed a fictional interview with a Brinkley girl, "The Queen of Hearts," by Alphonese Duval:

> "Are you not," I ventured, "The Nell Brinkley girl?"
> She smiled an affirmative.
> "I believe that I have met you often," I continued, "in the columns of my evening paper. I have often wanted to talk to you and ask you certain questions...."
> "It was such a nice day," she explained, "that I couldn't resist the temptation. You see, I have ventured out of the newspaper and been recognized."

Nell was even known overseas. In 1911 the British newspaper *The Sketch* reprinted her panels under the title "Nell Brinkley Girls: The Rage of America." As a newspaper cartoonist, Nell was accepted as "one of the boys"—

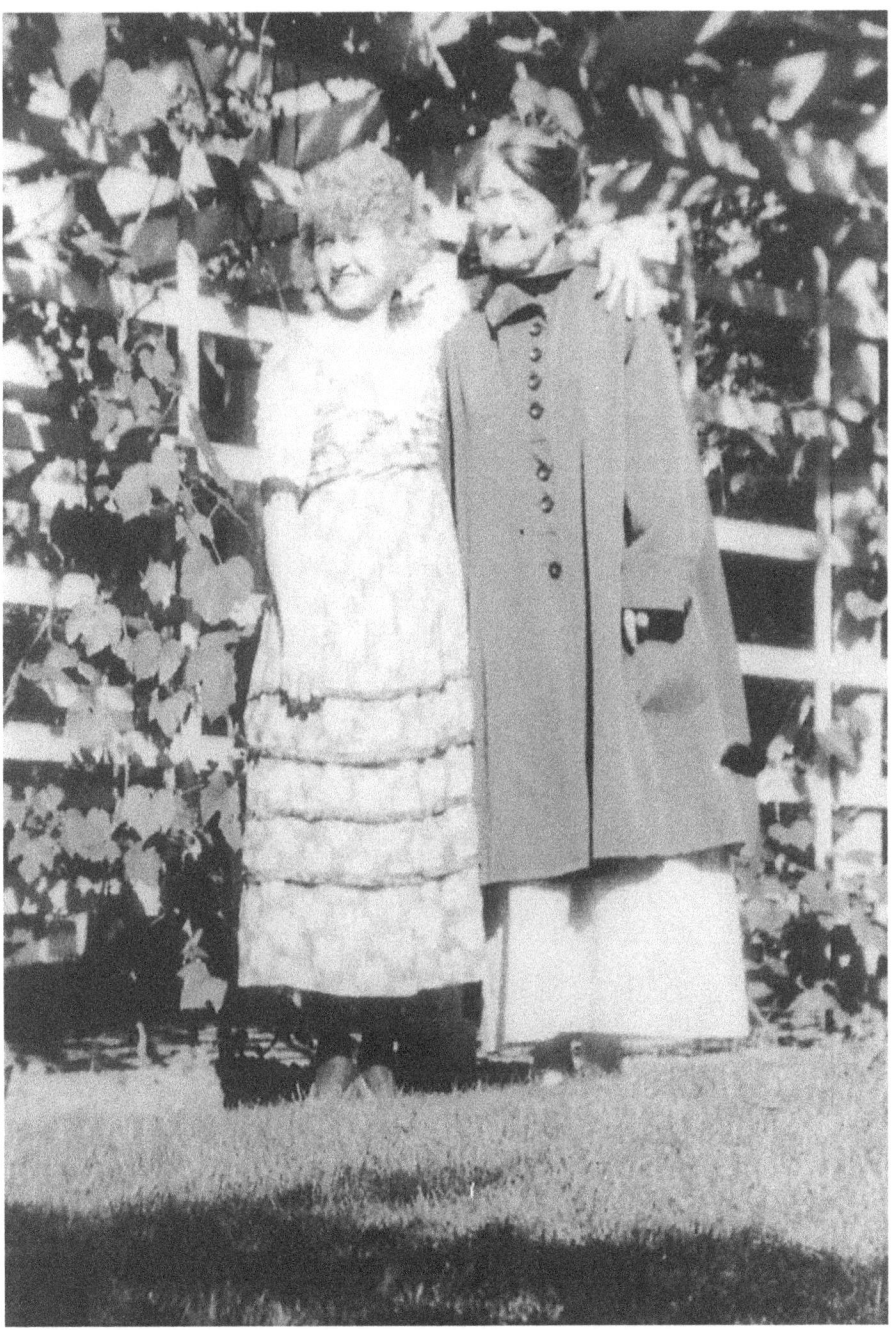

Nell and her mother, May, circa 1910.

DENTISTS AGAIN DISCUSS FREE CLINICS

The second day's sessions of the Panama-Pacific Dental Congress opened this morning in the Civic Auditorium.

While discussions of free dental clinics were continued and the issuing of dental diplomas to nurses and governesses were resumed, the more intimate affairs of the dental congress as an organization appeared.

The election of officers will be one of the most important matters to come before the congress.

The establishment of a free dental dispensary, the largest in the United States, as a foundation by George Eastman, camera manufacturer of Rochester, N. Y., held the interest of the congress. Dr. Benedict S. Hert of Rochester declared Eastman would spend

PRETTY GIRLS? S. F. FULL OF THEM, SAYS NELL BRINKLEY, HERE

Nell Brinkley, creator of The Call and Post's "Brinkley Girl," who is in San Francisco marveling at the beauty of San Francisco girls.

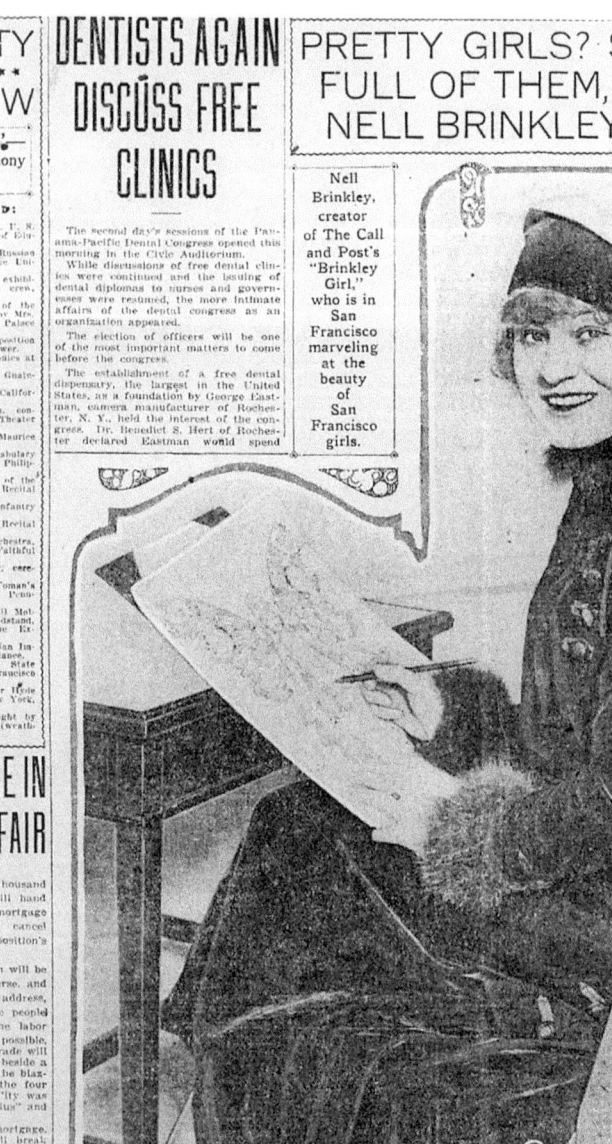

Prefers Writing to Drawing; Artistic at 2 Years, but Never Studied Art

and for the most part, the other cartoonists *were* boys. In 1917, W.R. Allman drew a strip for the *Cleveland Press* in which his wife reads out their Christmas list, consisting of every major newspaper cartoonist in America. Nell is the only woman on the list.

As early as 1913, scores of copycat cartoonists, mostly women, emerged from the woodwork with imitations of Nell's style. The May 1926 issue of *Circulation*, a magazine for newspaper makers, called her the "most copied artist in the world." Like Nell, her copyists sprinkled their work with cupids and comparisons of blondes versus brunettes. Eleanor Schorer, one of the best Nell clones, named her boy and girl couples Bessie and Bob instead of Betty and Billy. They all copied the breathless sentimentality of her writing style. In his 1924 panel, "When You're in Love," Walt Van Arsdale, one of her few male imitators, wrote:

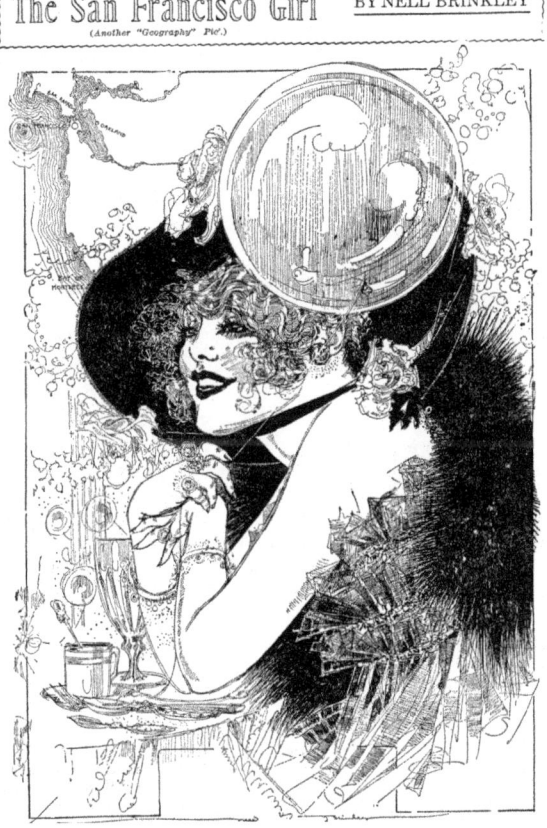

"The San Francisco Girl," 1915.

> Those who love tread the earth and yet are never on it. In the clouds, close by a castle in sunny Spain where warm ocean breezes are wafted through the air, in an old-fashioned garden where birds sing and the air smells sweet—these are the lands in which loved ones dwell, away—far away—from the rest of the world!

Opposite: **The *San Francisco Call* announces Nell's arrival in the Bay Area, August 31, 1915.**

April 12, 1911   THE SKETCH.

NELL BRINKLEY GIRLS: THE RAGE OF AMERICA.—VI.

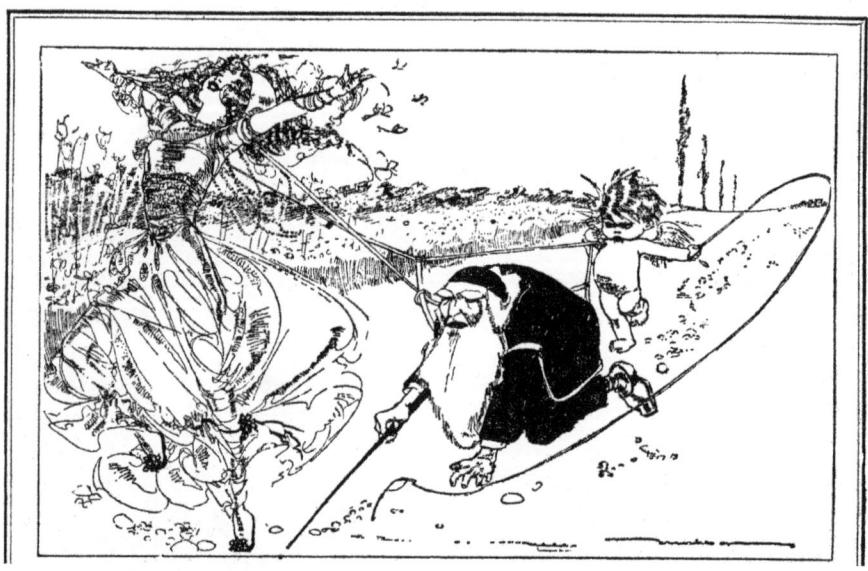

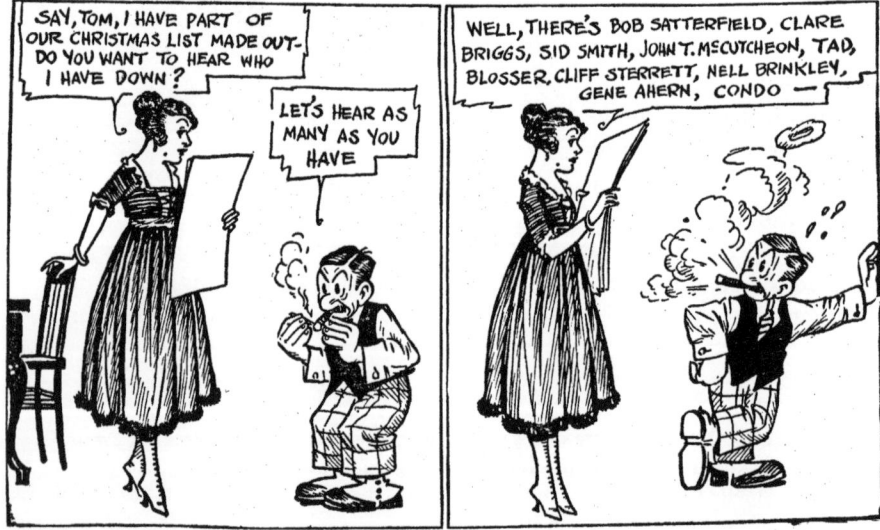

ALLMAN in Cleveland Press

Top: "Nell Brinkley Girls: The Rage of America," 1911. *Bottom:* A cartoon from W.R. Allman, the *Cleveland Press*, 1917. The artist's wife lists every major cartoonist in America, including Nell.

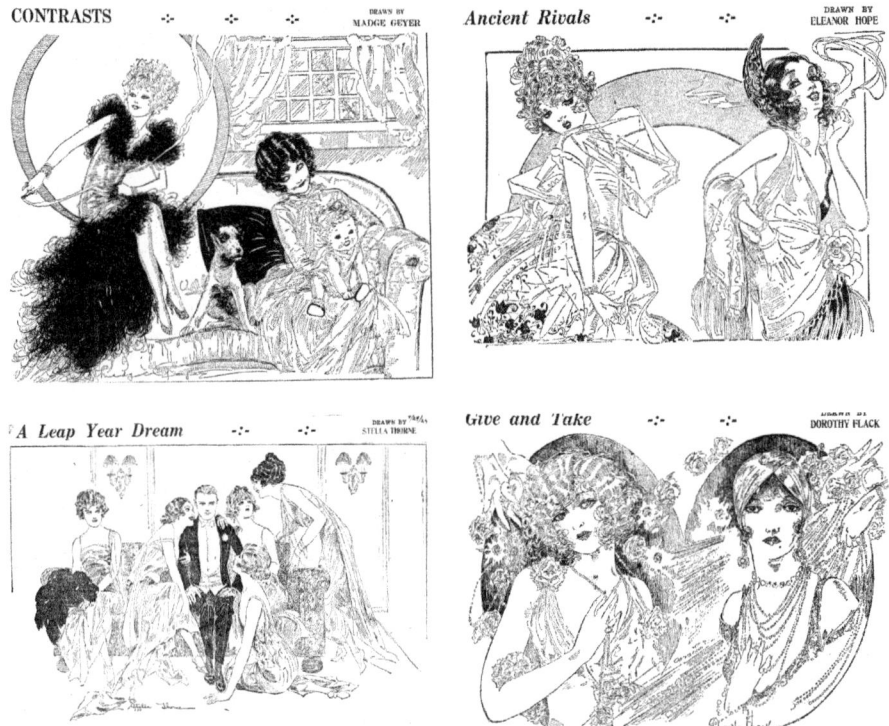

A gallery of Nell Brinkley imitators. *Top, left:* **Madge Geyer**; *top, right:* **Eleanor Hope**; *bottom, left:* **Stella Thorne**; *bottom, right:* **Dorothy Flack.**

None of them ever made any statements that could be construed as feminist or political. None achieved Nell's success, either.

Nell was realizing her dreams, including one that often popped up in her work: flight. In 1914 she went up in a plane, an experience that most people of that day, male or female, would never know. "Nell Brinkley Tastes Joys of Real Freedom Soaring in Clouds," ran the headline of the May 11, 1914, *San Francisco Examiner*, "Glides Over 3500 Feet on Floating Silence 'Till Earth' Arrives."

Europe was at war, and although America would not enter it for another three years, the country was already gearing up, and the biplane Nell flew was about to be transformed into a fighting instrument:

> I have flown. I flew—I did ... in the great dragon-tailed bird that is now (this day or two after) being dissected and picked apart bone by bone and built over into a thing of war—to carry ugly little gray bombs to Mexico,

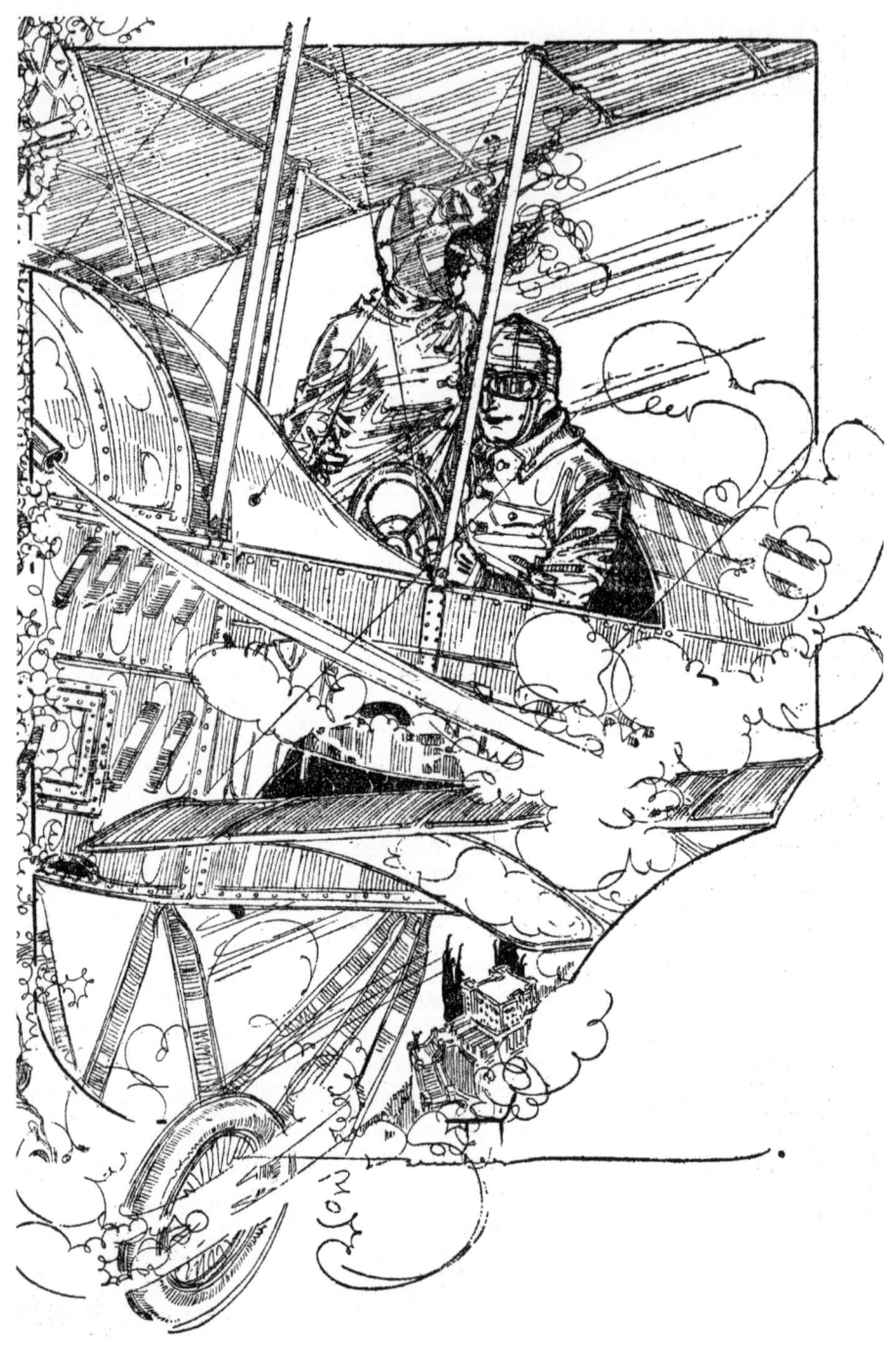

Nell's "great dragon-tailed bird," the biplane she first flew in, 1914.

instead of girls—for Uncle Sam, who is "stacking his drygoods" and rubbing his palms in the dirt. The dragon-fly is slipping its iridescent sheath and taking on the feathers and talons of the eagle. And I have had the great luck to ride it for one splendid half-hour before it went on the operating table, for its shedding.

And now ... I know how the tiny heart of the princess Badroulbadour tightened and her slant eyes widened to hold the great sights when her geni-spun palace took wings to itself and flew from a place in China to North Africa.... I know how Icarus longed for the sun when he took wing from the sea-cliffs of Greece; how the prince who bestrode the winged horse leaned and found the green plane of the earth just as a grandmother's "crazy-quilt made of bright bits of silk pieces." I know all of this.

The same year that Nell flew, she could afford to winter in California. She purchased a house in Long Beach, to which she returned yearly. In February 1914, she wrote about California:

> It's been a long year since I left this soft blue sea to go back to the gray one three thousand miles east on the other edge of the United States.... I've worked like a tow head (which I am) to get back again.

Nell did indeed work "like a towhead" for her fame and success and for the money that bought her New Rochelle home and her California vacations. May took care of the household duties and managed Nell's career so that all her daughter had to do was draw. Nell produced a page a day for the Hearst newspapers,[3] and turned out illustrations for magazines like *Harper's Bazaar*, along with the occasional sheet music cover and advertising art on the side. By the late teens, she was drawing advertisements for cosmetics like Djer-Kiss face powder, and by the early twenties her art sold Hennafoam shampoo. By the twenties she had also lent her name and her art to Nell Brinkley Hair Wavers and Nell Brinkley Bob Curlers, which could be bought for ten cents a card. Typical ads for these products featured Nell's curly-haired Betties wearing various hairstyles: the Water Wave, the Marcel Wave, the American Wave, the Horseshoe Wave, and the Bob. The copy, headed "My New Bob Curler Curls the Hair from Tip to Top!" was actually signed by Nell herself:

> Hundreds and hundreds of bobbed-haired girls have confided to me the difficulties of curling their hair.... So for these girls I have designed this absolutely new and flexible curler.... You will find as I have (yes, my hair is bobbed) that the little arm of my curler is like an extra hand which holds the hair securely while your own two hands are busy rolling up the curl.

Best Pal :-: :-: :-: :-: NELL BRINKLEY

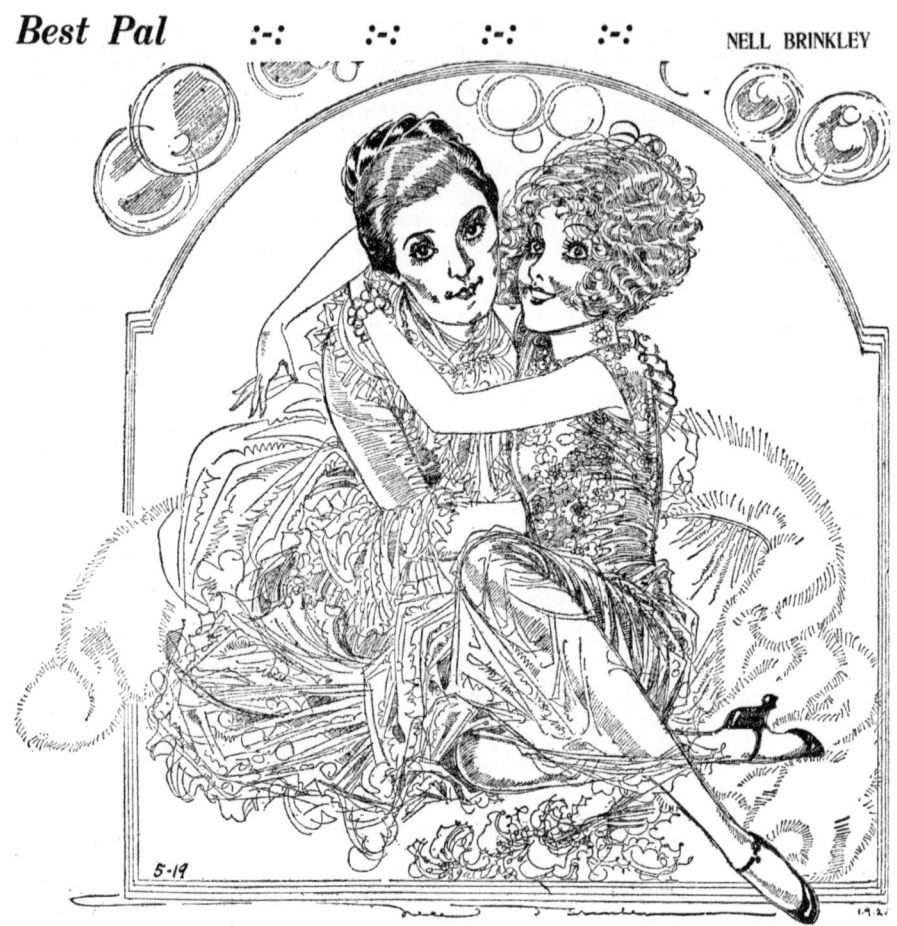

"Best Pal," 1925. A portrait of Nell's mother.

With such a workload, it's no wonder that Nell recycled some themes. One subject she drew throughout her career was similar to her *My, How Funny* series. Called variously *Can Such Things Be?* or *Point of View*, it featured a stylish Brinkley girl from the past and an equally stylish contemporary Brinkley girl regarding each other with amused wonder. Again, this was a great opportunity for Nell to draw beautiful antique costumes, which in some cases weren't really that antique to her. In her 1913 "Point of View, or, The Pot Calls the Kettle Black," three fashionably dressed women in a museum laugh at a painting of a high-wigged belle from the court of Louis XV. Years later, in Nell's 1934 "The Point of View!" four museum-going Brinkley girls now laugh at a portrait from 1913!

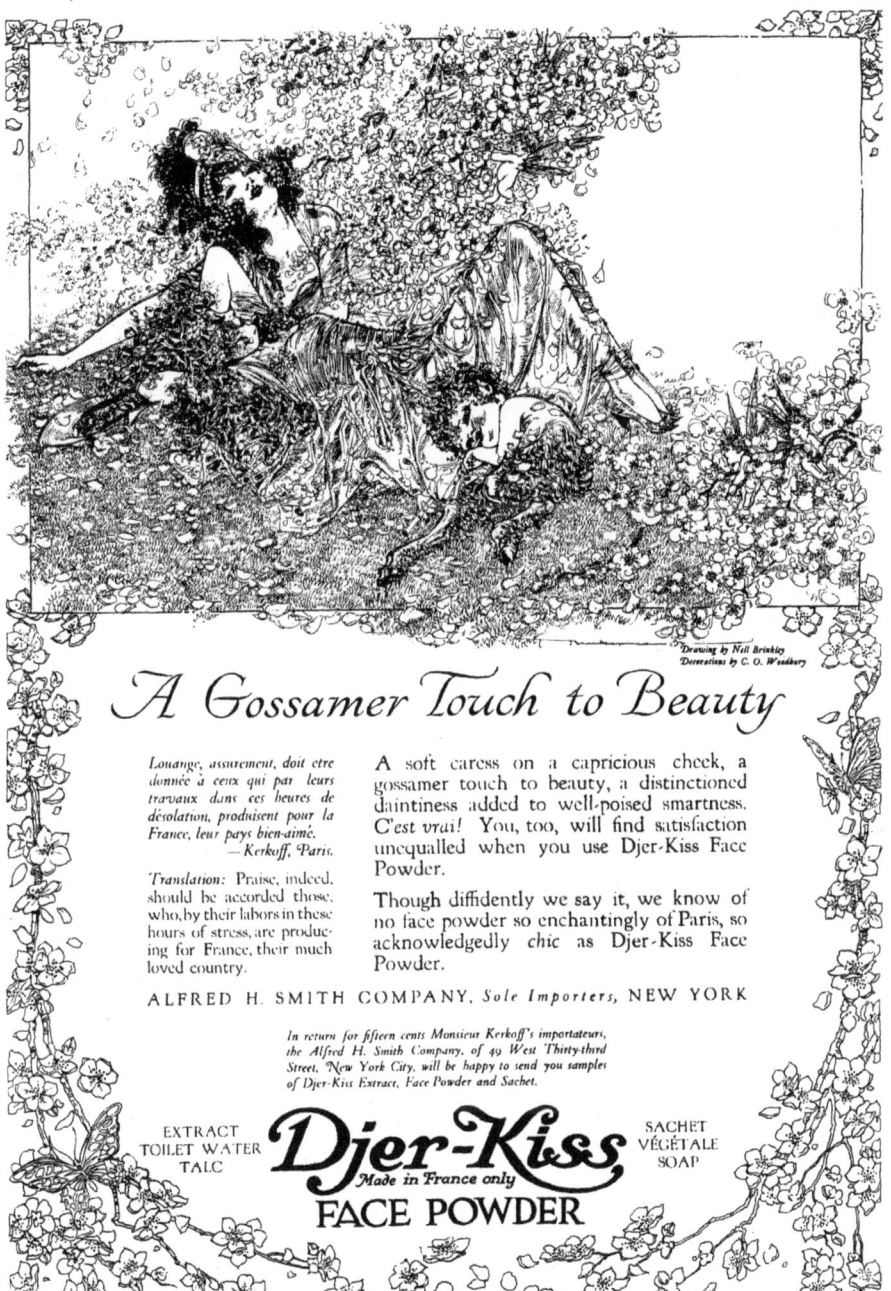

Djer-Kiss advertisement, 1918.

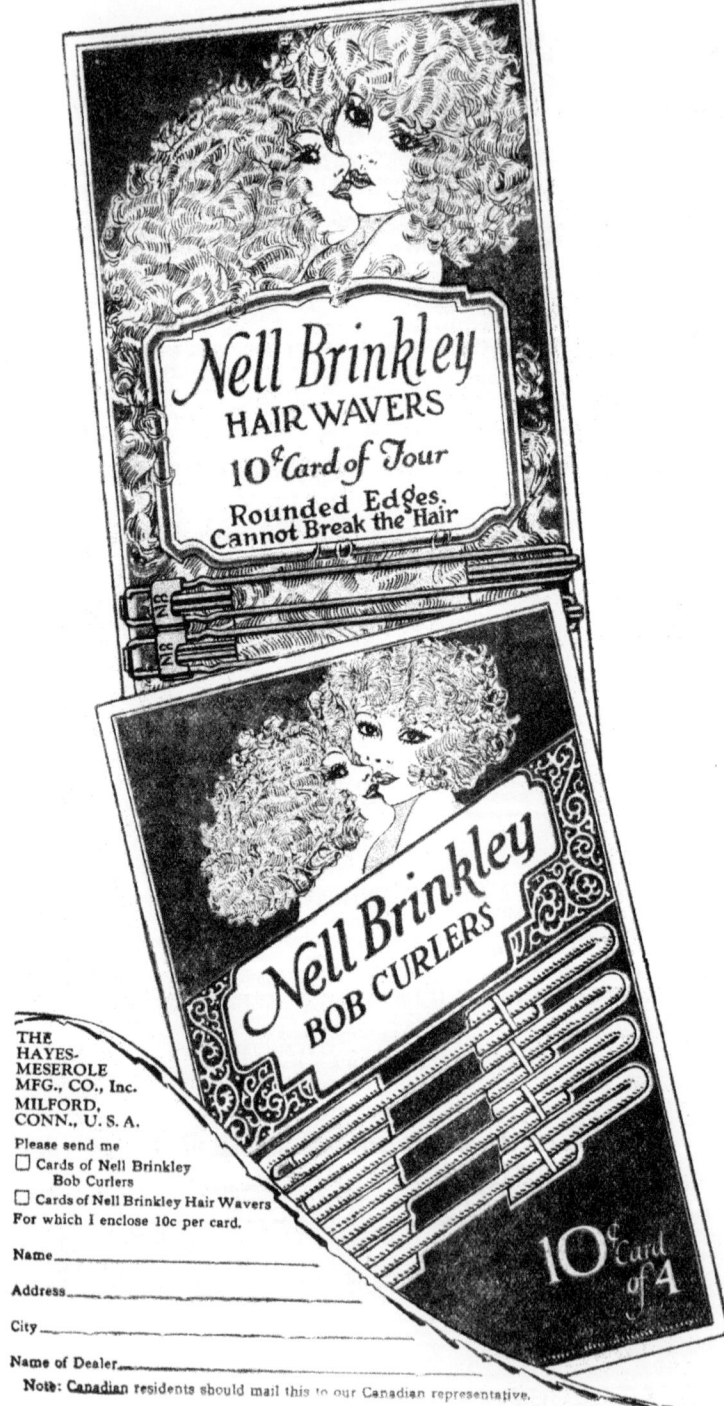

On occasion, Nell even cut out characters from earlier drawings and pasted them into new settings. She used a 1912 panel called "Cinderella," in which the pretty young maid watches her ugly mistress dressing up for a ball. In 1913, the very same maid appeared opposite an equally pretty rich young thing, herself recycled from yet another earlier panel, with a puzzled cupid hovering between them. This time the title was "Cupid in a Quandary," and like the earlier panel it favored the poor working girl. The text ran:

> Cupid is in a quandary these days—with all the advice that has been given about mistresses and maids. Sometimes he is tempted ... to take the little maid in preference to the daughter of the house, who lords it over the shrinking girl who waits on her.
>
> Cupid knows the maid is better natured than her mistress and is every way more desirable for a life partner.

And in 1921, another time when Nell couldn't make her deadline, she recycled half of a panel she'd produced seven years before. "Coming and Going!" had consisted of two panels: a winter scene of girls ice-skating and a summer scene of girls surfing. For June 4, 1921, Nell used only the surfer girls and retitled it "Joy 'Twixt Land and Sea." The swimsuits on her Betties look a trifle dated—a fashion revolution had occurred in those seven years—but presumably her fans didn't mind the occasional lapse in style.

When Nell was stumped for ideas, there were always faces to draw, pretty Brinkley girls that she could probably grind out in her sleep. Sometimes she drew a blonde and a brunette and made comparisons between them: "The Dark Side and the Fair Side." One of her best, from 1915, is subtitled "Blue-Eyed Fay, Love Me or I Die; Black-Eyed Fay, Love Me or You Die." Or her daily panel might simply consist of the face of a generic Betty, to which she would add a sprinkling of Brinkley cupids, a handsome Billy or both, and a title such as "The Girl He Left Behind," "The Coquette," or "The Girl Who Might Have Been."

Around 1913, Nell's daily panels show that she had started to become aware of working women. As a hard-working woman herself, she must have related to them. Of course, as drawn by Nell, they could not be anything but beautiful. Nell might have been talking about herself working "like a tow head" when she described shopgirls sympathetically in her August 1913 "When the Whistle Blows":

Opposite: **Nell Brinkley hair curlers, 1924.**

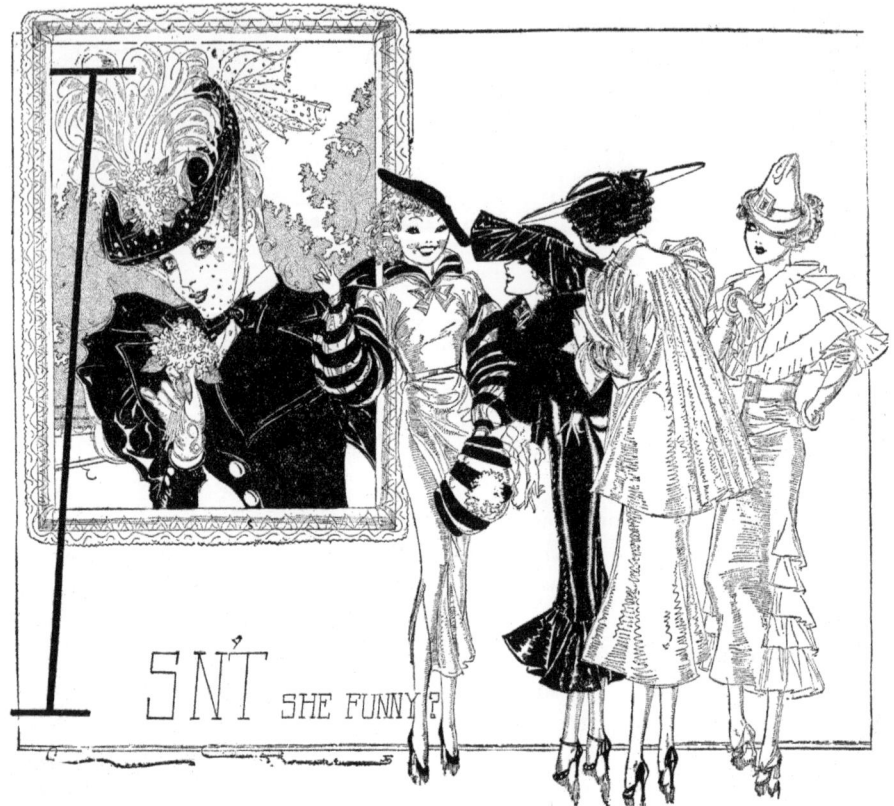

"Isn't She Funny?" 1934.

Six o'clock! And the girls who smile all day long as steadily as any chorus girl is bidden to do, who haul down enough yards of stuff in a day to tie a sash around this vain old world, who try debutante dancing frocks on fat relics who've seen 40 Summer moons or more, who get down endless "middies" for lean little girls, whose too flat pay envelope is sometimes the fortune of the family.... All these bits of womanhood who go to make up the brave army that work in shops pour out of the employee's door and out under the clamor of "six by the clock!" ... And PRETTY! Have you noticed that?... They'd have a heap of excuses not to be that, too—what with trying to stretch a bill longer and greener than it is, and standing on their two feet all day long, and smiling long and sweet at grouches.

A month later, Nell tackled the career girl, whose life may have been a little closer to her own, and whose desire to be recognized and taken seriously Nell, still teased by Tad, must have understood:

Four. The Teens

❧ Cupid in a Quandary ❧ ❧ By Nell Brinkley ❧

And Cupid knows not whether to advise his clients to take for their own the Daughter of some proud house or the Maid who waits so demurely.

"Cupid in a Quandary," 1913. The figure on th right is probably recycled from "My, How Funny She Looks!"

> Here in my inky fist I hold a letter ... from one of the valiant army of girls who do battle shoulder to shoulder with the men.... Plain and square and typed, smelling of just clean air, the very sign and symbol of the trim, black-and-white, sane and cleanly sort of brainy girl it came from. [The] girl had just covered a mile, more or less, of city streets on a stout pair of pumps.... The square white letter says—courteously and appealingly— "Make if you please once, not the splendid creature of leisure and plenty, but just the plain business girl! There are a lot of us, you know."

There were indeed a lot of women in the workforce by 1913, and Nell identified with them. She was growing up and realizing that there was something in the world besides pretty girls. But in a 1912 *Los Angeles Examiner* interview, when asked her opinion on the women's suffrage movement, it still seemed that only if they were beautiful were feminists okay with her.

> The fame of California as a suffragette state has reached Miss Brinkley's ears. She said she was just crazy to meet some of them.
> "They say some of them are very pretty out here in the West," she exclaimed.... "The same can't be said of suffragettes back east. There they

Such Is Love — 'Blue-Eyed Fay, Love Me or *I* Die' / 'Black-Eyed Fay, Love Me or *You* Die' — BY NELL BRINKLEY

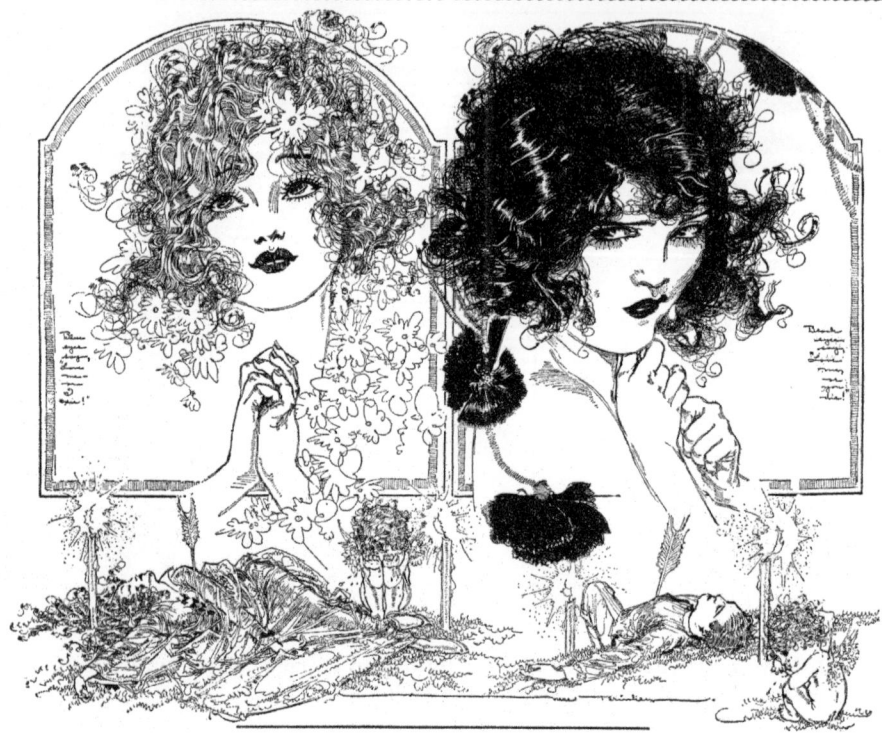

"Blue-Eyed Fay, Love Me or I Die; Black-Eyed Fay, Love Me or You Die," 1915.

are tall and some of them are frightful looking things. I can't say I like suffragettes. Suffrage is all right, but oh, the products."[4]

Still, Nell would have been the first to insist on a woman's prerogative to change her mind, and a year after her anti-suffragette statement, she did indeed change her mind. In 1914, she drew the modern working woman, "Miss 1914," sitting at a desk loaded down with books on art, architecture, law, finance and political economy. On the floor at her feet is a book on medicine. Behind her on the wall, a sign announces that she is a real estate agent. Of her, Nell writes,

The girl—THE GIRL—in this stunning age of "Hello!" clear across the continent and "How-dy-do?" across the gray waters from Germany to New Jersey coast on the wings of electricity, of "movies" and radium ... is an

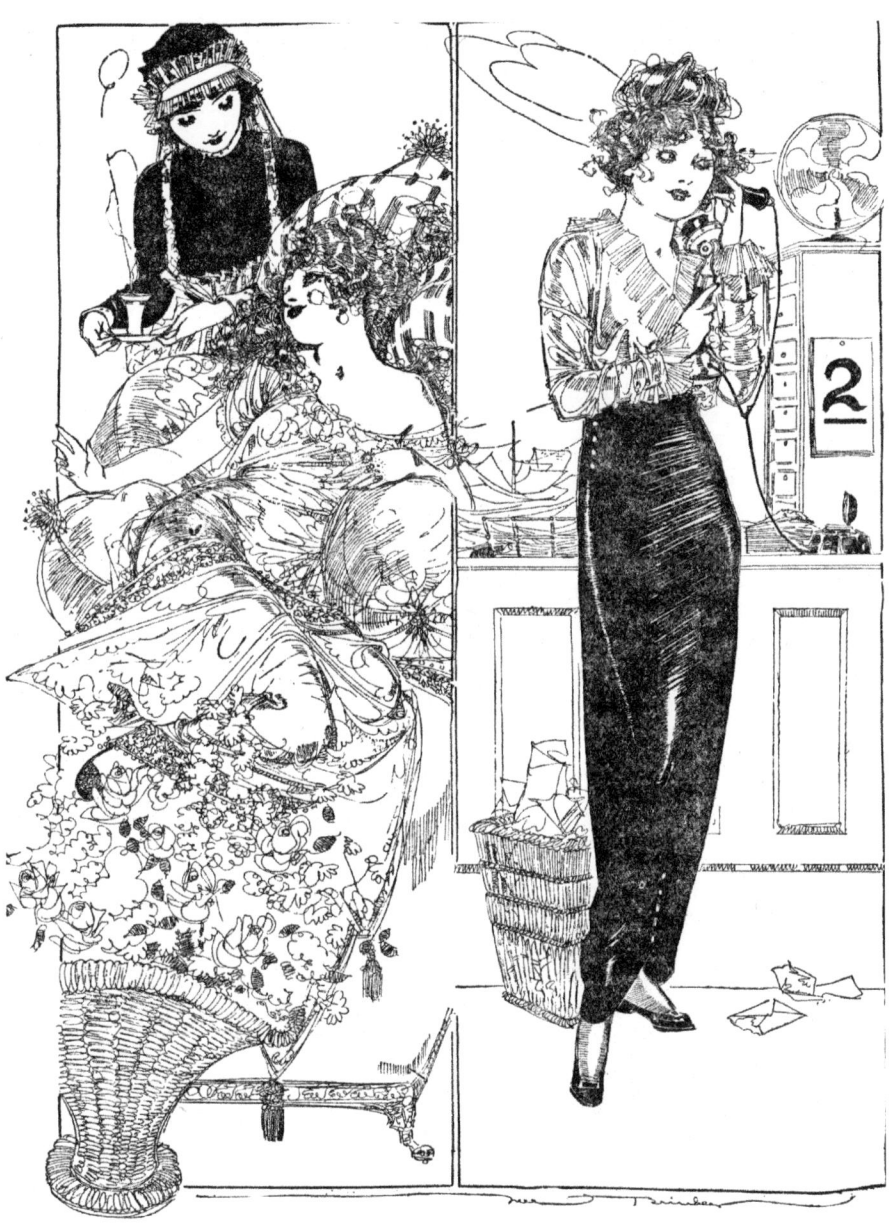

"A Business Girl," 1913.

amazing young creature, let me tell you. She's up to her neck, all under but her pretty head, in a heap of THE BUSINESS OF THE WORLD. Her pretty fingers are dabbled in everything that a man can do—and the fingers are agile and skilled, too, my friend.

"Too Busy"

By NELL BRINKLEY

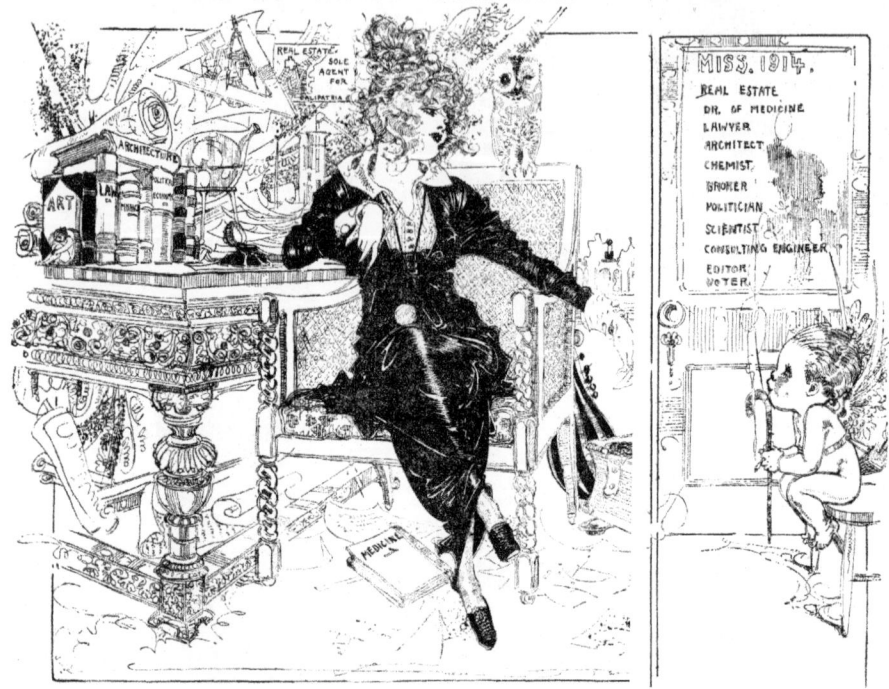

"Too Busy," 1914. Outside the door of the New Woman of 1914, Cupid awaits, smoking.

On the door to Miss 1914's office, Nell has printed a list of her vocations: "Real estate," "Dr. of Medicine," "Lawyer," "Architect," "Chemist," "Broker," "Politician," "Scientist," "Consulting Engineer," "Editor." And to the bottom of the list, she added "Voter."[5] Of course, the ever-romantic Nell drew Cupid waiting outside the door.

Nell worked from nine in the morning until sometimes after six at night,[6] yet she had to find the time to attend and review openings of plays and musicals. She drew the stars of the day, like Will Rogers, Irene and Vernon Castle, and the Dolly sisters. By the early teens she added films to her repertoire. In her 1915 advice, "Burning the Candle at Both Ends," she again talks about herself as well as the working girl. She is one of them.

> If you are one of the great swarm that fills the early morning trains on the way to the hive—if you peg away in crowded, humming offices and shops all day long—burning your candle—please believe me, for I know—

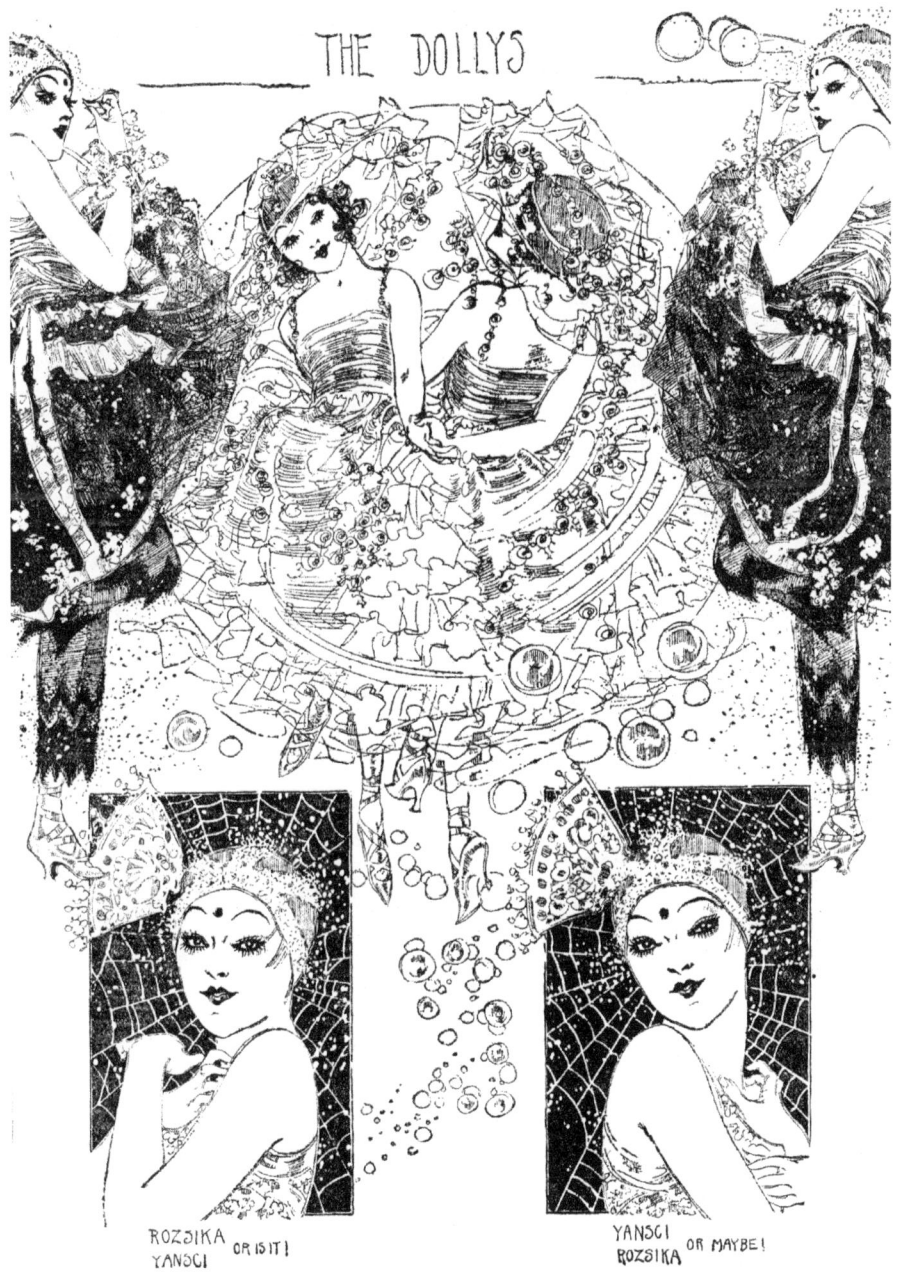

The Dolly Sisters, from the Ziegfeld Follies of 1916.

A GISH SKETCH -:-   -:-

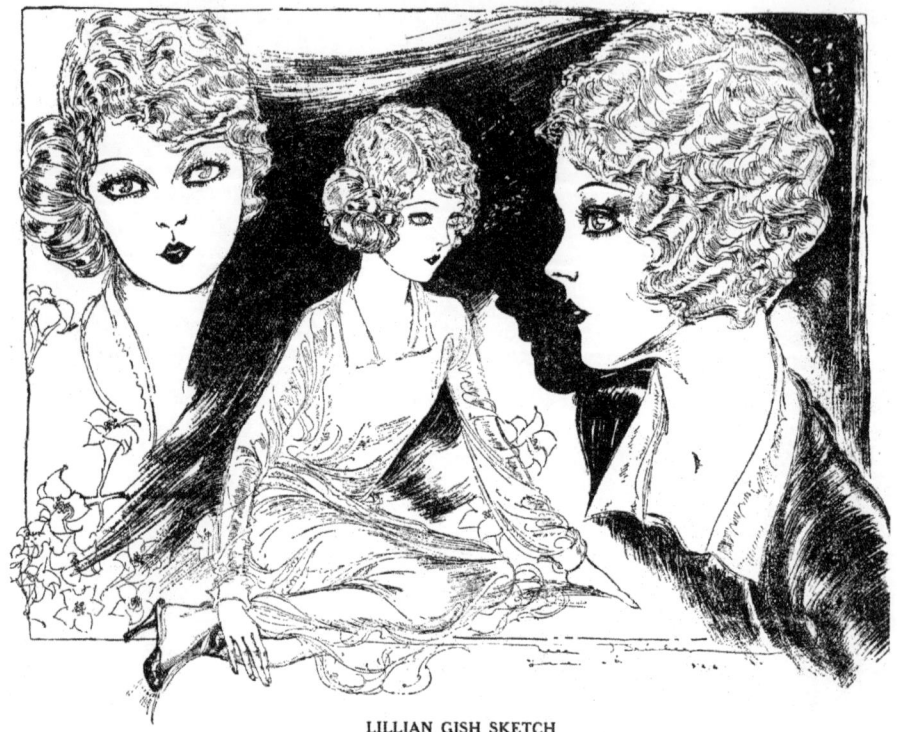

LILLIAN GISH SKETCH

Lillian Gish, 1926.

at its highest and brightest from eight in the morning until five and six at night—so your little shine may stand as high and as steady and make as big a circle of light in the working world as the other candles that burn—then leave one end in the firm socket and leave your candle dark most nights. For if you work—and aren't there a lot of us—what?—and get a step nearer the heights your eyes are on—if you even *keep* the shelf you have won—you have to burn your candle all day long. And you can't burn it at the other end, hard and bright, half the night long, without getting to the middle in a hurry—or else the working end goes out.

And in her 1916 panel, "Awfully Busy," she again relates herself to the working girl:

The little person who beats a typewriter all day long, or the pleasant, so-many-times-pretty girl who spreads everything she has from behind the counter for your pleasure, looks sadly at the unmended blouses and stockings with little ladders of dropped stitches going down them, and says, "If I wasn't so busy!"

The man who rolls your ashcans from your cellar door these cold mornings enunciates from his board-like lips, "Terrible *busy*!"

The artist who scratches away in black-and-white, and is looked upon enviously by the ashcan man, groans while he ('r *she*) "gets out" a drawing while all the rest of the world is asleep, "I can't get time to write to my own father—I'm so *busy*!"

In yet another 1915 panel, "The Tug of War," Nell draws working women, identifiable by their plainer, more serious office clothing, involved in a tug of war against rich society girls dressed in ruffles and feathered hats. The rich girls laugh—it's all a lark to them—but the working women are dead serious, even grim.

Hardworking Nell knew exactly which side her bread was buttered on: her editor and her fans wanted Betties and Billys and cherubs and romance, and she gave them what they wanted. But by the 'teens, for every twenty sentimental Brinkley girls without a care in the world, she commented on women in the workforce. For most Americans of that time, the only proper career for women was still that of wife and mother, and heaven forbid that sweet Nell should offend her audience! In "Careers," from 1916, she managed to give a flowery nod to motherhood and still express herself in her usual exuberant run-on sentences. In the center of her panel sits the traditional adored and sainted mother, a halo above her head, a babe at her breast. She is flanked on either side with women in the arts: a musician and a potter, a writer and a singer. The lowly shop-girl is not present in the picture, but Nell writes about her:

> Loyally we put the mother-career where it belongs—under a halo, in the full, fair shine of the "spotlight": but in these days you dare not sniff at any of the others that girls aspire to. Because—these are times when girls are expected to, and expect to, care for mothers and fathers growing old; when girls dream of mother having the silk dress and petticoat that are her beau ideal, and go out to earn them; when girls lift their eyes to some coveted ease for the Dad that has trudged, machine-like, back and forth on the same trail in an endless circle of seasons; when girls toss at night with the unrest of ambitions that used only to stir boys' hearts—the dream of uplifting head and shoulders above the level; when girls educate and help dress small sister and brother nestlings; when girls—more often than I like to believe—keep an open purse for the dipping hand of a broad-shouldered brother or two—a small, soft Atlas with the great lump of an idle world on her shoulders! So put a finger over your lips when next you begin to whisper disdain of any girl-career that is not the mother one.... Is she so different from you—a fellow—now that she's taken the trail 'long side of you? She has the same aspirations, the same spurs that rowel her

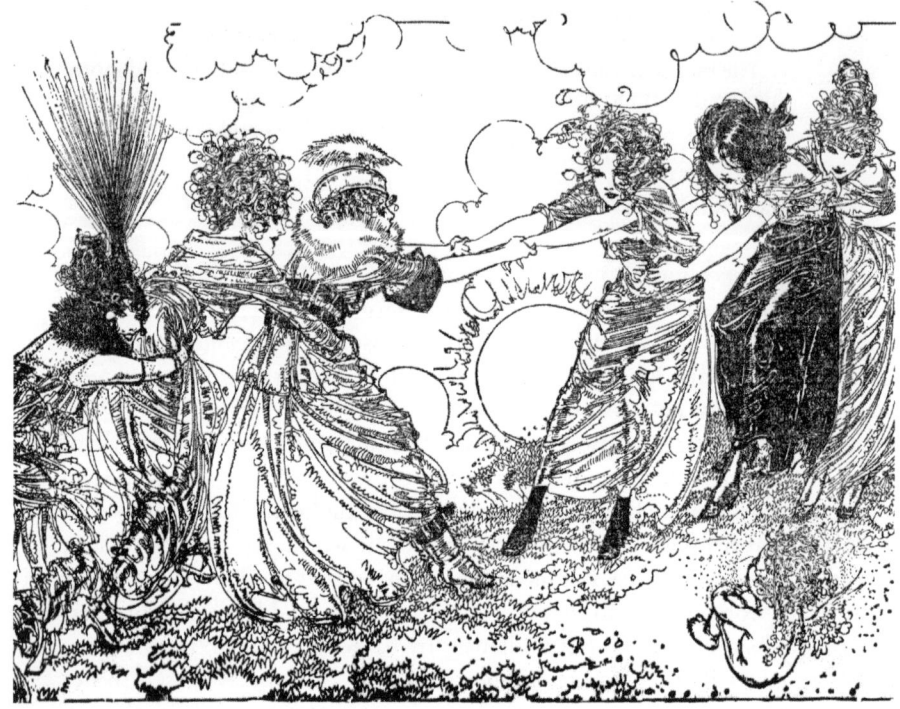

"The Tug of War," 1915.

ambition and send it up and up, the same weariness, the same rewards. And just as you do, she gets money for the talent she markets.

Notes

    1. Florida State University English professor W. T. Lhamon, Jr., writes in his book *Raising Cain: Blackface Performance from Jim Crow to Hip-Hop* that such music was "a tool of cross-race sympathy and identification."

    2. The Tuesday, August 31, headline read: "Pretty Girls? S.F. Full of Them, Says Nell Brinkley, Here."

    3. During her career, Nell churned out over 10,000 drawings.

    4. The reference to California as a "suffragette state," means that in 1912, California women already have the right to vote. Women were granted suffrage in California in 1911.

    5. Nevada granted women the right to vote in 1914. National women's suffrage, however, didn't come about until 1920.

    6. "Who's Who in New Rochelle," an interview in the New Rochelle, May 7, 1932.

CHAPTER FIVE

The Great War

> Goodbye Broadway, hello France, we're ten million strong,
> Goodbye sweethearts, wives and mothers, it won't take us long."
> —"Goodbye Broadway, Hello France," C. Francis Reisner, Benny Davis, and Billy Baskette, 1917

In 1917, America entered the war, and Nell abandoned most of her other themes in favor of a fierce patriotism. Romance was given a patriotic theme, and all the men she drew were in uniform. A drawing of a couple eloping was called "Over the Top." To illustrate "Another Air Raid," cupids in flyers' goggles descend from the sky. For "Doing Her Bit," a loving couple (he of course in uniform) cuddles on a grassy bank near a bridge. Nell writes:

> You see, "guarding a bridge" is most dull and doleful duty ... no thrill, no glory, no ardor of comradeship in battle.... So, if the last butterfly and a patriotic girl come gaily by, and tarry a tiny while to brighten the dull fabric of his "plain duty," will anyone tell his superior?

Men were encouraged to enlist. Nell makes it clear that girls said "yes" to *boys* who said "yes." "I could not love thee, dear, so much—loved I not honor more," she quotes. She portrays women flocking around the doughboy and ignoring the unhappy civilian. He skulks in a corner of the picture,

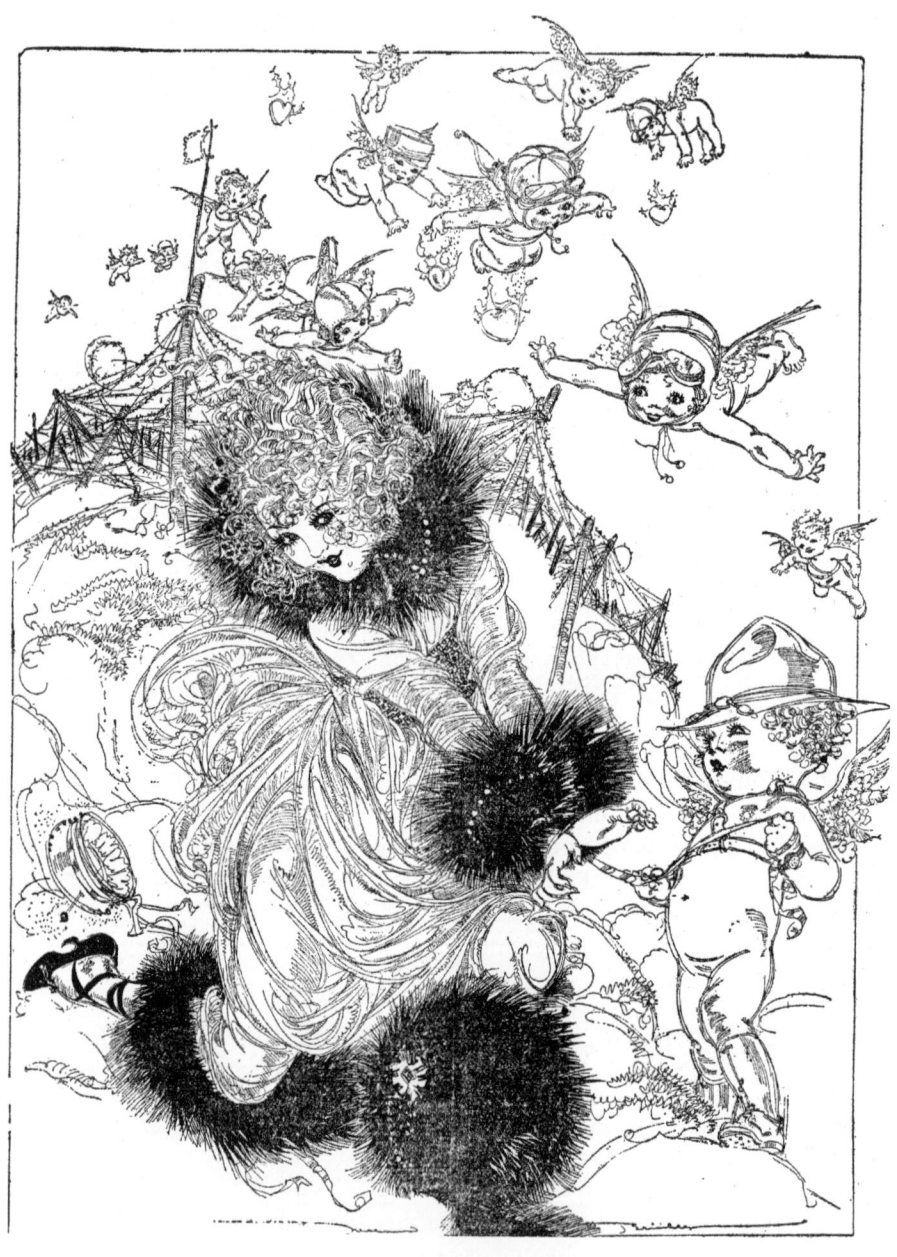

"Another Air Raid," 1917.

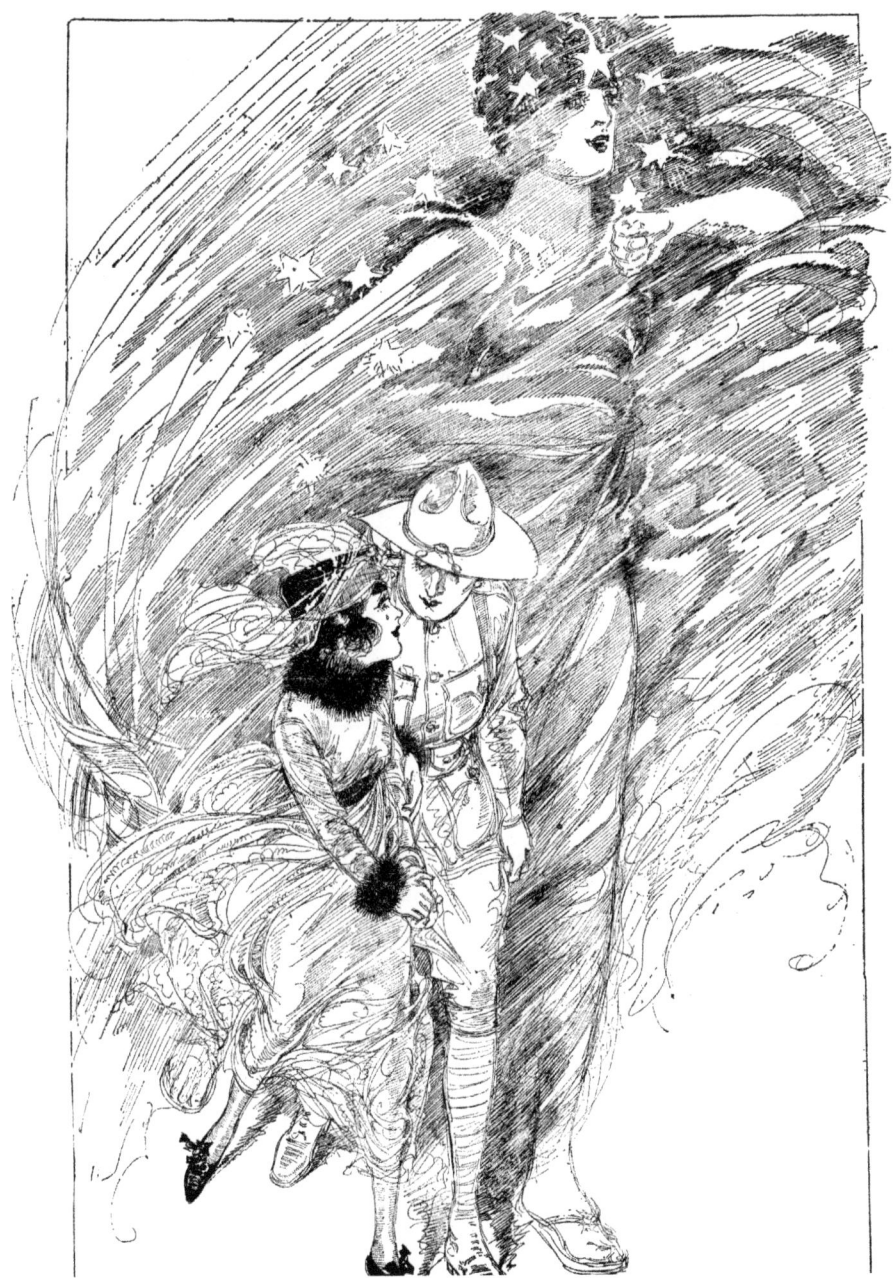

"The Silent Partner," 1917.

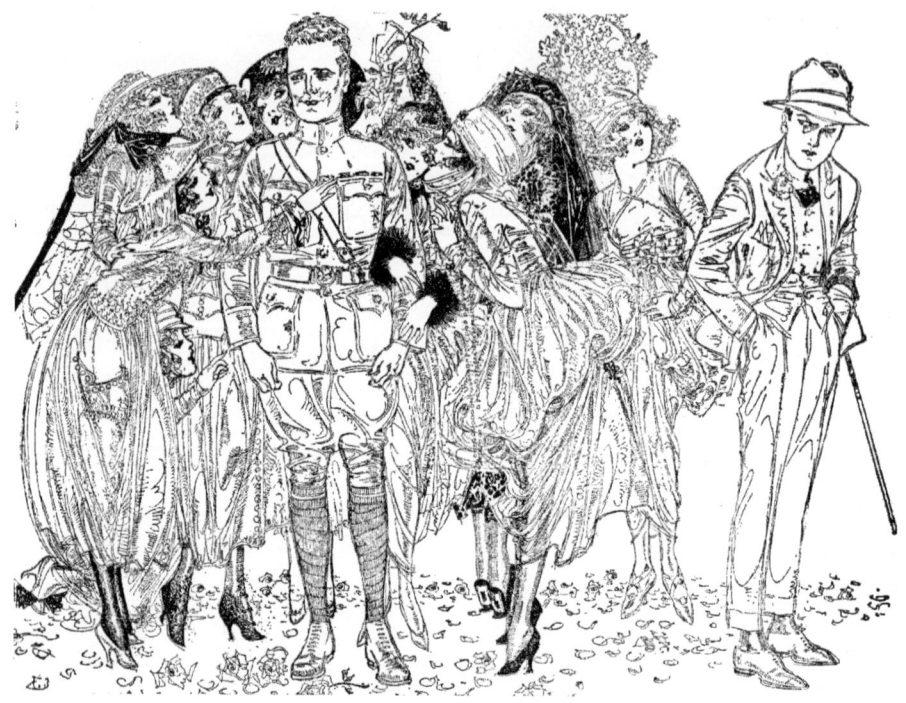

"Summer in Chicago," 1917.

glared at by one of the women from the adoring crowd, in disgrace because not in uniform. In another drawing, five men propose to a Betty, but she chooses the soldier. In "To the Navy," beautiful Brinkley girls toast a sailor: "Our shores are clear of disaster because he has gone down to sea in a ship." She titles still another drawing, "All the World Loves a Lover—But It Loves Him a Patriot More."

Nell's Betty sits on the beach, knitting socks and sweaters for her boyfriend overseas. She adds a military theme to her latest fashions. Betty's photograph, in a silver case kept close to his heart, saves Billy from a fatal wound: "'It was a near thing, old boy. This bit of leather and silver and femininity from home kept it from being your *heart*—and you've just got a bad old gouging!'" In yet another scenario, Billy brings home a French war bride.

In case Betty wasn't enough, Nell created another girl, Babette—perhaps inspired by the French war bride? One of her funnier panels from this period, "You Have a Soldier at the Front!" shows a gypsy telling Babette's fortune:

"Sister Susie"

SHE SEWETH SHIRTS FOR SOLDIERS By NELL BRINKLEY

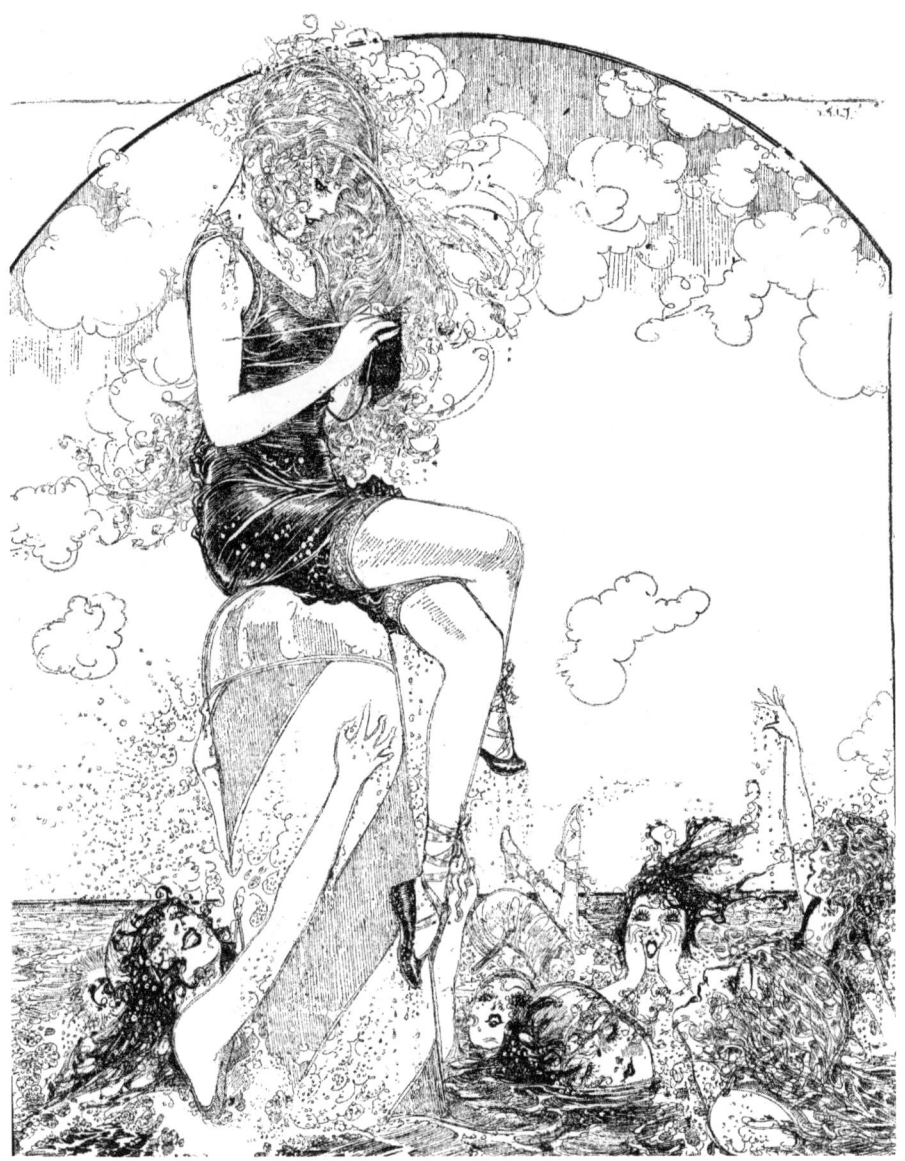

"Sister Susie," 1917.

And Babette, with ardent-telling eyes—her knitting—a knot of the precious red white and blue in her buttonhole, and a letter rustling in her bag when she stirs—with all these telltales, Babette opens eyes and mouth and says to you, says she: "You know, I don't believe such things—but really, you know, it's queer how she knew!"

To Keep a Man Safe
By NELL BRINKLEY

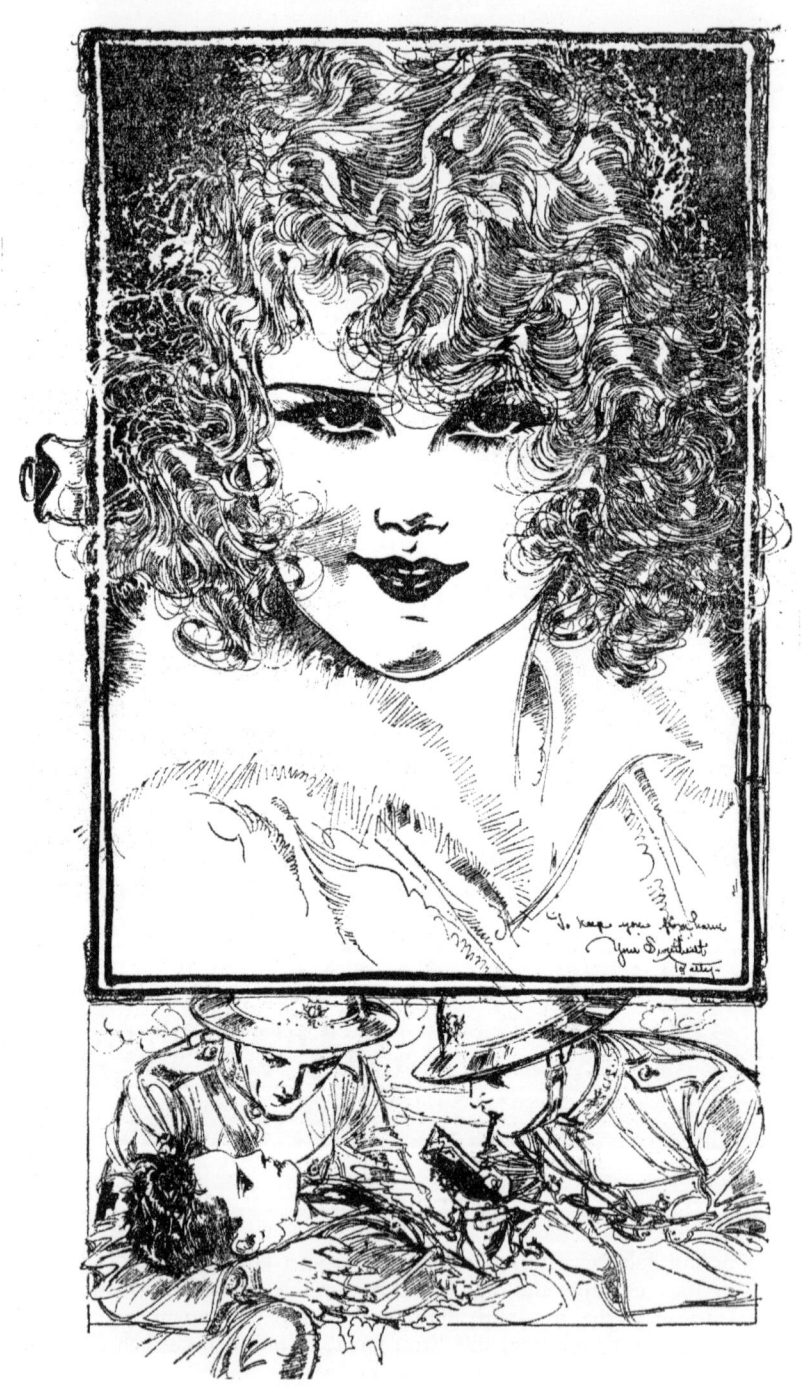

Five. The Great War

In directing her attention upon the war, Nell had not turned her back on working women. As they would again in 25 more years, young women were pouring into Washington, D.C., to take over the jobs deserted by enlistees, and Nell came up with a series called *Girls Who Work for Uncle Sam*. She makes a point of telling us that for all their important State Department jobs, these young women are just nice American girls with boyfriends "over there." When she draws Sadie May Lack, reporter in the office of the solicitor, Nell makes sure to include Sadie's sailor boyfriend, and to show her knitting. Of Marian Hoffer, she writes,

> She is a little girl, with a pair of clever hands and head that her Uncle Sam is needing so right now.... And she is a good, splendid American, for she herself is in Uncle Sam's states' relation service, Department of Agriculture, busy every day in his service, and, besides—she has a soldier boy in France!

And for Miss Mildred Morris, Department of Agriculture, Nell writes:

> Lovely Miss Mildred Morris is a Washington girl and never worked at all for anybody else until Uncle Sam began to call aloud for the help of his women folks' soft, but dexterous, hands. "But now," she volunteered, "since I know what it is to be busy all day—to be needed by so big a man as Uncle Sam—I wouldn't go back and be home all day with nothing to think about but a lunch with somebody, and a matinee...." She confessed to a soldier boy already in France—proudly—with a warm color in her cheeks.

All was not hunky-dory for the girls who worked for Uncle Sam. There was a severe housing crisis in Washington. Young single women were regarded with suspicion and landlords would not rent to them. In "Uncle Sam's Girl Shower," Nell draws bright-eyed young women floating through the air to land at Uncle Sam's feet in Washington, ready to go to work for their country. But off to the side she shows us a Betty, suitcase in hand, staring at a sign that reads, "Apartments. No Dogs Children or Girls," while another Brinkley girl curls up against a wall to sleep and a third, exhausted, leans against a lamp-post. In her coyest baby-talk style, Nell pleads for decent housing:

> What you goin' to do about them, Uncle Sam, your eager little daughters of your own true blue, of your own white honor, who are falling in on you at Washington at YOUR call, to be your clerks and help you win the war? You goin' to let them curl up on park benches with their little

Opposite: "To Keep a Man Safe," 1918.

"You Have a Soldier at the Front!" By NELL BRINKLEY

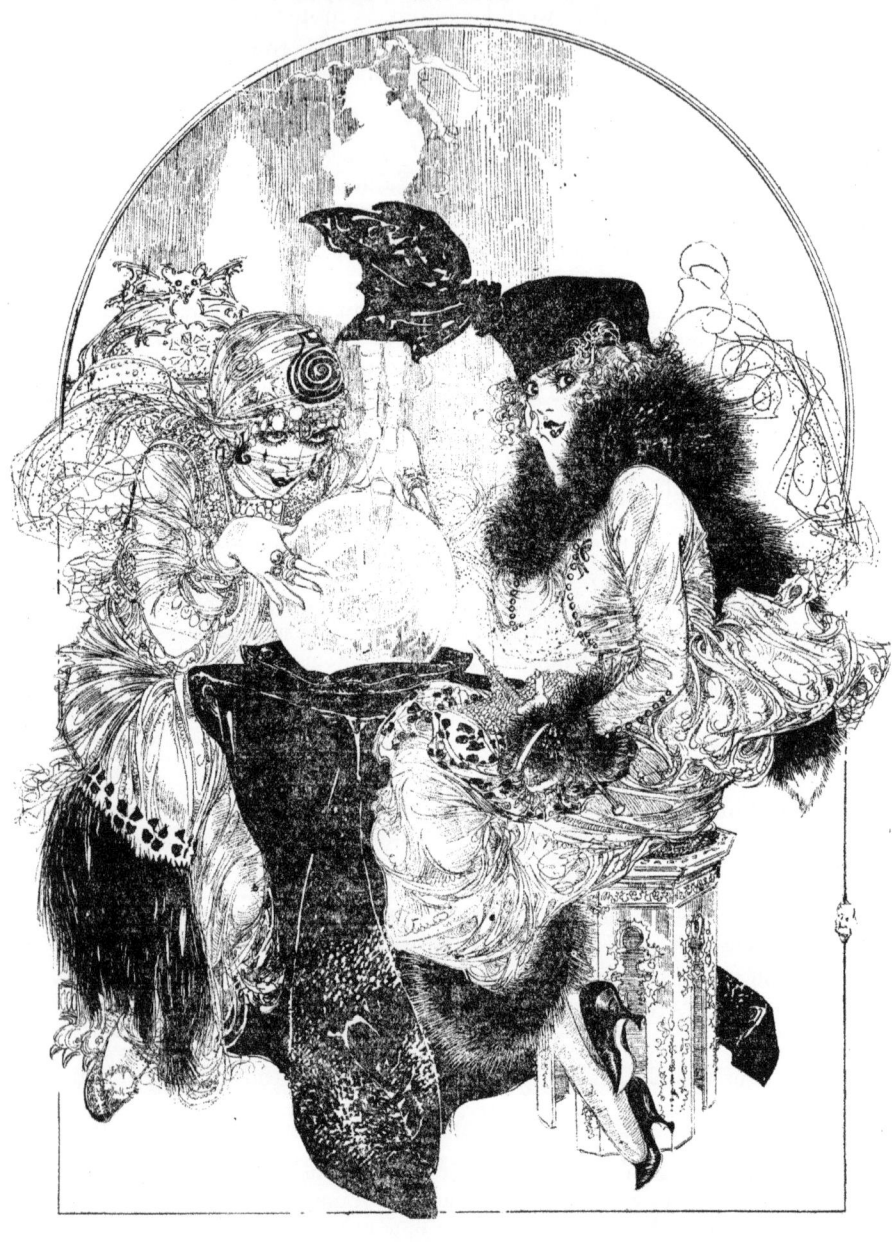

"You Have a Soldier at the Front," 1917.

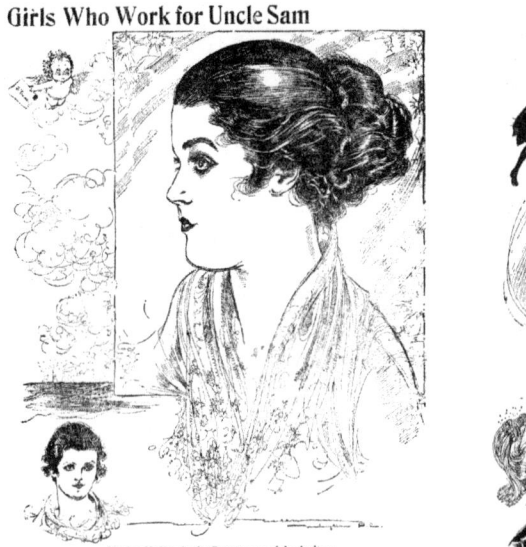
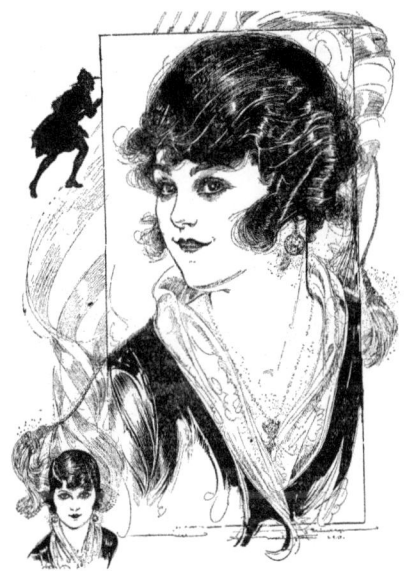

Left: *Girls Who Work for Uncle Sam*, "Marian Hoffer, Department of Agriculture," 1918. Right: *Girls Who Work for Uncle Sam*, "Miss Mildred Morris, Department of Agriculture," 1918.

> chins in their muffs to spend their first night in your great, white town? You goin' to let them lean on a lamp-post barricaded with grips and bags and knitting bags all of a cool Spring night? You don't believe one ever had to do that, do you? You goin' to let them run into the barbed wire entanglement apartment house sign that says in black-on-white, "Apartments to let. No dogs, no children, and no YOUNG LADIES?" When you goin' to put up against the lovely blue of your soft Southern air a barracks, as you do for your soldiers?

The more serious the problem, the more Nell sugar-coated her demands for justice. But she demanded justice, nevertheless. Washington's new women workers received lower salaries than the men, and no pensions at all. In "Uncle Sam's Schoolgirls," Nell even brought up the heretical possibility that not all women would marry Mister Right and live happily ever after:

> These are Uncle Sam's little schoolgirls! Did you know he had so many, many, many? Don't you think, as I think, that they deserve good pay—these little clerks, brown-eyed Southerner, and blue-eyed Westerner, and a pension, after Uncle Sam is through with them, and they with him, after good years of service, so that if the dream they all dream of—a home and a man and a child and Love dwelling with them, does not come true—his schoolgirls will be taken care of?

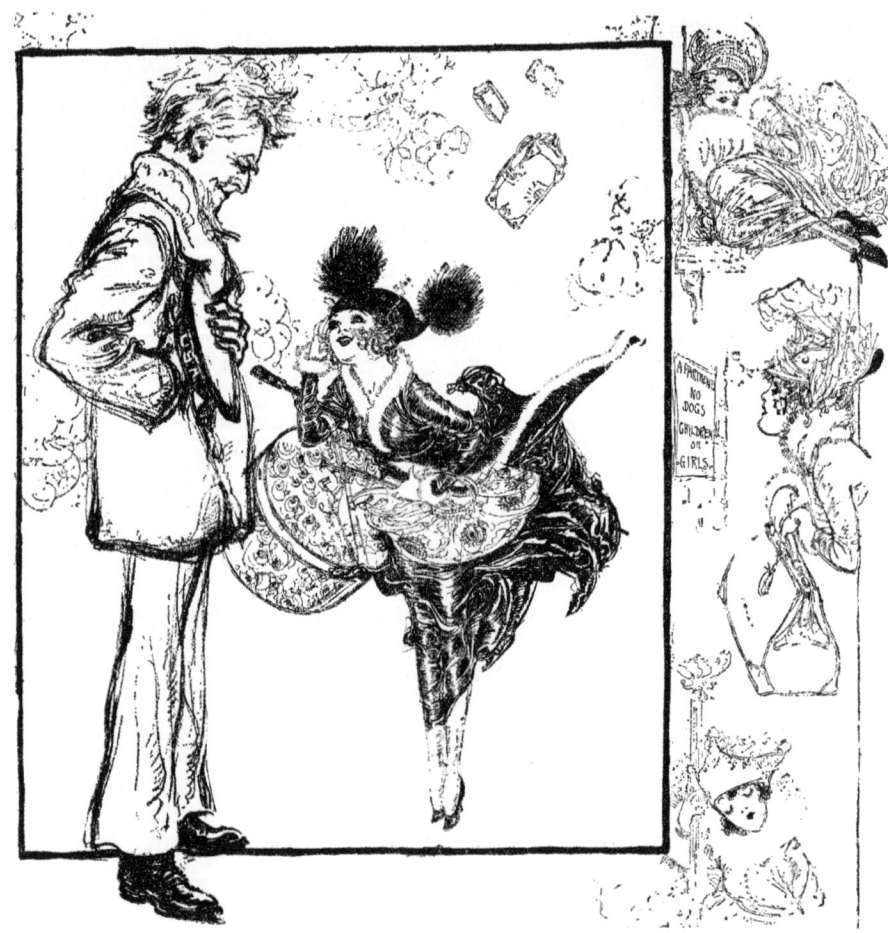

"Uncle Sam's Girl Shower," 1918.

In 1918, Nell, who thought and wrote in color, but had been printed in black and white, was finally given a regular full-color Sunday page in the newspapers. It was not her first color page; she had done a cover for the *American Sunday Monthly* magazine as early as 1913. Titled "An All-Year-Round Peach," the magazine cover had depicted a Brinkley girl as a ripe peach hanging from a tree, and featured some of Nell's most incongruous early writing:

> In Summer the peach is in myriads everywhere. They take to the shimmering surf—they climb mountains—and grow in tennis courts—and dance the tango under the moon. You will find it lovely in the fashion colonies—and just as rich of bloom and sweet in a tenement hole.

Five. The Great War

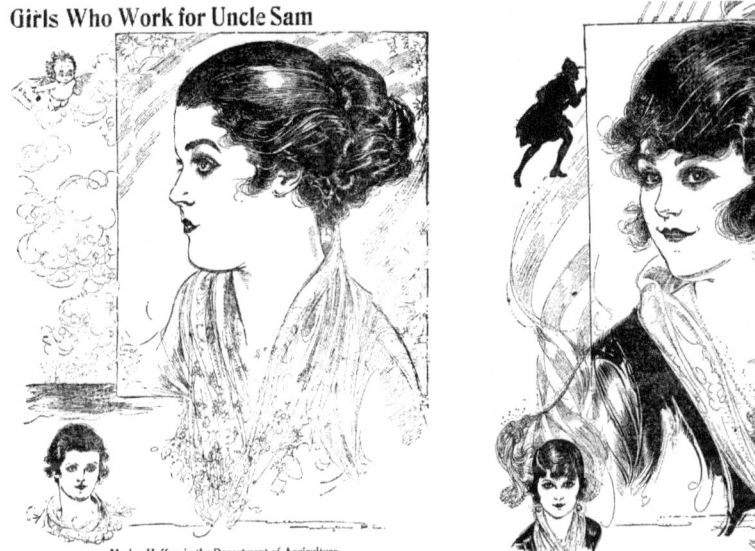

Girls Who Work for Uncle Sam

Marian Hoffar, in the Department of Agriculture

Left: *Girls Who Work for Uncle Sam*, "Marian Hoffer, Department of Agriculture," 1918. Right: *Girls Who Work for Uncle Sam*, "Miss Mildred Morris, Department of Agriculture," 1918.

> chins in their muffs to spend their first night in your great, white town? You goin' to let them lean on a lamp-post barricaded with grips and bags and knitting bags all of a cool Spring night? You don't believe one ever had to do that, do you? You goin' to let them run into the barbed wire entanglement apartment house sign that says in black-on-white, "Apartments to let. No dogs, no children, and no YOUNG LADIES?" When you goin' to put up against the lovely blue of your soft Southern air a barracks, as you do for your soldiers?

The more serious the problem, the more Nell sugar-coated her demands for justice. But she demanded justice, nevertheless. Washington's new women workers received lower salaries than the men, and no pensions at all. In "Uncle Sam's Schoolgirls," Nell even brought up the heretical possibility that not all women would marry Mister Right and live happily ever after:

> These are Uncle Sam's little schoolgirls! Did you know he had so many, many, many? Don't you think, as I think, that they deserve good pay—these little clerks, brown-eyed Southerner, and blue-eyed Westerner, and a pension, after Uncle Sam is through with them, and they with him, after good years of service, so that if the dream they all dream of—a home and a man and a child and Love dwelling with them, does not come true—his schoolgirls will be taken care of?

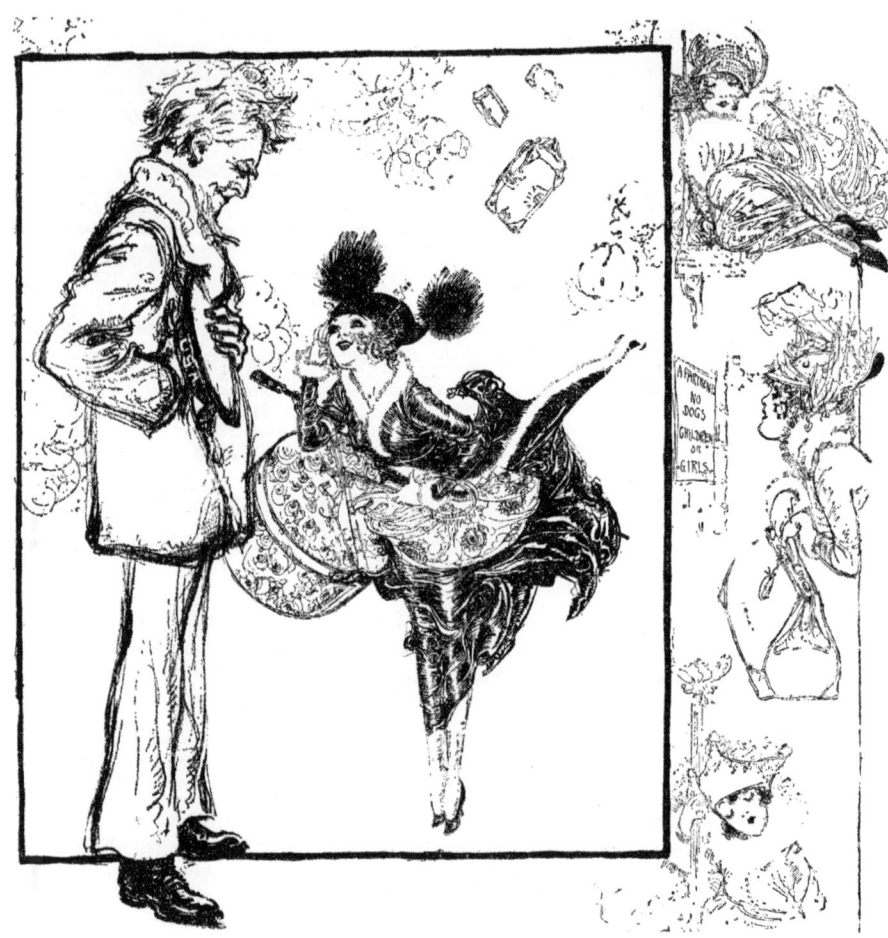

"Uncle Sam's Girl Shower," 1918.

In 1918, Nell, who thought and wrote in color, but had been printed in black and white, was finally given a regular full-color Sunday page in the newspapers. It was not her first color page; she had done a cover for the *American Sunday Monthly* magazine as early as 1913. Titled "An All-Year-Round Peach," the magazine cover had depicted a Brinkley girl as a ripe peach hanging from a tree, and featured some of Nell's most incongruous early writing:

> In Summer the peach is in myriads everywhere. They take to the shimmering surf—they climb mountains—and grow in tennis courts—and dance the tango under the moon. You will find it lovely in the fashion colonies—and just as rich of bloom and sweet in a tenement hole.

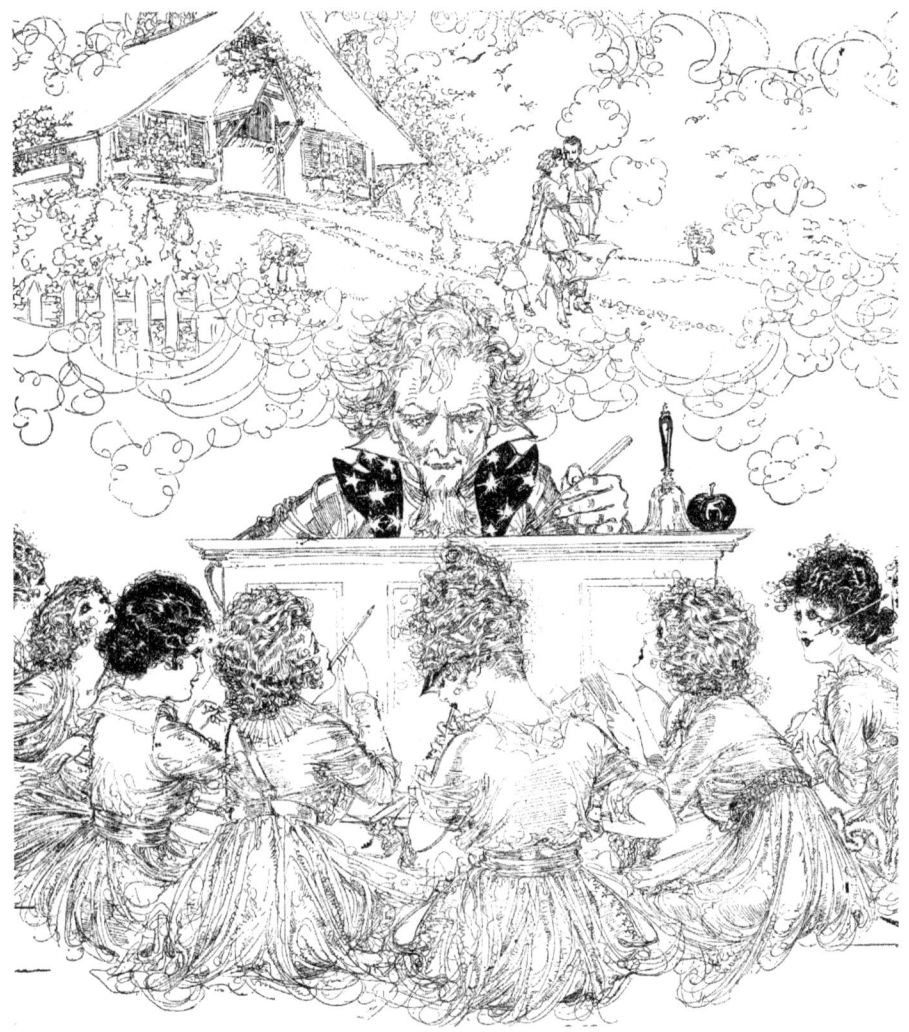

"Uncle Sam's Schoolgirls," 1918.

But this time she outdid herself, with a serial about the war in 15 weekly chapters, running from April 1918 through February 1919. *Golden-Eyes and Her Hero, Bill* reads like the then-popular Pearl White silent film serials, with adventure, romance, a plucky heroine and her even pluckier collie named Uncle Sam. The addition of color renders her full page art lusher than ever. In Chapter 1, "Golden-Eyes Asks, Have You Bought Your Liberty Bond Yet?" we meet the heroine, Golden-Eyes, and her collie. She stands, symbolically, on a pedestal, her military-style dress and cape billowing in the breeze, her golden curls escaping from beneath a military hat. One hand rests over her heart. Beside her stands the noble Uncle Sam, her handsome collie, carrying a Liberty Bond in his mouth by its red, white and blue ribbon. In the foreground a cupid, wearing a doughboy's hat, beats on a drum.

Golden-Eyes' sweetheart, Bill, sporting a jaunty mustache this time, is fighting overseas. Feeling the need to help, she sells Liberty Bonds, but this is not enough. Wanting to do even more for her country, she goes overseas herself, commencing a series of adventures. She plays Mata-Hari and vamps a German officer, stealing his secret plans. In exquisitely overwrought style, Nell describes the scene:

> Schwartzenburg's senses swam slowly to the surface and he struggled to his feet to find: an open tunic, like a wound in his heart—a triumphant girl with the coquette gone out of her eyes and ... nothing but a loathing "Yankee" looking out.... In his open breast he thrust a violent, fearful hand; and found no papers there!
>
> His reports! his orders; his superior's communiqués! the strength of his division; movements of troops and guns! Fury and fear fought together in the Hun's breast ... and before his eyes she glimmered—the *enemy woman!* A despised *American*—the "female" of the hated and dreaded Yank army, who "honored their women and did not understand that they were servants and slaves and dolls!" And she had outwitted him! The loss of his papers was a ruined career and a suicide....
>
> He dragged Golden-Eyes to the top of the trench. He would shoot her before the eyes of the American sentries of their lines three hundred yards away! Erect above the mud and turf the slim figure stood—a tiny silk flag of her own country clutched close to her heart—her game up!— but her lips smiling! She had fought hard for love and life—but honor remained—hers and her army's. So she smiled!

Golden-Eyes is rescued at the last moment by both Bill and her collie, of course, but no sooner are they reunited than the lovers part again. Bill returns to the battle and Golden-Eyes opens an abandoned chateau to one hundred little war orphans. Chapter 12 finds her in the uniform of a red-cross nurse, in No Man's Land with her faithful collie. The writing is vintage Nell:

> *Hearing voices* in a rough, lowered tongue with the hated guttural hissing, dog and girl dropped and crawled, slowly, fearfully, nearer and nearer, their two hearts thumping on the rough ground they hugged. Once Golden-Eyes' medal, worn in pride at night ... tinkled faintly on a stone, and the two fainted near dead away!
>
> Out of sight, dug in from wind and enemy, Germans were talking low of a coming big raid on the trench their own Bill held!

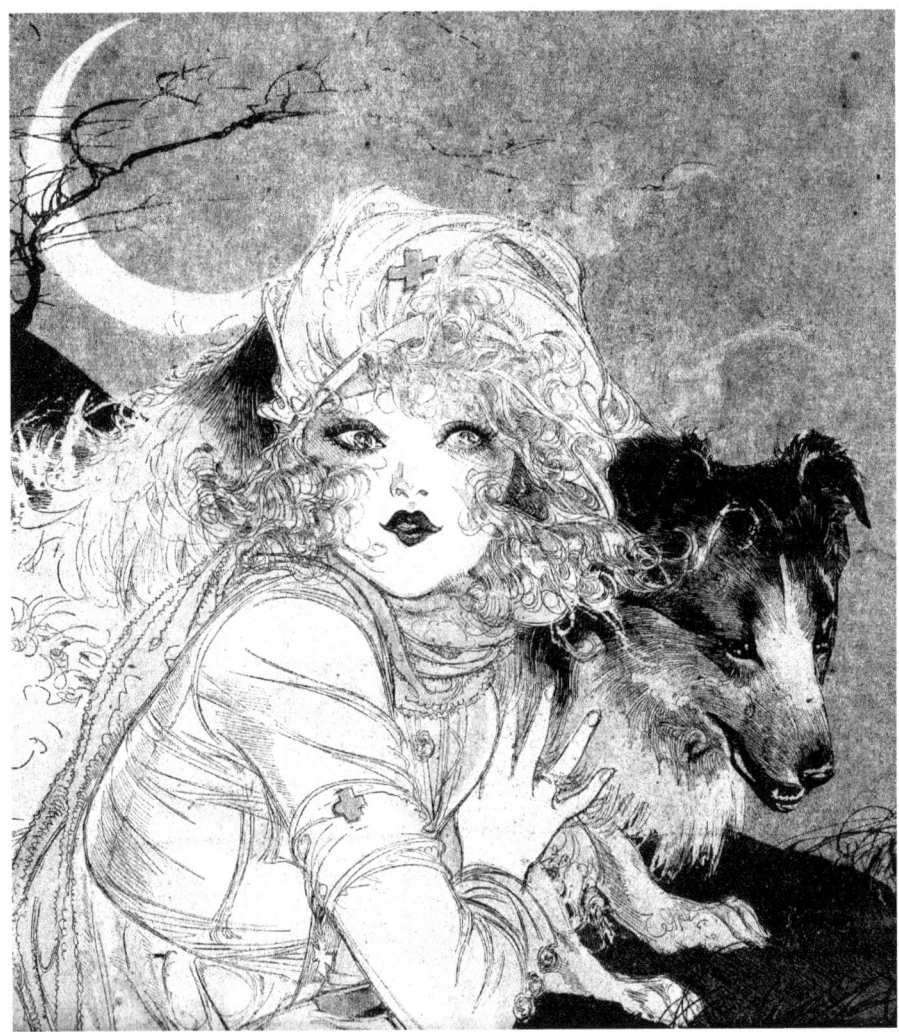

Golden-Eyes and Her Hero, Bill, "Over There," 1918. Golden-Eyes and her collie, Uncle Sam, crouch in No-Man's Land, overhearing German plans.

> Later the ghost-moon saw two wild figures ... running—running—reckless of barbed wire and holes.... "We *got* to be on time, Doll-dog!" panted Golden-Eyes, gone ungrammatical and caressing with excitement.

The next episode describes the battle: "Devils they are—our dough-boys—to that army who ravished the children—the women—the fruit trees—of God! Saints they are to little children, and the old...."

But "somebody had seen Bill fall, and hadn't seen him again after that." Golden-Eyes and the collie search for Bill, and *the dog* relates (sounding suspiciously like Nell):

> Others we found. Sometimes she sobbed cold tears into my collar and beat her little hands together.... At last ... in a smother of snow, we found him. He had bandaged his leg, dug himself in, lighted a cigarette—and fainted. Once under Golden-Eyes' face he opened his eyes, whispered, "I got mine in the leg," and was gone again. We dragged him back to safety and a first-aid *abri*—we two—leaving a red badge in the snow where we rested, like the ensign of the Red Cross.... And I had to stop sometimes and get out of the way—for Golden-Eyes dragged her mate like a cavewoman.

This was only the first of many regular Sunday color pages Nell would produce throughout the coming years, but she never surpassed the mix of astonishing feminism and patriotic fervor of *Golden-Eyes and Her Hero, Bill*.

CHAPTER SIX

The Twenties

Just hop on a train at the Grand Central Station,
Get off when they shout "New Rochelle."
—"Forty-Five Minutes from Broadway," George M. Cohan, 1906

When young Nell still lived in Colorado, she would sit in the balcony of Denver's Elitch Gardens theater to watch performances by then-famous British stage actor Bruce McRae. The two became friends, and the older actor told the young artist, "If ever you should go to New York, I want you to look up my boy and take him out golfing with you."[1] Years later, now famous herself, Nell bought a house in New Rochelle next door to the McRaes' summer home. "One day," reported the *Denver Post*, "out sailing in her own little craft, Nell went to the assistance of a youth whose boat gave signs of turning over—the youth was Bruce McRae, Jr."

Bruce Jr. possessed the classically handsome actor's looks of his father. Nell was a star, at the height of her career. The two were married on her birthday, September 6, 1920, the same day that the article appeared in the *Post*. He was 22, she was 34, and had been representing herself as two years younger since her 1907 arrival in New York. On December 15, 1923, their son, Bruce Robert McRae III, was born. Nell's panels make it clear that she had long wanted a baby. A recurring theme of hers was the rich woman who had everything except children of her own, and her envy of the poor

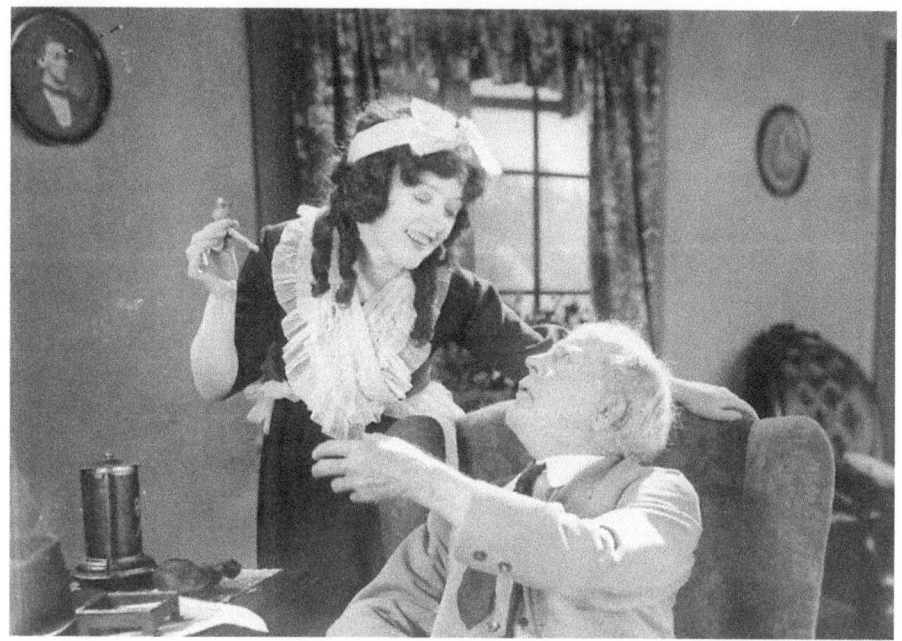

British actor Bruce MacRae on stage, circa 1920.

woman who was nevertheless rich because she had children. As early as 1910, she had drawn an elegantly dressed woman on the subway, looking enviously at the poorly dressed (but, beautiful, as drawn by Nell, of course!) immigrant mother and baby sitting opposite her. She wrote,

> On one seat a woman—rich-garmented, satin-shot, her bag of linked pearls fat with bills ... in the perfect repose of a natural born ... aristocrat. I watched her because she was so handsome.
> Into the seat opposite slipped a shabby little foreign woman with a darling fat lump of a baby.... And then I saw the coveter. The woman across slid forward on her seat, ... a mist came over her widened eyes, and ... I was permitted a sight of a divine, enthralling passion for a short ten minutes.
> And so they faced each other—the woman to whom God gave everything but the one thing she wanted, and the woman to whom He gave that thing.

A year after her son's birth, Nell was still expressing that sentiment in her art. In "Rich Girl, Poor Girl," she drew Barbara Bachelor and Betty Benedict. Betty sits, surrounded by her children, in a simple housedress, tendrils of hair artfully straying into her eyes. Betty, dressed to kill in pearls and fur, covets her humble sister:

Six. The Twenties

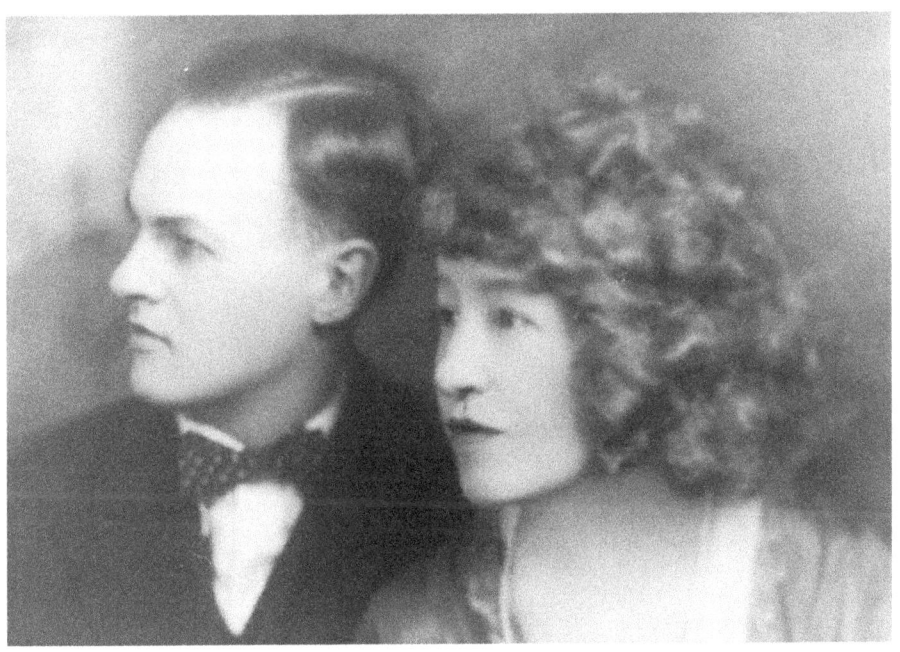

Bruce MacRae II and Nell, circa 1920.

> Barbara is Betty's older sister—older in years and worldly wisdom. Barbara is a "business lady." She lives in a very charming apartment with another handsome bacheloress.... She wears smart clothes, sees all the shows, has all her time to herself.... There are no baby finger marks, either, on her windowpane or on her heart. None, save Betty's babies.... Who's envious? Who sighs and turns in bed after a day with Betty? Who says, "She hasn't a minute to herself! ME, I'm free," and then suddenly, wildly longs for all that Betty has.... In the stillest hour and the blackest of the night she says, "I have nothing! I have missed everything, and I am poor! Betty has the world, and she's richer than Croesus!"

After Nell finally had a baby of her own, she made her new son the subject of one of her newspaper panels. This self-portrait of Nell and her baby is signed with Nell's married name, Nell Brinkley McRae. After she married, Nell sometimes added her married name to her signature, depending, it seems, on her subject. Domestic subjects such as "Rich Girl, Poor Girl" tended to be signed with her married name; the name signed to her fashion panels remained simply, Brinkley.

Newspapers across the country carried photos of mother and child. A comparison between a published photo of new mother and baby with Nell's drawing shows she based her art on the photo, and also shows how

Rich Girl, Poor Girl — NELL BRINKLEY

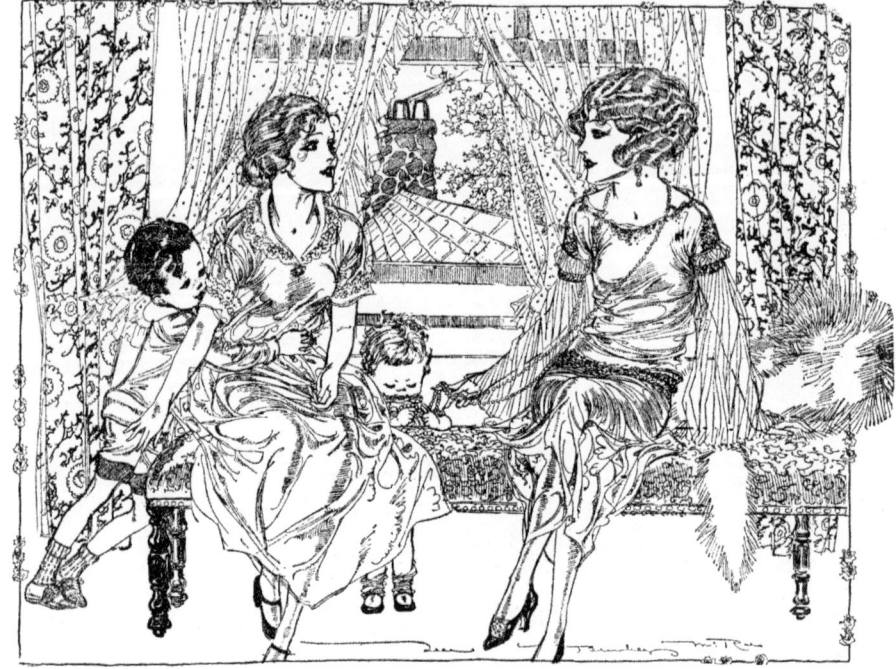

"Rich Girl, Poor Girl," 1924.

she romanticized reality: she has turned the lace collar on her dress into something far lacier and frothier and beautified herself and her son. However, Nell really *did* wear her hair that way. How she got it to stay up like that is anyone's guess; perhaps she used her own curlers.

In 1926, Nell, Bruce, little Bruce and May, who still lived with them, moved to a new home on Pryor Terrace, in the elegant Beechmont neighborhood of New Rochelle. A 1934 article in the *New Rochelle Standard Star* describes the home as filled with color and expensive antiques:

> Everywhere is the warmth of rose or red and blue and gold. In a little room on the third floor originally intended as a studio, are several antiques, pieces she sometimes uses as models.... These pieces include a spinet made in 1700. Crow-quills instead of hammers bring a sweet tone from the strings of the old instrument.... It is almost a duplicate of one now in the Victoria and Albert Museum in London.
>
> A Governor Winthrop desk is another antique which occasionally does its bit in pictures.

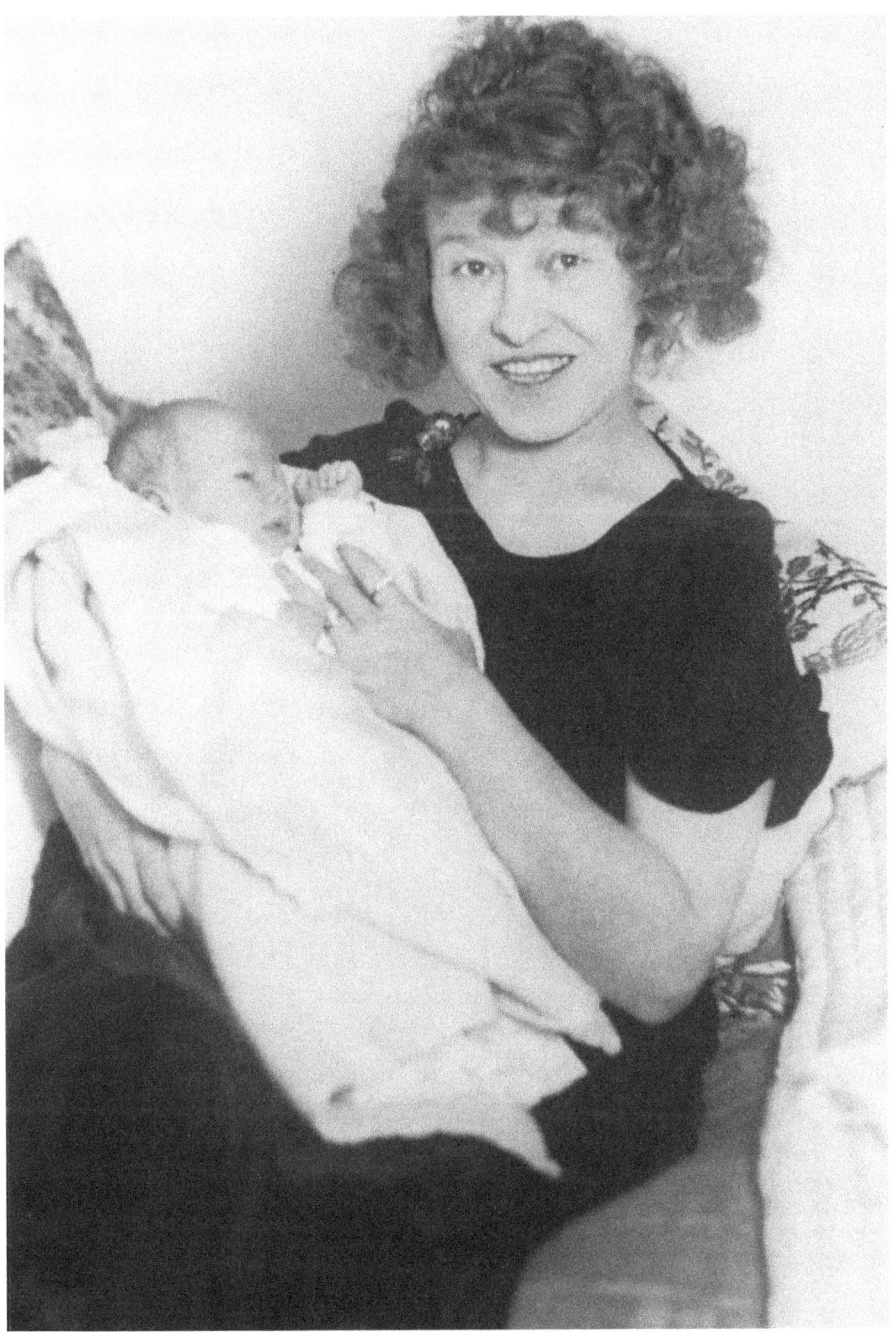

Nell and her new baby, 1923.

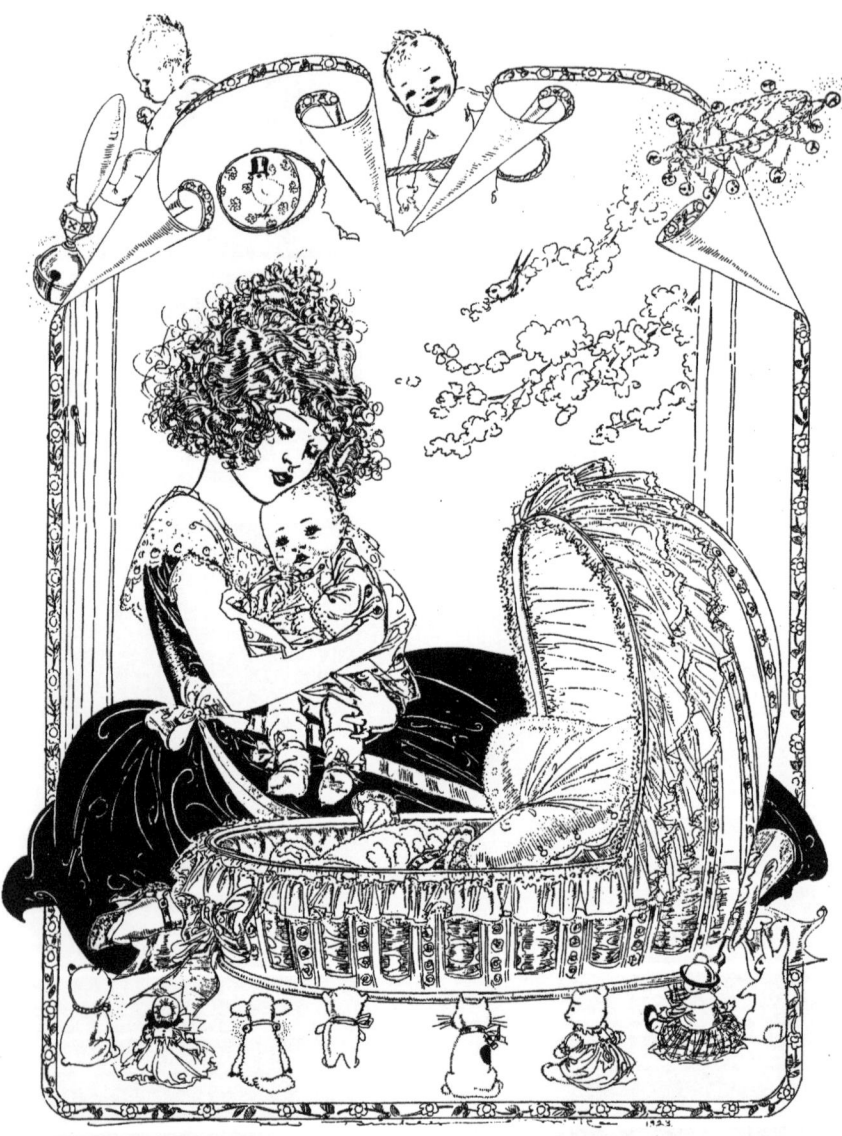

ART'S RIVAL
By NELL BRINKLEY McRAE

A WOMAN once wrote to me and told me I didn't know how to draw babies—that if my little "Loves" were meant to be like them they were all wrong. Well, she can't criticize me now; I'm sure to get them right—the wrinkles in the right place and all. However, though I once had the hardihood to write about babies, and knew nothing of them, now, when I do know about them and feel deeply about them—I am smitten dumb, with a head full of thoughts like white butterflies.

"Art's Rival," 1923.

Six. The Twenties

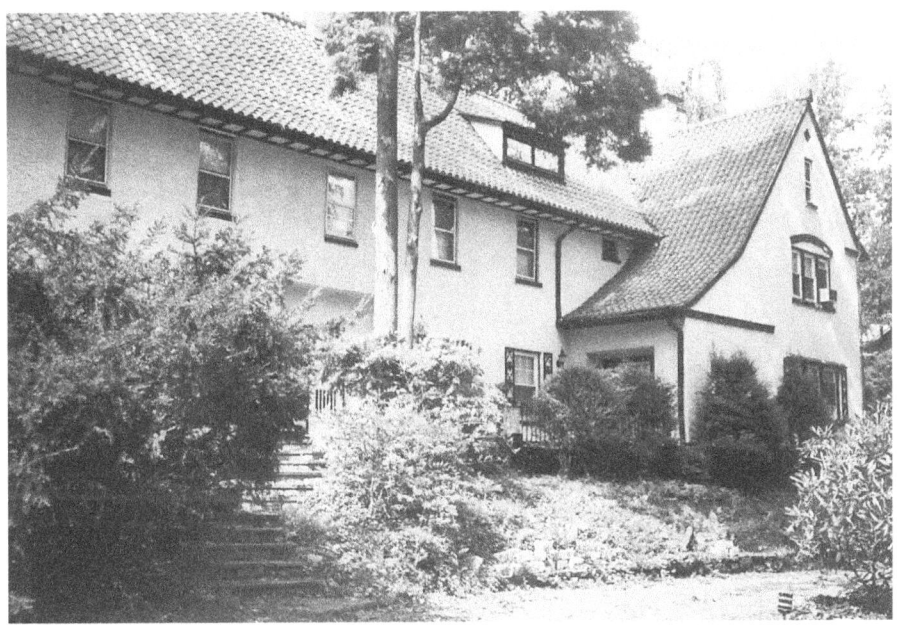

Nell's house on Pryor Terrace today.

The stately house on Pryor Terrace still stands amid landscaped surroundings in an exclusive gated community behind Iona College, looking much as it must have in 1926.

A husband and baby did nothing to slow Nell down. Her mother continued to take care of any daily home or business-related problems, freeing Nell to produce a page a day. May and Nell had devised an elaborate system whereby Nell could get her work to the New York newspaper offices without ever having to leave home. A chauffeur would drive Nell's finished page, rolled up in a cardboard tube, to the New Rochelle train station in time to meet the one o'clock train from New York. The brakeman would receive the page through the train window and carry it back with him to Grand Central Station, where a courier from the paper waited to bring the art back to the newspaper offices, in time to be published in the next day's edition.

To meet her intense schedule, Nell continued to recycle ideas and themes. Perhaps her most bizarre recycled theme was based, either consciously or subconsciously, on a painting by Pre-Raphaelite artist William Holman Hunt. *The Light of the World* shows Jesus carrying a glowing lantern, knocking on the wooden door of, presumably, the human soul. Prints of this painting were extremely popular at the end of the 19th century and

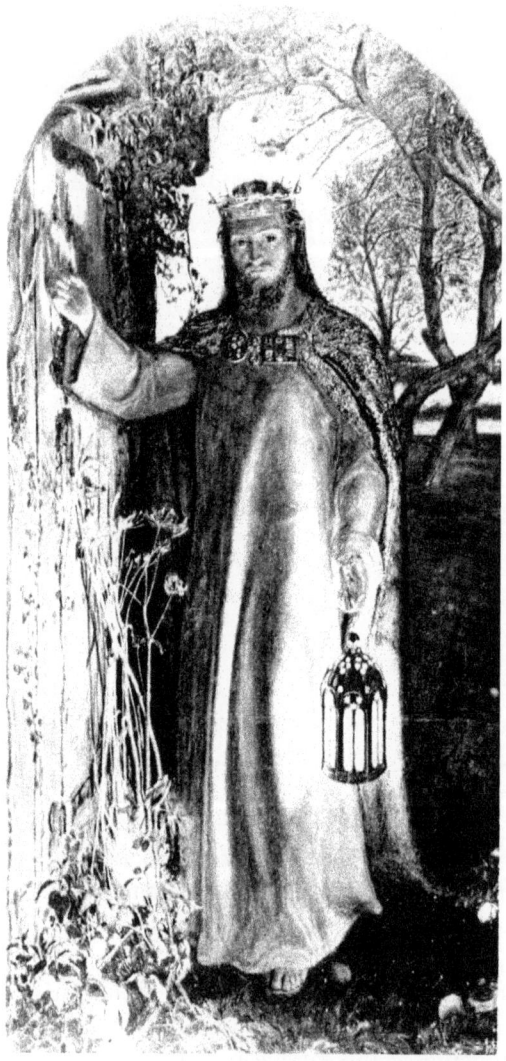

Light of the World, a painting by William Holman Hunt.

the early 20th century, and hung in most churches and schools, as well as in a great many middle-class American homes. It's very likely that Nell grew up with one of those prints. In her 1921 "Who Knocks in the Dead o' Night?" cupid knocks on the door, while standing inside is a Brinkley girl. Her pose is a mirror image of Jesus in the Hunt painting, and instead of a lantern she holds a lit candle. In "The Fraidy Cat," from 1923, cupid, copying Jesus' pose, knocks on that same wooden door. The oddly sacrilegious, and even pagan, aspect of substituting cupid for Jesus leads one to believe that Nell's parodying of the Hunt painting was probably subconscious.

Another of Nell's constant themes was women and sports. As early as the teens she had portrayed her Betties ice-skating, swimming, skiing and riding horses, but as real-life women grew more active, so did Nell's girls. Nell, who in a 1913 newspaper interview had said, "I like fluffy, trailing females,"[2] had grown proud of her boyish sisters of the 1920s. Indeed, these were good times for women: the 19th Amendment, passed in 1920, had granted women universal suffrage, the war was over, and the country was experiencing financial boom times that would last until the end of the decade. The financial boom times meant enough jobs for everyone, and no one looked askance at working women anymore. The flapper of the twenties held a good office job (although she was paid less than her

Six. The Twenties

By NELL BRINKLEY

"Who Knocks in the Dead o' Night?"

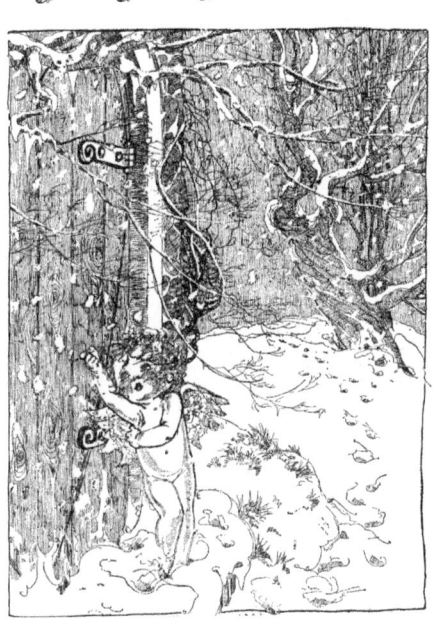

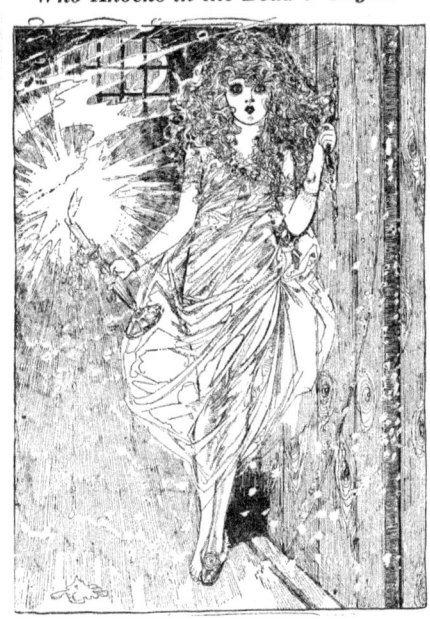

"The Fraidy Cat" -:-

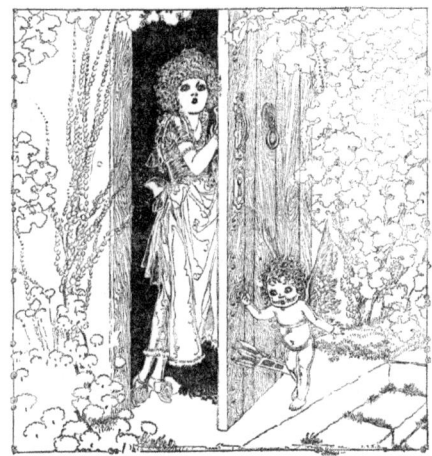

Top, left and right: "Who Knocks?" 1921. Above: "The Fraidy Cat," 1932.

male coworkers). She smoked cigarettes, drank bootleg liquor and considered herself men's equal in every way, and so did Nell, who made comparisons between the modern woman and the woman of the last century. Her 1928 panel "A Little Ghost and the Flapperettes" is a variation on her "Can Such Things Be?" theme. The shade of a mid–19th century woman watches with delight as short-skirted flappers have a snowball fight:

I wondered what it would be like to be one of those little maids of another time if she could move forward, a bright little ghost, to a modern scene, and witness the freedom of our girls and their knees!

Myself, I think she would wish to live another life—right now. The girl-girl would envy the boy-girl. And buy herself a short skirt straight off!

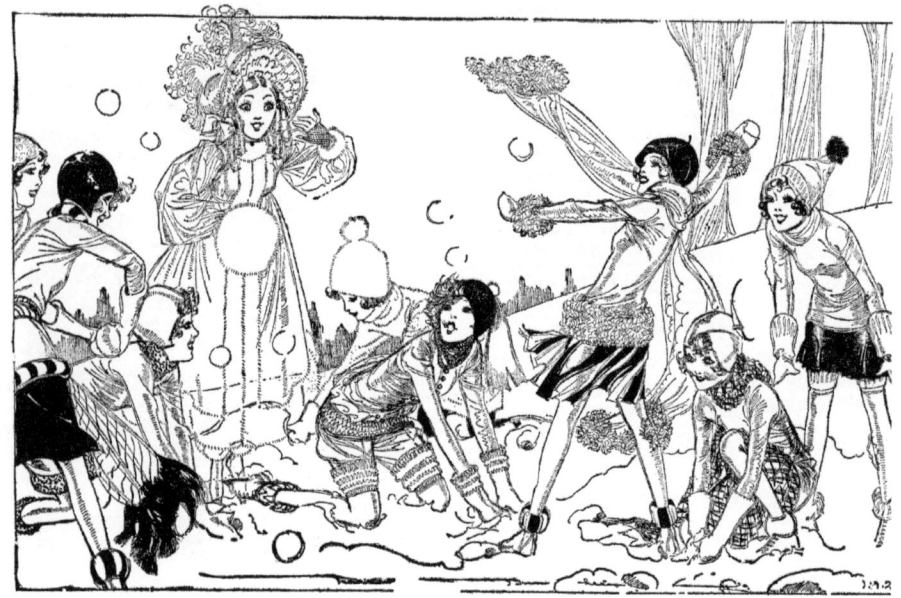

"A Little Ghost and the Flapperettes," 1928.

Eighty years before there was a Year of the Woman or a National Women's History Month, Nell was drawing panels called "The Day of the Girl." Her June 15, 1915, offering was subtitled "The Campfire Girl," and read, "She tramps the pine woods and the hill in knickerbockers and middy-shirt; her waist free of corseting and her limbs of skirts; her pack on her shoulder; and never missing man!"

In 1916, Nell drew another "Day of the Girl" panel, this time the girls were horsewomen playing hockey:

> Was a time when Miss would have held up two mitted hands had you ever told her that her little granddaughter would some day pound down the field with the best of 'em after the ball with a long croquet mallet, would stand about rosy and unconcerned in snow-white wingey breeches and tall, glittering black boots, her soft woman's hair sleeked up comfortably under a helmet, right in the daytime, with no cloak on!

In 1921, another "Day of the Girl" panel again pictured horsewomen: "This is the day of the girl, when a girl may exercise her body as the maidens of ancient Sparta did free-limbed, with mind and face open to the clean air and the sun."[3] Nell was fascinated by the "maidens of Sparta," liked to compare them to modern women, and used them as subjects for her drawings. For a 1922 panel titled "Back to the Spartans," she wrote,

Six. The Twenties

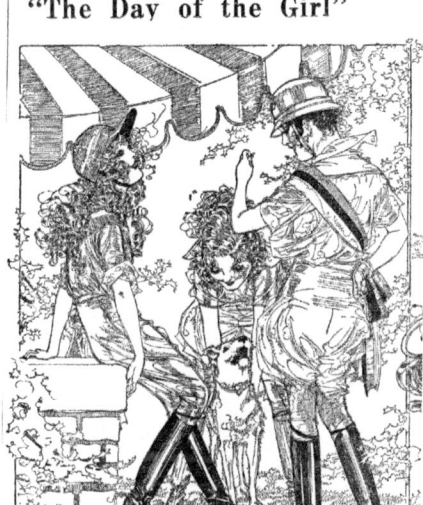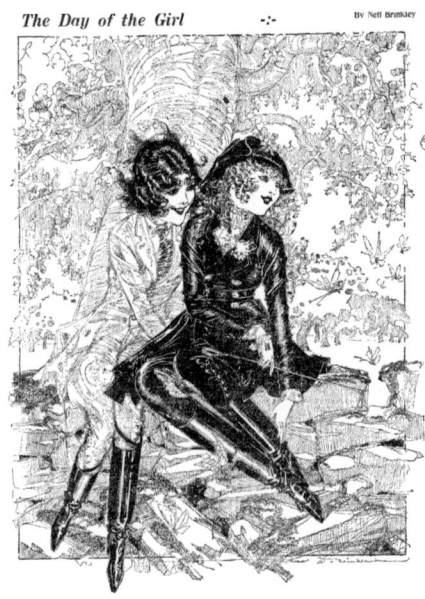

Left: "The Day of the Girl," 1916. *Right:* "The Day of the Girl," 1921.

> The girl ... who runs and vaults, swims and rides, throws the discus, plays baseball and skates, from the top of her head to her flat-heeled sandals, even the cut of her bathing costume with its narrow shoulder straps, its loose waist, its brief little skirt, its long legs, all freedom and boyishness—she is a throwback to her ancient little athletic ancestor—the Spartan—who raced with her brother and thought it no harm to show a bare knee and arm to the wide world the same as he did. She beat him if she could. And he didn't care. She does now, too—and he still does not care!

Sometimes, rather than generic "maidens," Nell compared one specific Greek woman to the flapper. In her 1913 panel, "Diana on Peachtree," she drew the goddess descending from a limousine and reached the conclusion that, despite the efforts of contemporary clothing reformers like dancer Isadora Duncan, who affected filmy togas in her daily dress, ancient Greek styles were not right for modern times:

> Something awfully wrong. If the enthusiastic persons who long for the day when the beautiful and comfy dress of the ancient Greeks will be worn at luncheon—on the street—ever bring their dear hope true—the limousine will have to be banished and made over. Somehow sandals and pink toes climbing out on a rubber running board hurts!

However, in her 1928 panel, "Old-Fashioned Helen of Troy—Not for Long!" Nell sang a different tune. She drew Helen in the same pose as her

Back to the Spartans

DRAWN BY
NELL BRINKLEY

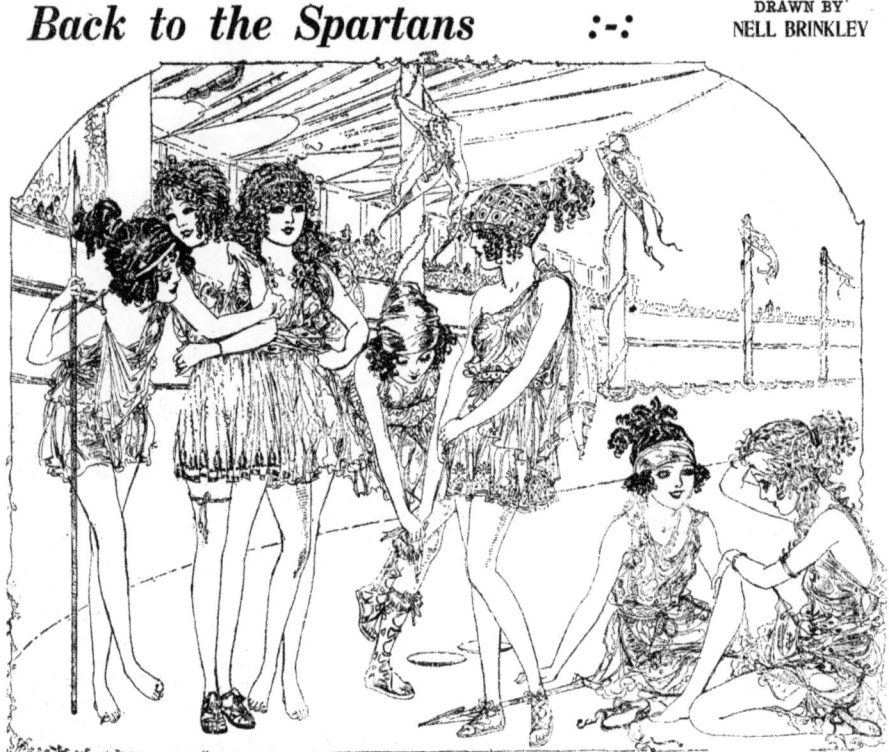

"Back to the Spartans," 1922.

1913 art, descending from a taxi, but this time her Greek heroine gets a haircut and buys a new hat, but, writes Nell, "She would never have had to change her Greek nymph's dress! It was just right."

Nell had come a long way since her 1912 comment that "[suffragettes] are tall and some of them are frightful looking things. I can't say I like suffragettes. Suffrage is all right, but oh, the products!" In a 1920 panel titled "Clothes Don't Always Make the Woman," she depicted two women on a subway train, a confused cupid sitting between them. One is a "fluffy, trailing female," encased in a fluff-trimmed dress, and with a matching fluffy dog by her side, her hat topped with a giant bow. She reads *Essays in Political Economy*, described by Nell as "a thin volume of high-brow dope." The other woman is Nell's 1912 cliché suffragette. A stern woman clad in a man-tailored suit and fedora, pince-nez perched upon her nose, she reads *Young Love, A Novel*. Nell now understands, as she writes, that "judging by appearances is all wrong when you come to what's behind the cover."

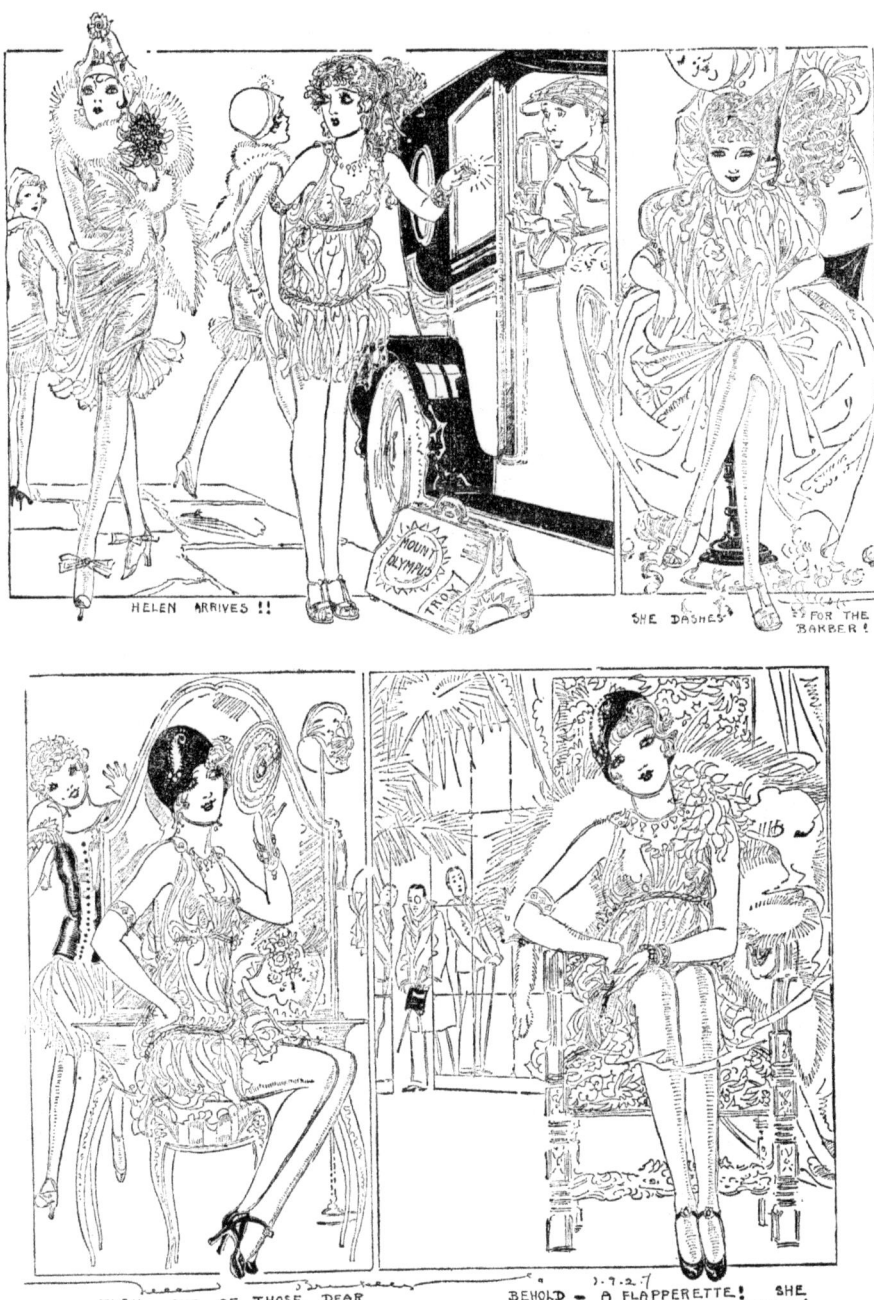

"Old Fashioned Helen of Troy—Not for Long!" 1928.

Clothes Don't Always Make the Woman

By NELL BRINKLEY

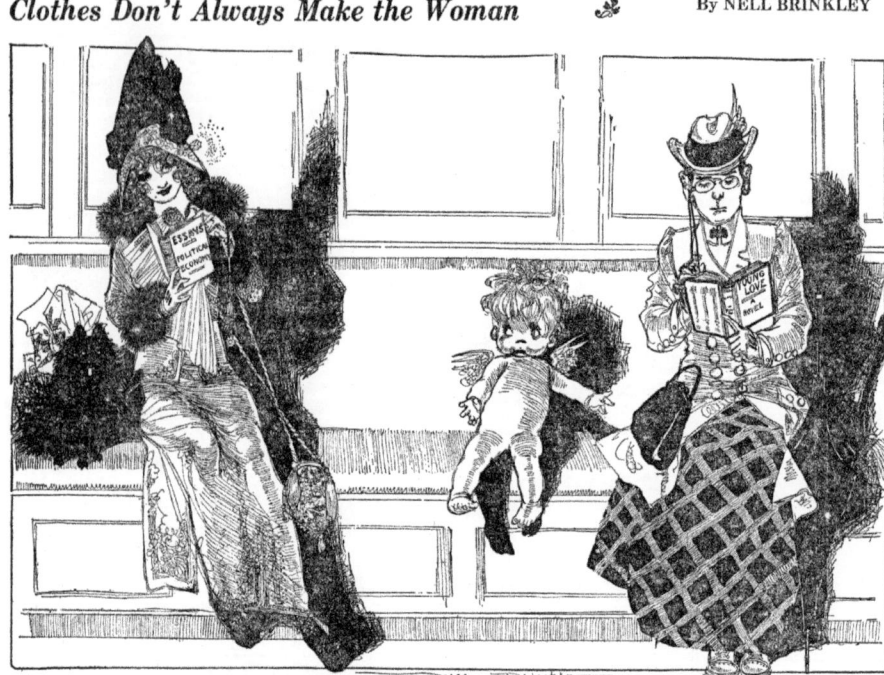

"Clothes Don't Always Make the Woman," 1920.

Nell could also be contradictory and just plain ornery. She was such a celebrity that wherever she went, local newspapers interviewed her, usually asking her opinions on women, romance, and fashion. One gets the impression that, tired of always being asked the same questions, she sometimes answered off the top of her head, not necessarily meaning whatever it was she said. Thus the 1913 interview, done during a period when Nell's work was at its frilliest, was headlined, "Nell Brinkley Scorns Dictates of Fashion: Too Many Frills: Lack of Individuality," and in a 1929 interview for the *Denver Post*, Nell, who now glorified the modern woman, is quoted as saying, "In the process of winning her equality, (the modern woman) is losing something precious, her charm.... After many years of postwar disenchantment, women are at last beginning to realize that the demure femininity of their grandmothers had its solid compensations."

Now that she had a family, Nell shared her life with the reader. She had put herself into her art before—a 1918 panel, titled "Here's Nell Brinkley Drawing Beauty from Life," showed the artist surrounded by pretty girls—but her writing became more personal, and by the twenties she gave the reader a peek into the life of Nell, the artist. In a 1927 panel titled

Six. The Twenties

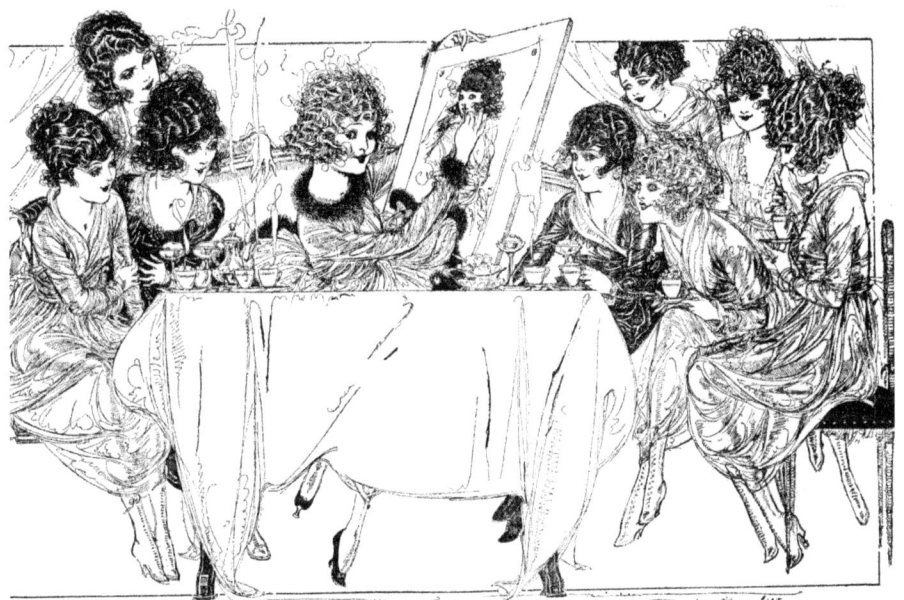

"Here's Nell Brinkley Drawing Beauty from Life," 1918.

"Fame: The Dream and Reality," Nell portrays herself hunched over the drawing board, still working well into the night. She tells the reader that "even after Fame is your partner, it isn't all indorsing [sic] checks and going to teas with other famous people.[4] It's still just plain old WORK!" And a month later, she portrayed herself showing young hopeful artists how to draw Brinkley girls. The girl described in her 1924 panel "East Is East and West Is West" as "Young Miss Colorado," is also obviously Nell herself, having her first experience with the ocean: "And when she saw the first tiny breaker—knee-high, coming foaming along, she squatted—and JUMPED it—and then ran like a jackrabbit for shore!" Years earlier, Nell had written,

> When you are a young lady who makes pretty girls, whose business it is to show you all the frills and romance and the moonshine and the happy things in the world instead of the mournful, the homely and the funny, what a great temptation it is when you make a picture of yourself. If it should be that I am homely, I wouldn't make it that way, would I? But one white truth I have given you, the bump on my nose.

Photographs from the period show that young Nell was very pretty. Nonetheless, the Nell in all of her self-portraits until the end of the twenties

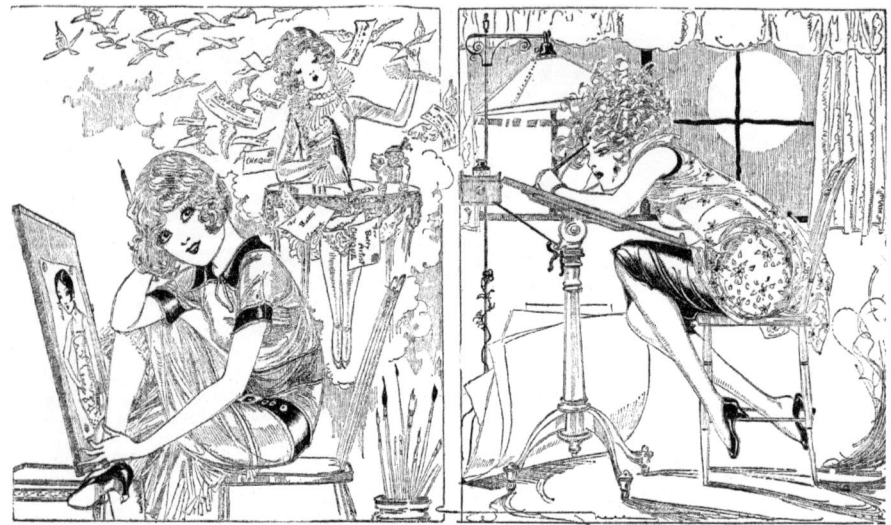

"Fame: The Dream and Reality," 1927. As Betty imagines checks floating down to her, Nell, the real artist, works well into the night to meet her deadline.

is just another pretty girl, a Brinkley girl. Thereafter, the reader can recognize the artist herself in her art. As the decade progressed, Nell's art style had changed from the delicate spiderwebbed multi-lines of the tens and teens to a newly-fashionable cleaner, more art deco style. And even though her earlier drawings had been gorgeous enough to make her world famous, there had been small problems. Her perspective had not always worked, and she sometimes had trouble mooring her characters to the ground; in certain drawings, they seemed to float in the air. But Nell's art matured during the twenties. By 1929 she was producing realistic portraits of herself, nose bump and all.

Her writing style also had matured. Although she never lost her breathless tone of girlish enthusiasm, Nell developed a whimsical sense of humor and had long since ceased writing, "Oh di mi!" In her 1929 series, *Westward Ho!*, Nell shares with the reader her first trip back to Colorado in ten years. The art in this series is a masterpiece of realism, in which not only Nell, but her husband, son and mother, are all perfect portraits.[5] None of Nell's whimsy is lost in the realism of her rendering, however. As the four of them rush to meet their train, she draws her short self, holding on to the hand of her tall husband, flying through the air.

Despite the glimpses into Nell's private life that she now allowed her audience, the majority of her daily drawings still featured the subjects her

WESTWARD—HO!

DRAWN BY
NELL BRINKLEY

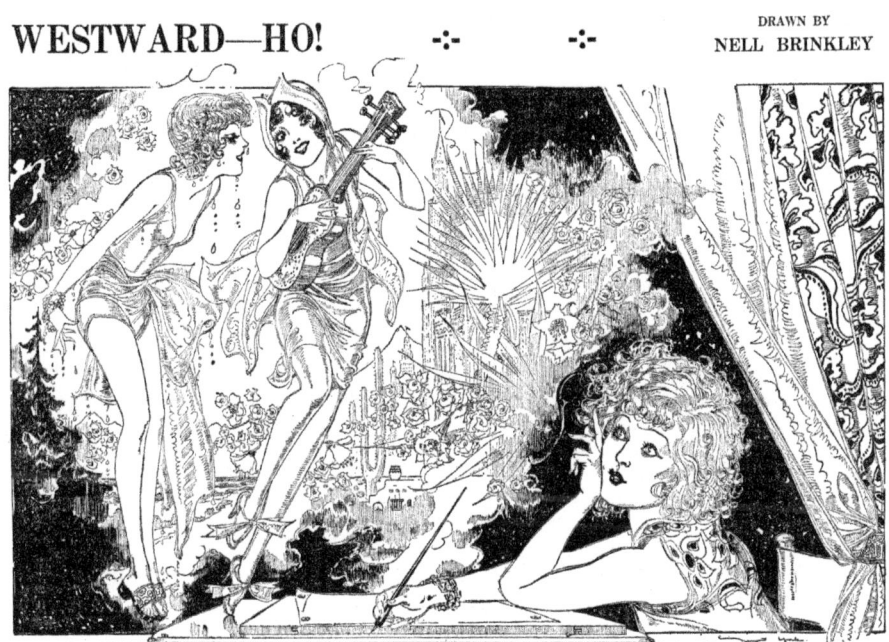

'WESTWARD HO!' 'The World for to See!' :: Drawn by Nell Brinkley

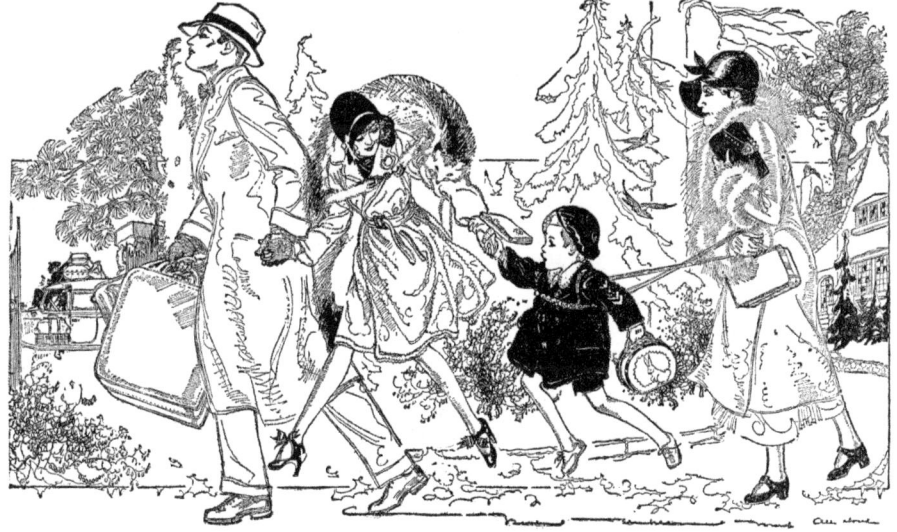

Top: *Westward Ho!* April 8, 1929. Bottom: *Westward Ho!* "The World for to See!" May 1, 1929. Along with portraits of herself and her family, Nell has drawn her house on Pryor Terrance into the picture.

public most expected from her: romance and fashion. Some of Nell's funniest work during this period dealt with fashion, and she started producing long panels in which several drawings appeared in continuity, sometimes even in frames, like comics strips. In fact, they *were* comic strips. One of the funniest, "Milady's Battle of 1925," shows a Brinkley girl going through contortions as she tries to put on the newest style, a buttonless dress that slips on over the head. "Getting in a buttonless dress is bad enough for young Bettina-Bob," comments Nell, "But did you ever try to get out of one?... It's the hook-and-ladder a lady needs!"

"The Invitation; or, A Modern Story Without Words," from 1926, is even more like a comic strip. The art consists of pictures in panels and a punch line. After six scenes of Betty getting ready for her date, it ends with Billy being told that "she can't be here because she hasn't a thing to wear!" Nell, who had once refused to draw comics, threatening to go back to her "good daddy in Denver," was drawing comics.

She was also producing exquisite full-color full-page art for the newspapers' Sunday color sections. *Golden-Eyes and Her Hero, Bill* had only been the beginning. She followed her war saga with *Kathleen and the Great Secret*, which ran for 18 episodes, from November 7, 1920, until March 13, 1921. *Kathleen*, another adventure in the tradition of the Pearl White serials, outdid the film serials in sensational thrills, chills, daredevil stunts and overwriting. Kathleen—"An American girl, of course!" writes Nell—has a fiancé, Jim, who appears to have discovered atomic power, or something very like it:

> Jim had reached with his dreaming into the mysteries that young scientists, equipped with a grounding of solid lore and the daring of visions, are plunged into. He had "tamed a star"; harnessed the Titan that blows the wind, rides a million worlds, walks the Milky Way, revolves the world on its axis, glares livid in the black storm-cloud; discovered a "star-dust" that would enable the world to do without coal. Jim had roped energy himself.

But Kathleen's cigar-smoking, tycoon stepfather wants the formula for his "Power Trust." He offers the younger man a fortune for the formula, more than enough to "buy a bungalow for Kathleen," but the idealistic Jim refuses. Kathleen's step-father locks her in her room, but she escapes "down a slender rope of knotted linen," drives to Jim's laboratory and discovers that he's been kidnapped. Still in the lab is "the woman," a red-haired vamp who may or may not be the brains behind the plot, with the secret formula clutched in her hands. A catfight follows, and "at last Kathleen's trembling fingers clutched the paper they sought, and she stood a victor, her opponent lying bruised and breathless at her feet."

Six. The Twenties

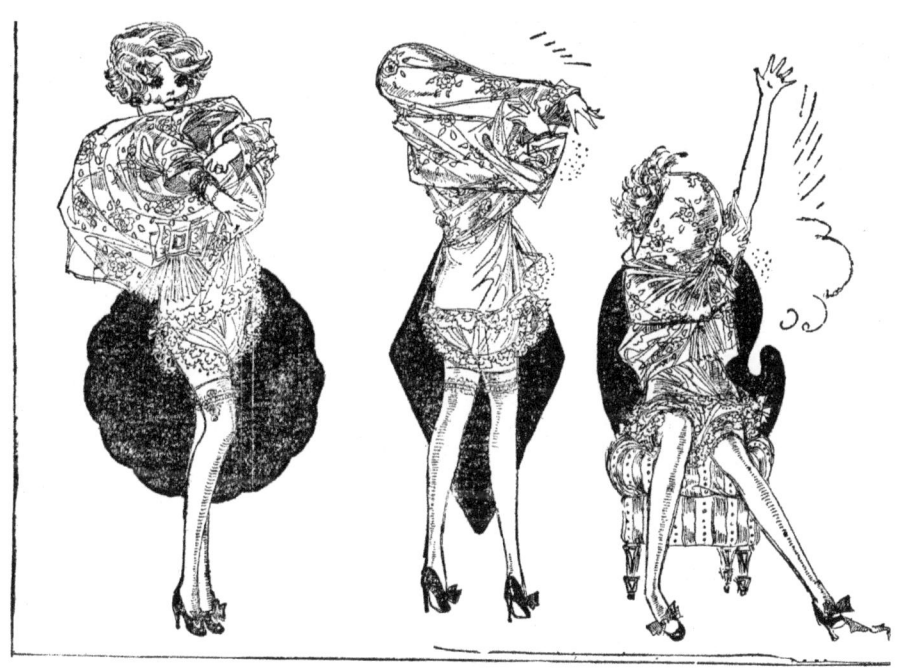

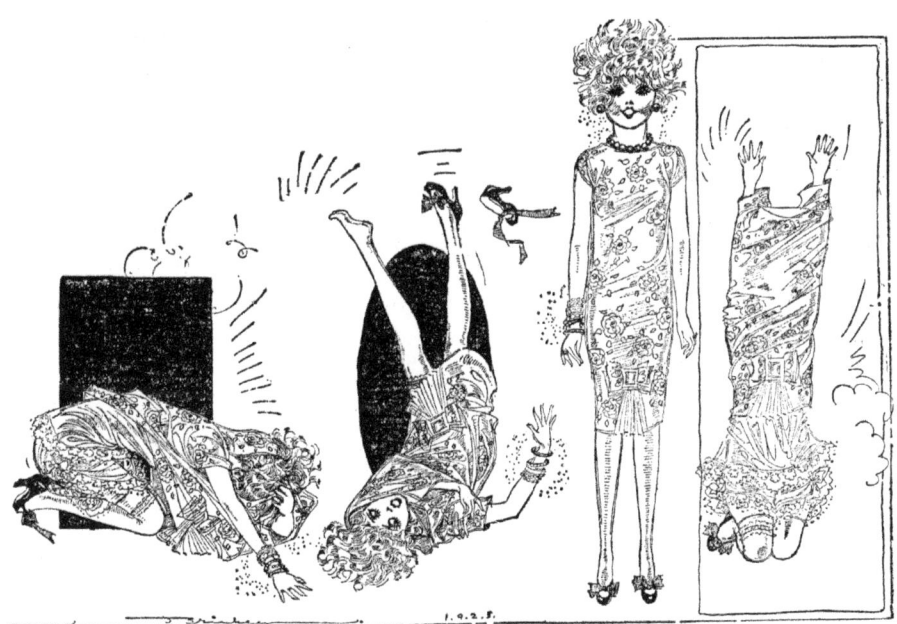

"Milady's Battle of 1925."

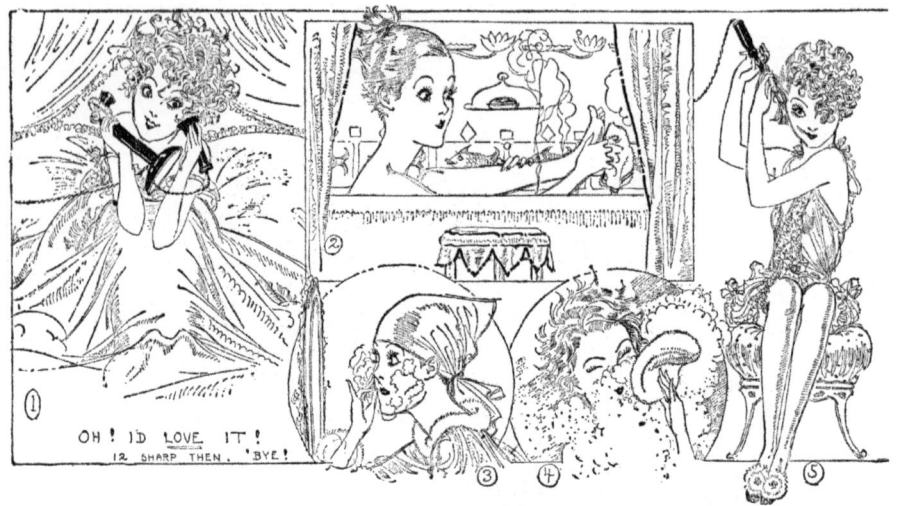

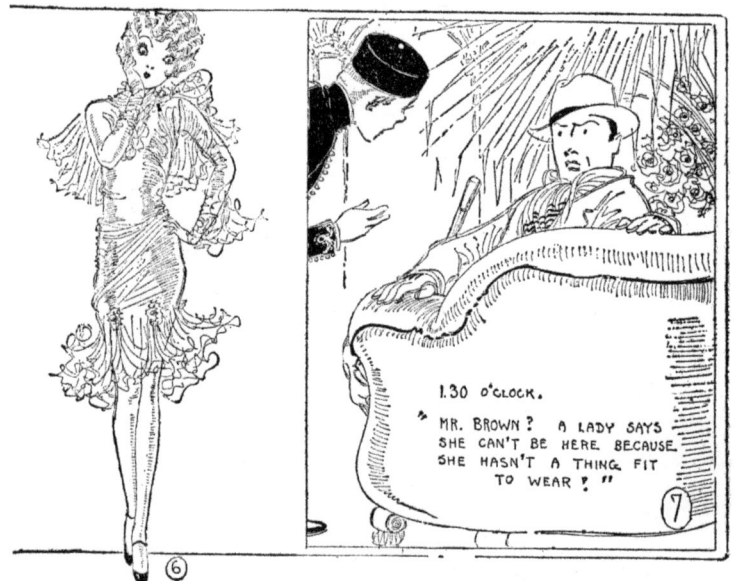

"The Invitation; or, A Modern Story Without Words," 1926.

But where is Jim? He's been taken prisoner on an ocean liner bound for the South Seas, presumably to get him out of the way.[6]

A wild, daring leap and Kathleen is out of her tiny boat and clinging for dear life to the rope ladder that swings perilously against the ship's wet side. Up and up, unheeding the terror of the black waters below, until at last her trembling feet feel the dock's firmness, and she and the secret are safe in Jim's enfolding arms.

As the ship nears Hawaii, the lovers slip overboard and swim to safety. Kathleen, her clothes "lashed to tatters by the surf," begs "a costume of a dusky native maiden...." This turns out to be a grass hula skirt and a neck full of leis. Nell's knowledge of Hawaii was pretty much on par with that of the average mainland American.

The odyssey continues: Kathleen and Jim are kidnapped by Chinese pirates, who think she is "a pretty native." They wind up in Mongolia, where a merchant chief plots to sell them into slavery. Before he can carry out his fiendish scheme, their caravan falls victim to a sandstorm in the Gobi Desert. Kathleen and Jim are rescued by soldiers from "an advanced British post set in a rocky pass on the arid borders of North India and Afghanistan." The British major confiscates the precious formula, Jim steals it back, and the couple hijack a plane and fly to safety—until the plane runs out of fuel and crashes in an oasis, where they are rescued by a tribe of Arabs whose sheik wants Kathleen for his wife. Their fortunes take them from there to Egypt, Venice and Switzerland before finally landing them back in America, where Jim gives his formula over to the government and Kathleen's stepfather says he's sorry.

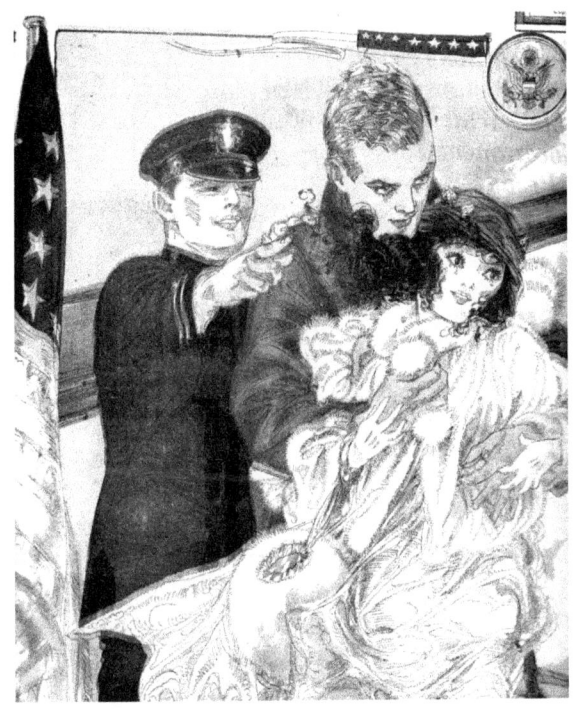

Kathleen and the Great Secret, March 6, 1921. Chapter 17, "Homeward Bound."

Kathleen and the Great Secret is definitely the pulpiest, most bizarre of Nell's serials, but the next one she did, *Betty and Billy, and Their Love Through the Ages*, is her most well-known, if anything by Nell can be considered well-known today. This series, which ran throughout 1922, is Nell at her most romantic. Compared to the Byzantine Kathleen and the dashing Golden-

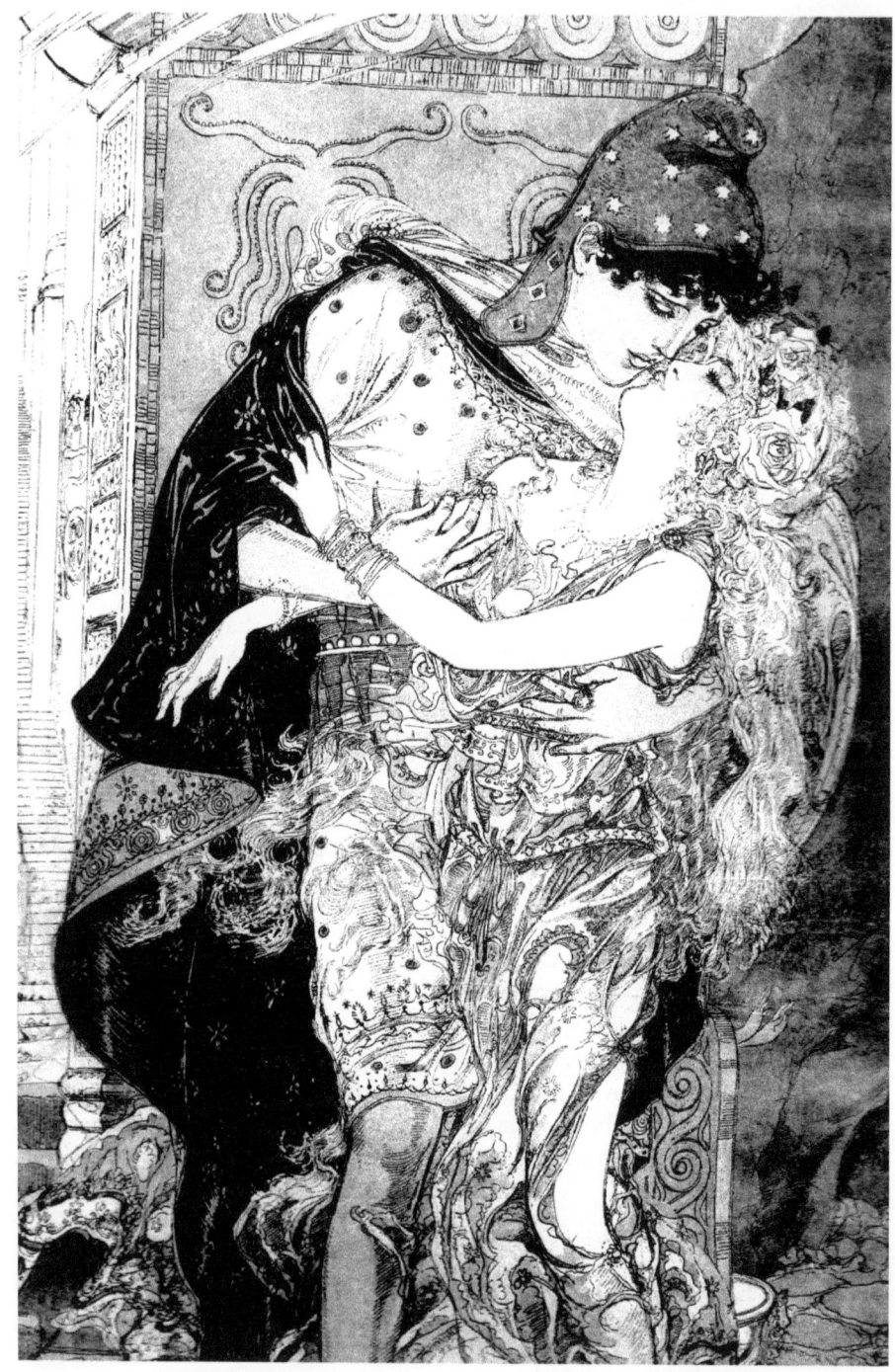

Eyes, the plot is simple: modern-day Billy and Betty see themselves through a crystal ball in all their previous incarnations, always lovers. They visit their past lives as prehistoric cave dwellers and Vikings; in the Arabian Nights, in ancient Egypt, Crete, Rome, and Celtic Ireland; among the Mongol hordes of Genghis Khan, in Renaissance Venice, as a Saracen maiden and a crusader knight, as an Aztec princess and a conquistador. The story isn't much, but the art is Nell at her lushest, fairly dripping with gorgeous costumes and exotic backgrounds. It's easy to see why this series is the most sought-after by today's small subculture of Nell Brinkley fans and collectors.

Throughout the rest of the twenties, Nell no longer wrote her own color Sunday pages. Most of them were written by Carolyn Wells, a prolific commercial writer who also produced numerous potboiler novels. Nell was no Dostoyevsky, but Carolyn Wells produced clichéd, shallow fluff, without even Nell's evident sincerity. The series, variously titled *The Adventures of Prudence Prim, The Fortunes of Flossie, Romances of Gloriette, Dimples' Day Dreams, Pretty Polly,* and *Sunny Sue,* follow a formula. The stories, told in verse, relate the mildly amusing adventures of a beautiful but airheaded flapper. The January 19, 1929, episode of *Pretty Polly* is typical: Polly decides to train as a nurse and starts a three-year course in nursing. A doctor calls her in to help him bandage the victim of a car crash, and Polly takes one look at the patient's bloody face, grows hysterical and faints.

Nell, creator of plucky heroines who dragged their lovers to safety on the field of battle and shinnied up ropes to reach ocean liners, must have hated illustrating stories that belittled women like this. Nonetheless her art, especially in the 1929 *Sunny Sue*, where the skinny, elongated arms and legs of her characters show a John Held, Jr.,[7] influence, is outstanding, proving that she could beautify even the most banal writing. The pages themselves, like her fashion strips from that period, consist of pictures, some even in panels, that tell a story using continuity, and they must be considered comics.

None of Nell's Sunday color pages from the twenties even approached the wonderfully fluffy feminism of her war epic, *Golden-Eyes and Her Hero, Bill*. In fact, Nell paid less attention to world happenings in the twenties than she had during the war, perhaps because nothing so earth-shaking as a World War occurred during this period. However, the 1922 discovery of King Tutankhamen's unopened tomb in Egypt prompted a 1923 panel of fashion advice, "Hobnobbing with Egypt," in which Nell draws three Betties

Opposite: Betty and Billy, and Their Love Through the Ages, **March 19, 1922. Chapter 8, "The Toys of the Minotaur."**

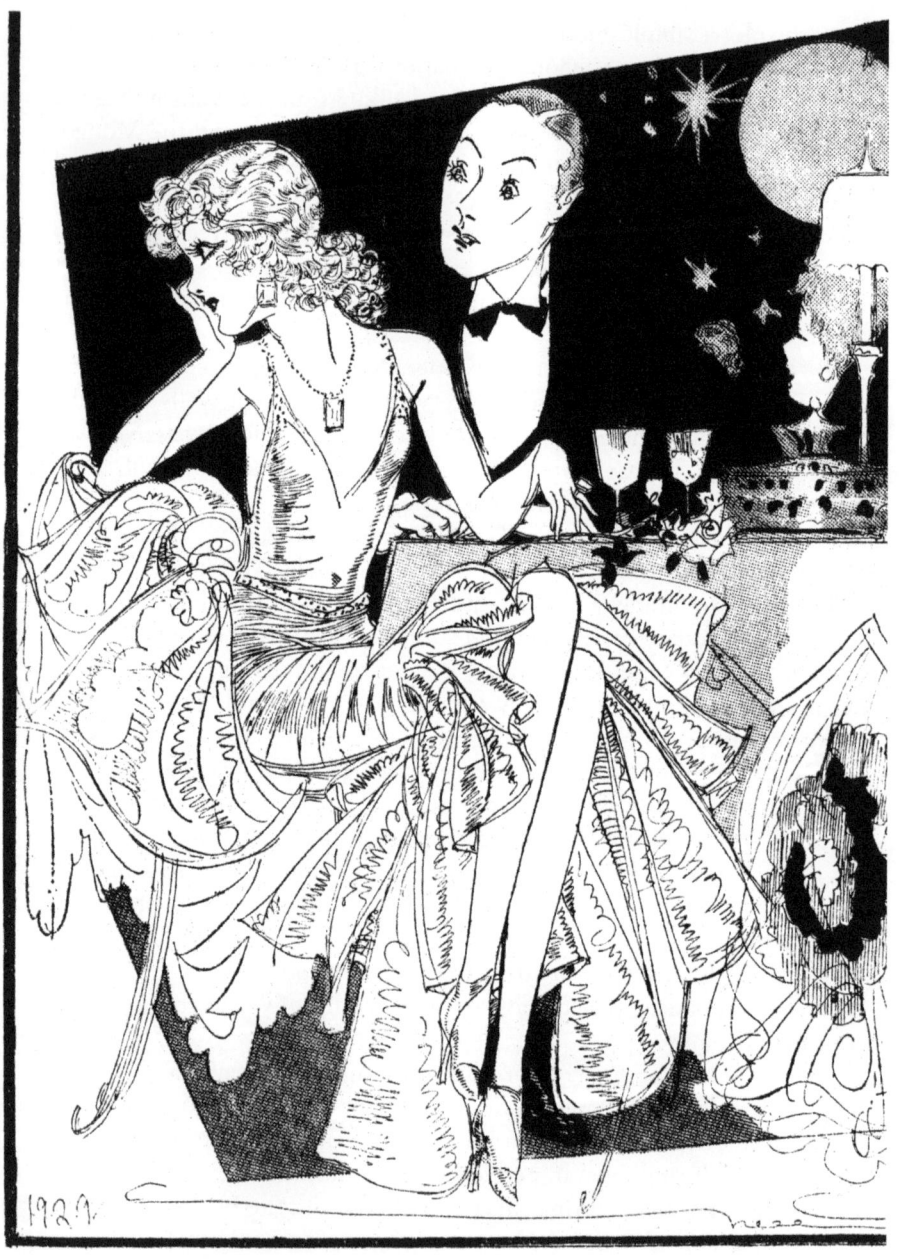

Sunny Sue, 1929.

Hobnobbing With Egypt

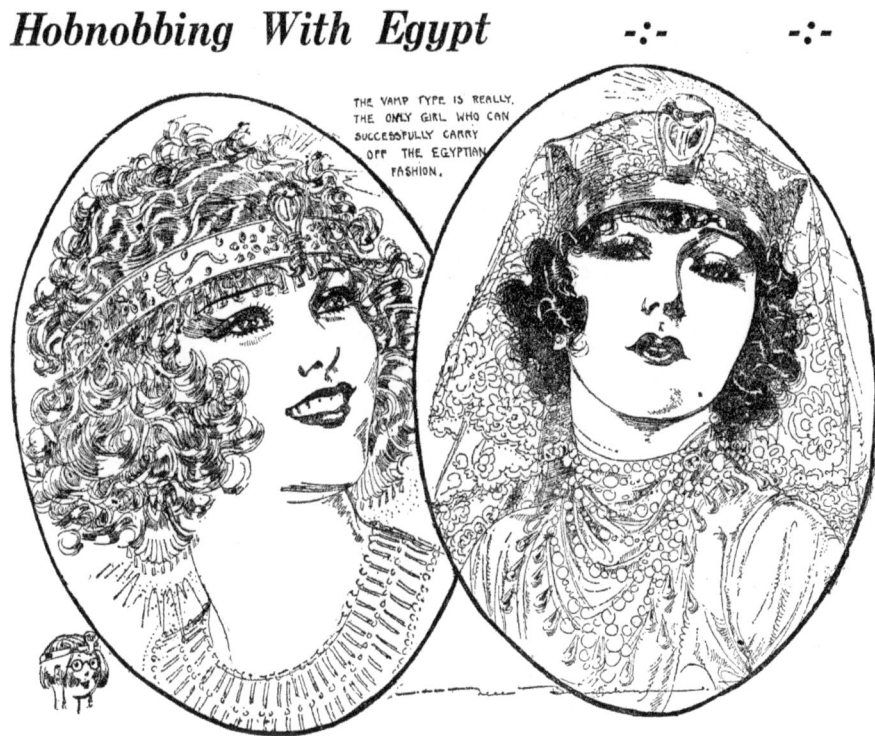

"Hobnobbing with Egypt," 1923.

wearing Egyptian head-dresses. She writes, "Our eager-faced little modern demoiselle is too jolly-looking, too frank and rosey. She would wear the queenliest head-dress on one ear!" On either side of the panel, she draws two cartoon-women—a rarity for Nell, who almost *never* drew in broad cartoon style—a fat lady and a girl in glasses, looking pretty silly in Egyptian hats.

The tomb discovery also inspired a series of 1923 panels about King Tut. For "The Return of Tutankhamen," she draws Tut in a contemporary nightclub, smoking a cigarette and applauding a nightclub dancer. On another part of the page, a forward young woman phones the Egyptian prince to ask him for a date. Nell writes, "He may have had flappers, but he never had one 'call him up!'" She concludes, "Behind the mask of the girl we know today looks out the girl of 3000 years ago—a girl with much the same longings, joys, griefs and desires!"

Ever fascinated by flight, Nell drew her hero—and the world's—Charles Lindbergh, in 1928, when he made his famous solo "Lindy hop" across the

Hobnobbing with Egypt :: King Tut Wasn't Always Old :: NELL BRINKLEY

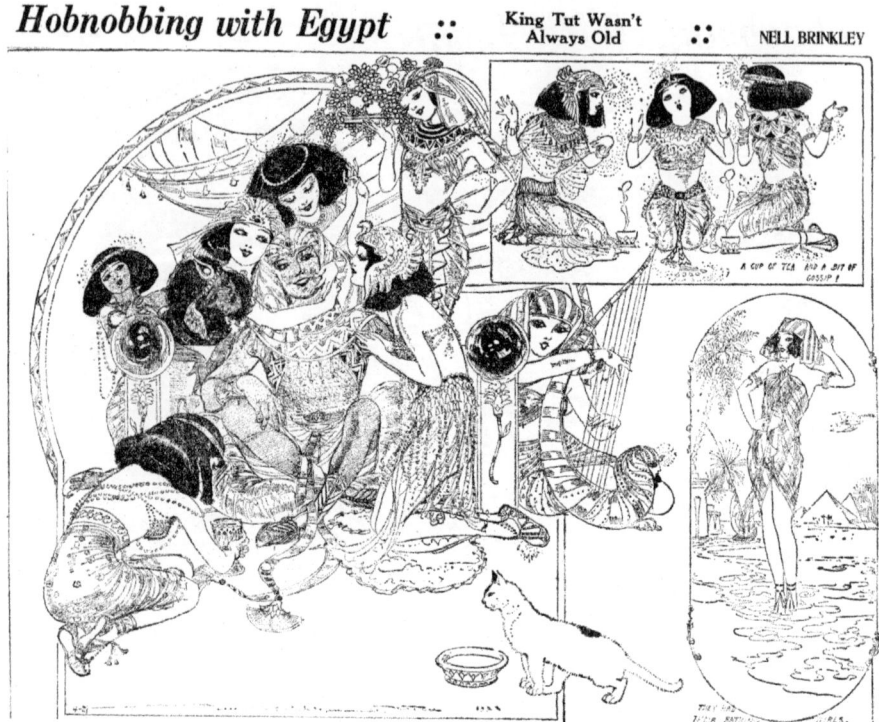

"The Return of Tutankhamen," 1923.

Atlantic. It was one of the rare instances in which Nell devoted her daily panel to a man. Beneath a barely idealized portrait—Lindbergh really was very handsome—she wrote:

> He is the world's hero, and our greatest national pride.... His modesty, his bravery and his character have spiritually and emotionally done good to a bored and bitter world. The spectacle of youth that is both honest and good riding the elements like a god helped the world's belief in the beauty and success of good and honest things.... Here's to the boy we can't forget!

The twenties was a booming peacetime decade, but occasional references to political subjects nevertheless crept into Nell's commentary. Her 1924 panel, "Worry, the Dragon," featuring a charming illustration of a tearful, sword-wielding Betty biting her lip as she battles a dragon, deals with financial stress: ... "Babies that need more and more. Mothers that never have one minute in which to 'invite the soul' and are trying to stretch dollars—and everybody knows that dollars won't stretch." Then she suddenly

"A BOY YOU CAN'T FORGET"

Drawn by Nell Brinkley

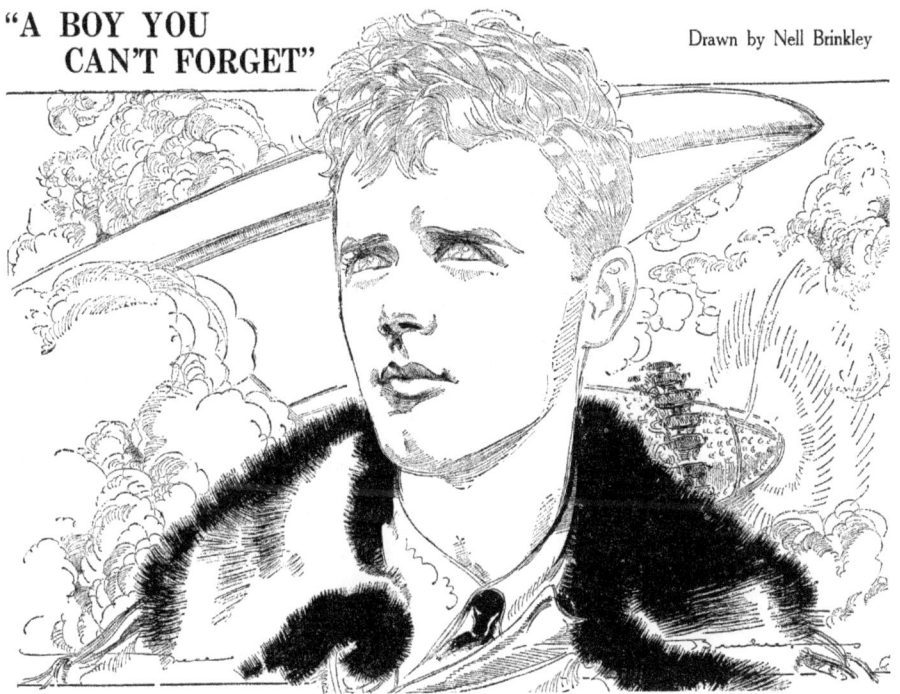

"A Boy You Can't Forget," 1928.

switches subjects and writes about child labor: "Some day maybe a perfect Government, the thing we dream of, the same government that will be in the hands of men of pity who will not allow a child to work, will be (the) Parfait Gentil Knight without reproach."

Nell cared enough about Ireland's revolution to draw a special St. Patrick's Day panel about it in 1922. Along with poetic rhetoric and a beautiful rendering of Ireland as an enthroned queen, her commentary includes a whopping typo:

> William Sharp, who loved the isles of Ireland ... has said, "The sweetest-voiced of the younger Irish singers of today—" meaning Keats "—has spoken of the Celtic twilight. A twilight it is but, if night follows gloaming, so also does dawn succeed night...."
>
> Ireland's morning star is high, her golden sun of dawn is rising, her twilight, her night have deepened, and lightened, and here is her dawning!

One as enthusiastic about Irish independence as Nell of course knew that "the sweetest-voiced" Irish singer was Yeats, but either she, through

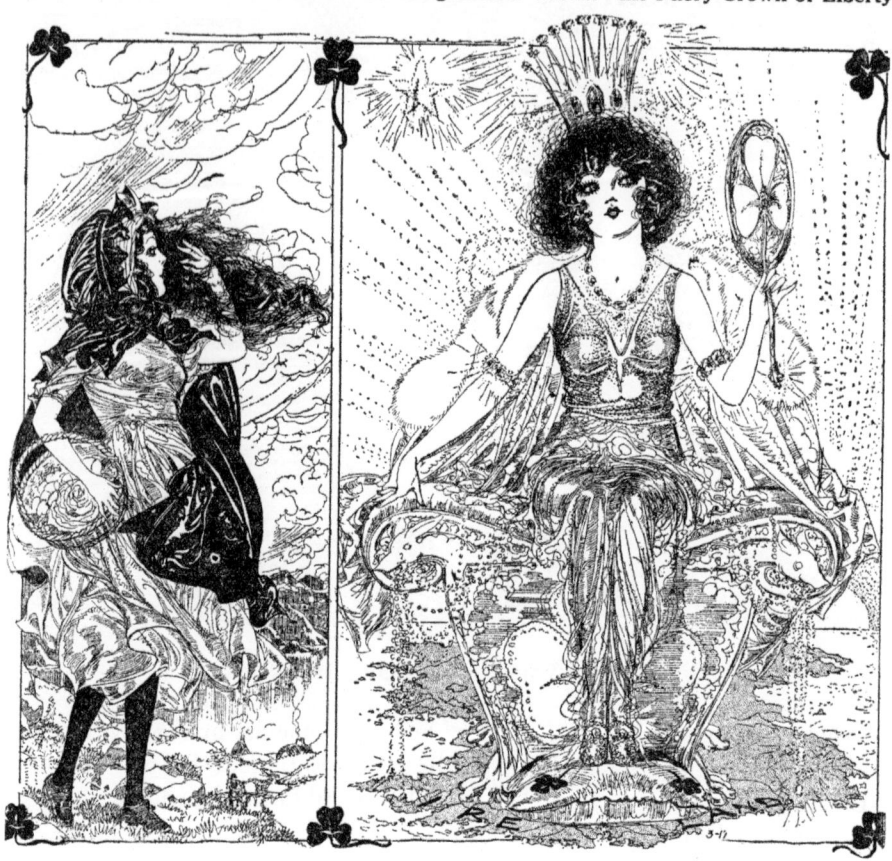

"St. Patrick's Day for Ireland," 1922.

carelessness, or some editor, not up-to-date enough on contemporary literature, changed the name to Keats.

She also continued to cover important trials, including the 1927 trial of Ruth Snyder and Henry Judd Grey for the murder of Ruth's husband. In her commentary, Nell makes her dislike for Snyder and Grey quite clear: she sardonically refers to them as "this priceless pair," and ends her description of the scene in the courtroom with, "She never looks at him nor he at her." Nevertheless, Nell manages to draw the murderess as an attractive woman.

Snyder and Grey were found guilty, and in 1928, Ruth Snyder earned the dubious distinction of being the first woman to die in the electric chair.

Nell Brinkley Sketches Moods of Ruth Snyder

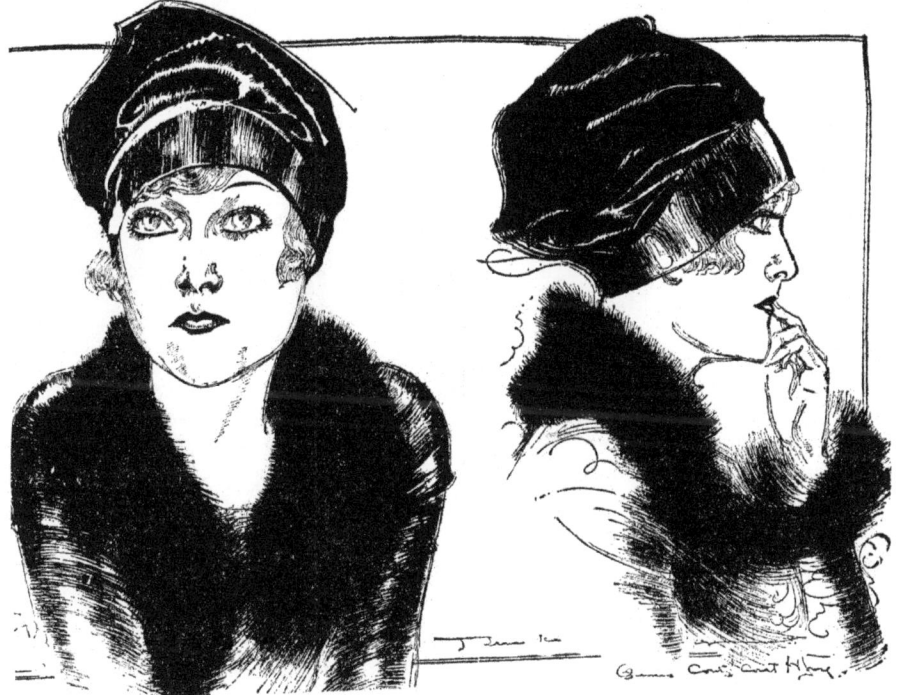

By Nell Brinkley.

"Nell Brinkley Sketches Moods of Ruth Snyder," 1927.

Snyder was also the first and only person actually photographed while being electrocuted. A reporter for the *New York Daily News* smuggled a camera into the death chamber by hiding it beneath his trouser leg to take the historic photo, which boosted the newspaper's circulation by one million.

Nell hobnobbed with the rich and famous; in fact, she was one of them. She reviewed silent films and made friends with the lead actors, like Mary Astor and Billie Burk, whom she reviewed.[8] It was not surprising that they sought her friendship; a good review by Nell of a Lillian Gish or Ala Nazimova film, along with a flattering portrait, carried considerable weight with the movie-going public. Ever shrewd, Nell took pains to give especially generous reviews to films starring William Randolph Hearst's mistress, Marion Davies. She had drawn Marion among the pretty girl cast of the Ziegfeld Follies of 1916, a year after Hearst first discovered her performing in the Broadway show *Stop! Look! Listen!*,[9] but had not mentioned her in the accompanying review. However, by 1922, Nell was rolling out her superlatives for the pretty blonde actress. The headline above her drawings of Marion in *When Knighthood Was in Flower* read, "The Greatest Motion Picture Ever Produced, As Seen by Nell Brinkley," and the copy beneath Nell's full-page, color drawing of Marion in *Little Old New York* read, "The part of 'Pat' is perhaps Miss Davies' greatest triumph." She headlined her drawing for *Janice Meredith*, Marion's 1924 film, "Here's the Picture You'll See Tomorrow." After Marion's other 1924 film, *Yolanda*, Nell described her as "a heaven-meant comedienne." "She proves herself delightfully able to look pretty and terribly funny ... at the same time," Nell continues. "She has an admirable willingness to offer up beauty to laughter."

For Marion's 1926 *Beverly of Graustark*, Nell's enthusiasm knew no bounds. Beneath the headline, "Marion Davies Is Riot in *Beverly of Graustark*," she raved:

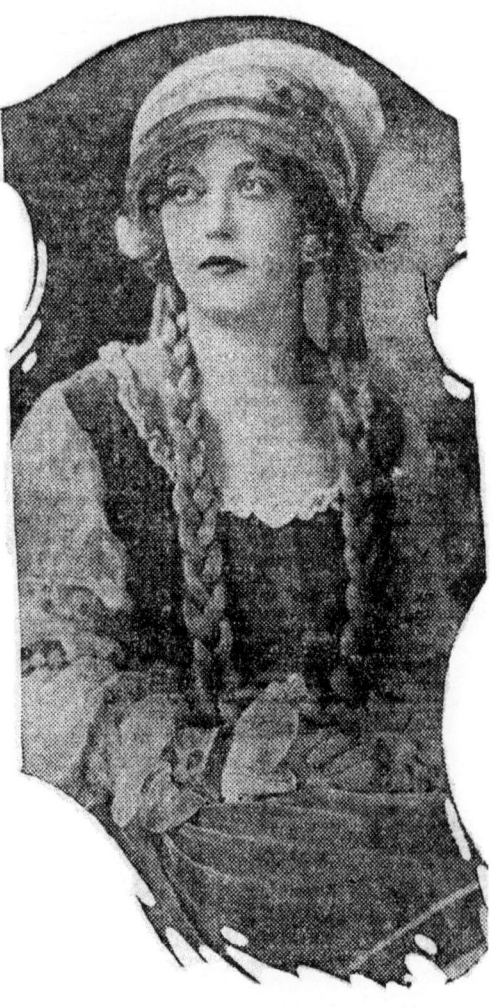

Marion Davies as Yolanda, 1924.

> Several years ago ... it began to dawn on some critical minds, from hilarious bits that the girl with golden curls and shiny blue eyes managed to smuggle into her performance ... that the young lady with the slightly retrousse nose who paraded so much as a fascinating lady was a comedienne, with a rich gift for laughable faces, a pair of feet that could stumble and spill her and still remain a pretty girl's feet, a genius for pantomime and boyish capers.... And she is having her big time in comedy—light,

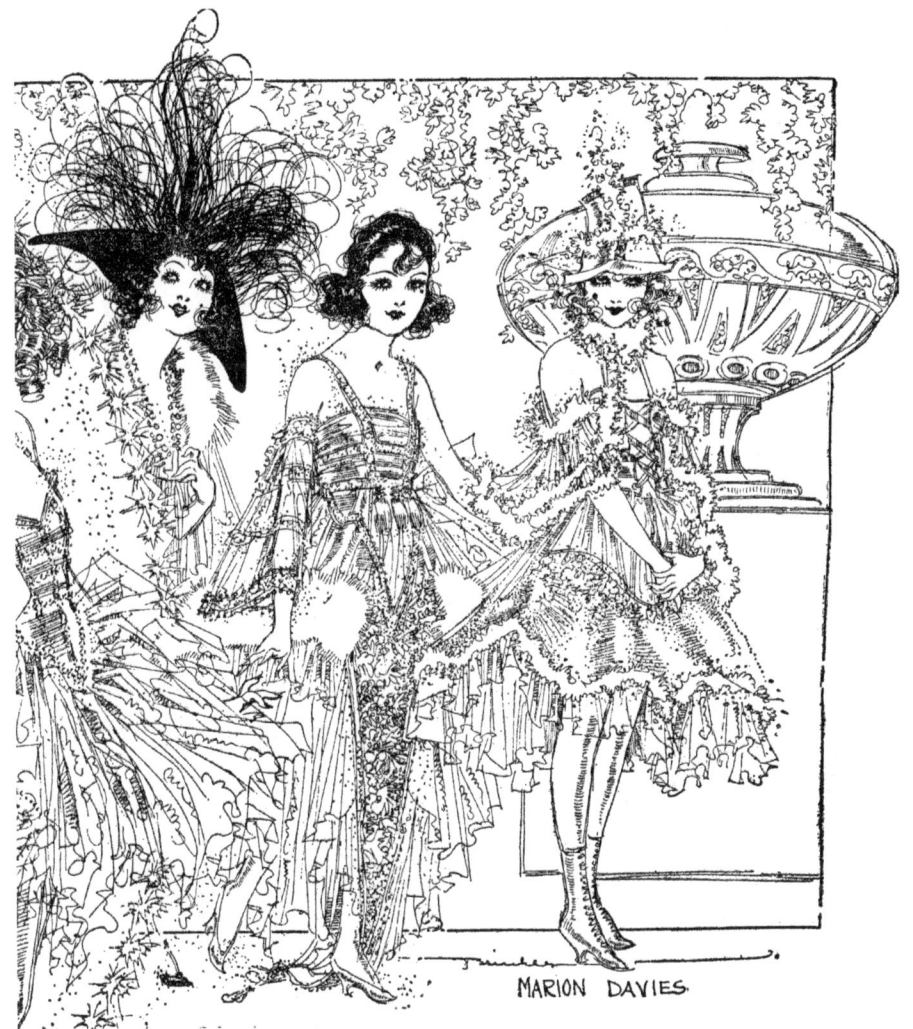

Marion Davies in the Ziegfeld Follies of 1916.

touch-and-go comedy.... In *Beverly of Graustark*, Miss Marion is a—just a—RIOT!

Nell ends her review with a statement that could not have been truer: "Marion's face is her fortune from beginning to the end."

Hearst showed his appreciation by inviting Nell to his 146 room castle at San Simeon, California. She was his guest there several times during the twenties.

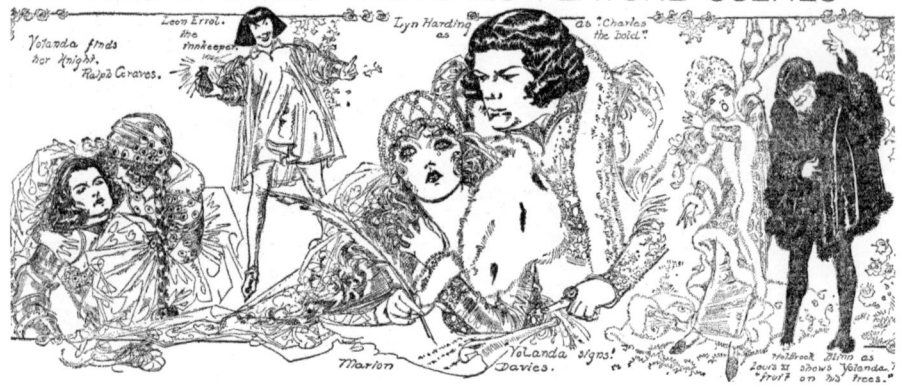

"Nell Brinkley Pictures Feature Scenes," Marion Davies in *Yolanda*, 1924.

And he even put her into a movie. Hearst had formed his own film company, Cosmopolitan films, largely as a vehicle for Marion Davies, but the actress was absent from his 1924 film *The Great White Way*. Instead, Hearst turned the lightweight prizefight-romance, adapted from H. C. Witwer's short story, "Cain and Mable," into a puff-piece for his newspaper empire, featuring famous cartoonist-employees George McManus, Billy De Beck, Fay King, Winsor McCay, Harry Hershfield, and of course Nell. Variety gave it this sardonic review:

> A glance at the cast ... and you get the idea of this picture. It seems to have been made with a view of the glorification of prizefighters and Hearst newspapers....
> On the screen you see the New York "*American*" and on the program it's mentioned the press room scene is from the Los Angeles "*Examiner*." ...
> Some of the captions drew laughs. Who wrote the others no one around knew or would tell. Maybe Hearst himself, William R. It's his picture, so no one could stop him; but if he did, William need never expect to be syndicated himself as a funny feller.

Nell did not fare much better. The *New York Times* wrote, "Nell Brinkley was to us extremely nervous, as if somebody told her that either the lights or the camera was going to bite her."

We can assume that Nell wept over this unflattering review all the way to the bank. In 1929, she also broke into the airwaves with a guest spot on the nationally syndicated *Breakfast Club*. Radio was the country's favorite pastime next to the silent movies; everybody listened to the radio. Being a

Six. The Twenties

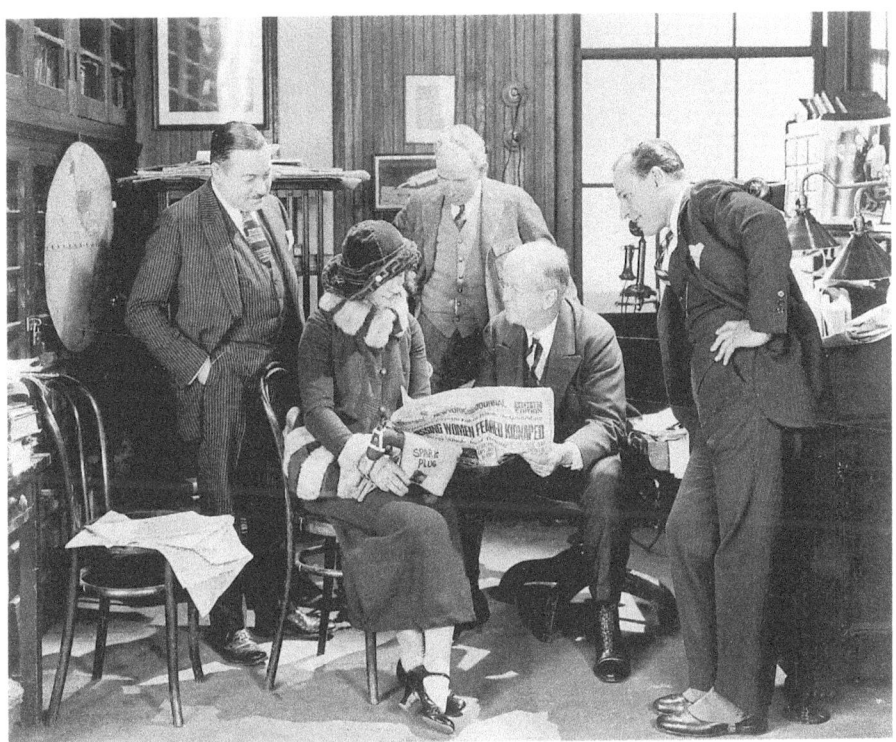

Still from *The Great White Way*, 1924. *From left to right:* George McManus (*Bringing Up Father*), Nell Brinkley, Harry Hershfield (*Abie the Agent*), Arthur Brisbane, Billy DeBeck (*Barney Google*). Nell has Barney Google's horse, Spark Plug, in her lap. (Courtesy of the New York Museum of Modern Art/Film Stills Archive.)

guest on the *Breakfast Club* was the equivalent of being a guest on the *Late Show with David Letterman* today. Nell was at her peak of fame and creativity.

Notes

1. *The New Rochelle Standard Star*, February 2, 1931.
2. *Los Angeles Examiner*, January 5, 1913.
3. Horsewomen were one of Nell's more common themes. Growing up in the West, she had always ridden and when she lived in New Rochelle, she kept horses.
4. Nell meant what she wrote about not going to teas with other famous people. She declined an invitation to join the Algonquin Round Table, a famed group of mostly writers and artists, including poet Dorothy Parker and illustrator Neysa

McMein, who met regularly, for tea and stronger drink, at New York's Algonquin hotel.

5. Nell had used her mother as the model in her 1925 piece "Best Pal." A comparison of that drawing and the May 1, 1925, installment of *Westward Ho!* makes it clear that this is the same woman.

6. Nell neglects to explain the reasoning behind Jim's being on the ship, as she also neglects to explain just how it is that Kathleen "by luckiest of chances picks up (Jim's) trail and follows it through dingy streets to the waterfront" and thus to the liner. Apparently fans of serials did not demand logic.

7. John Held, Jr., who also drew for the Hearst newspapers, was and is still considered the cartoonist who defined the Jazz Age with his drawings of flappers and their sheiks.

8. After writing up the scandalous Olga Nethersole in 1908, Nell and the actress had remained friends. (The *New Rochelle Standard Star*, October 23, 1944.)

9. After Hearst first saw Marion Davies on stage in *Stop! Look! Listen!* he attended every performance, buying tickets for two seats—one for himself and one for his hat.

CHAPTER SEVEN

The Thirties

Wait 'till the sun shines, Nellie, when the clouds go drifting by.
We will be happy Nellie, don't you sigh.
   —"Wait 'Till the Sun Shines, Nellie," Andrew B. Sterling and
Harry Von Tilzer, 1905

Nell's father, Robert Serrett Brinkley, died in 1930. Bruce and Nell paid $1,153 for a family burial plot in New Rochelle's Beechmont cemetery and buried him there, beneath a large, pink-veined, grey marble urn. In his later years Robert had been living in Orlando, Florida, where he operated another cigar store. Newspaper articles described him as having moved to Florida for his health. His wife had left him and followed their daughter to New York back in 1907.

It's clear that Nell loved and always missed her absent father. For a 1913 panel, "Puzzle—Who's Coming?" she draws a woman and baby, along with their cat and dog, all eagerly waiting at the garden gate for the man of the family to arrive home. She writes:

> He isn't in the picture, but it's a good portrait of him just the same—the sort of man that everything he owns is glad when he comes home!... When you pass a gate like this at twilight you don't need a picture of the man to know him. I know, because I have had much knowledge of such a man—my own dad.

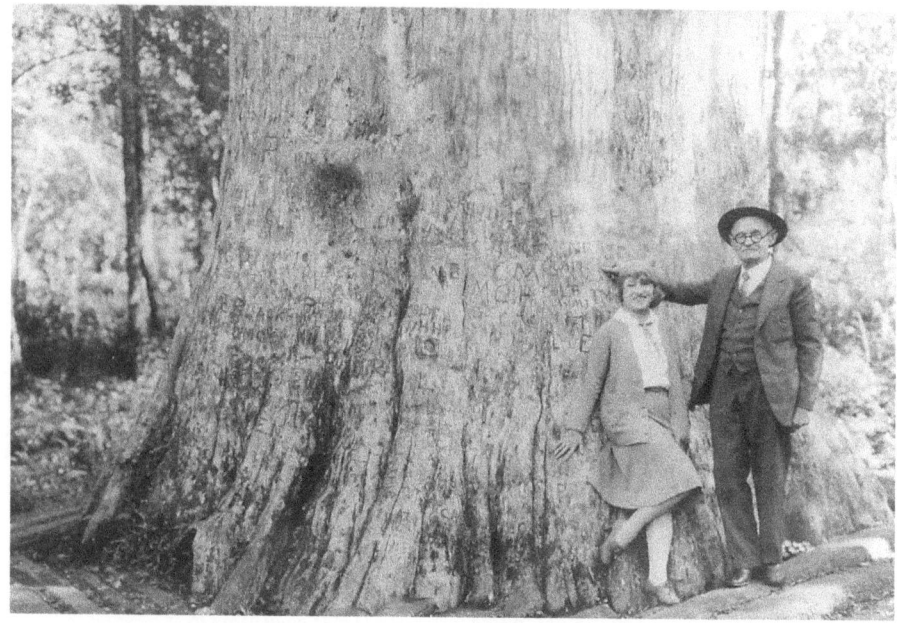

Robert and Nell at Sequoia National Monument, circa 1925.

Nell saw her father when she could. A photo from the mid-twenties shows father and daughter leaning against a giant sequoia tree during a visit to California's Sierra Nevada. Even in an old black-and-white snapshot, the joy that the two take in each other's company is palpable.

Engraved on the base of Robert's urn is a quote from British novelist Marie Corelli:

> I sail new seas and gaze on new lands where a perpetual light shines that knows no fading. We shall meet again, who have loved each other.

Nell probably picked out the quote. Although she had dropped out of high school, she was well-read. Her library consisted of over 2,000 books, some, including books by H. G. Wells and G. K. Chesterton, personally autographed to her, so it's very likely that she had read Corelli, a popular novelist with a mystic bent. In a 1934 panel, "Women—Two Kinds," she displays her erudition when contrasting four airheaded Betties of the thirties with renowned past women in the arts: Rosa Bonheur, Madame De Stael, Madame De Sevigne, Madame Roland, and Sarah Bernhardt.

The thirties was the decade of the Great Depression. During the ten years that followed the great stock market crash of 1929, 9,000 banks failed and 86,000 businesses went bankrupt. The country fell upon hard times.

Nell's panels commented on the mass poverty and unemployment she saw: she drew a worried woman, gazing out her apartment window to the city below, praying, "Please send my John a job!" She wrote, "There are hosts of children ... whose fathers, willing and anxious to do anything under the sun, ... cannot find work."

As always, she sympathized with working class women. In her 1932 panel, "I Know a Discontented Lady!" she chides a bored rich woman with the industriousness of farm women tilling their fields: "There are women in the world, Mimi, who help in the field. Did you know that? Women who have no 'change,' no beautiful things."

In 1932 an estimated 20,000 jobless war veterans

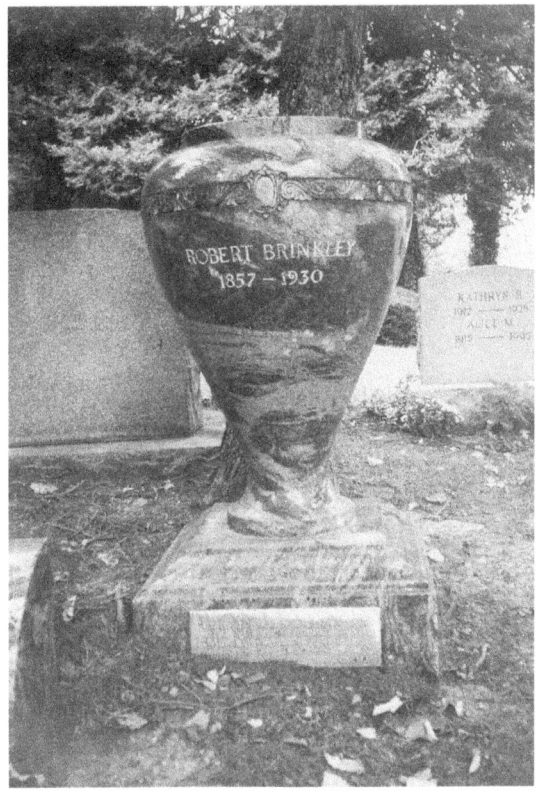

Robert Brinkley's grave, Beechmont cemetery.

and their families converged on Washington, demanding bonuses that the government had promised them. They camped out in the capital in what became known as Hoovervilles—squalid, unsanitary collections of makeshifts huts and tents, dependent on donations of food from churches and charities.[1]

Appalled by the treatment of men who had fought in the war about which she had been so very patriotic 15 years earlier, Nell reacted by producing her most serious panel and commentary. "The Man of the Hour," printed on June 29, 1932, is one of Nell's rare panels starring a man instead of a woman. In fact the art shows a typical Betty being hauled offstage, while being told, "Come my dear 'pretty-girl.' No one is interested in you just now!" A hand pulls aside a star-studded curtain to reveal the veteran alone onstage. Behind him is the Capitol building. He is handsome—Nell couldn't draw him any other way—but careworn, in his rumpled shirt and trousers,

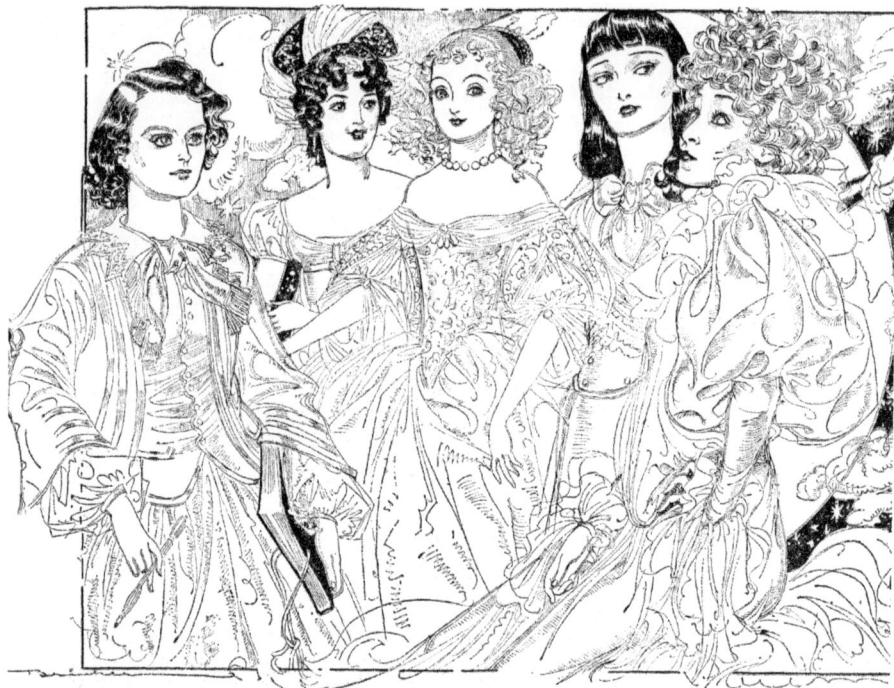

Rosa Bonheur—De Stael—De Sevigne——Madame Roland———Bernhardt

"Women—Two Kinds." *Left to right:* Rosa Bonheur, Madame De Stael, Madame De Sevigne, Madame Roland, Sarah Bernhardt, 1934.

carrying his hat and jacket. Unlike her earlier wheedling, in which she coyly begged for pensions and decent housing for Washington's wartime working women, Nell's tone is different.[2] She is angry:

> He was a patriot then (not every one of him felt a hero and WANTED to die—even as you and I—but he went just the same), and he is showing by a peaceful, wholly American attitude in the capital of our government that he still is one....
> The public DID back both its government and its soldiers during the war that changed us all. The public would like to see the government back the men it called heroes, now....
> We watched him one Winter day (of many days) leave his country, ten thousand strong.... We cheered, and wept, and bought bonds, and backed him up, with all our hearts. I REMEMBER!
> The public still backs him up. Will our Government let him be "a needy American"?[3]

Amelia Earhart's solo Atlantic flight of 1932 earned a more positive reaction from Nell. Beneath a portrait of the aviatrix crowned with laurels,

MAN OF THE HOUR

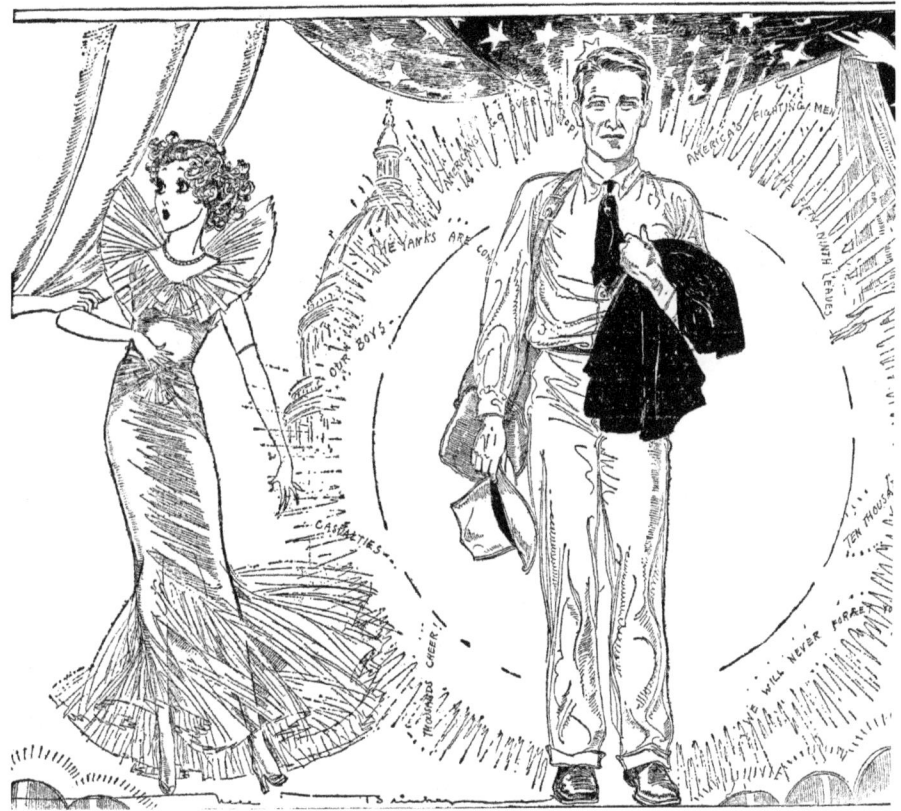

"The Man of the Hour," 1932. The Brinkley Girl is yanked offstage as the veteran takes the limelight.

Nell's text likened Earhart to Charles Lindbergh: "That the girl who looks so like our greatest and first conqueror of the sea between us and Europe, gentle like him, reserved and modest almost as he, should be the next across, and the first girl to do it, setting her name up besides his in history, is something to think about!... Even her mop of tousled hair is a sister to his."

In August of the same year, Nell turned one of her most enthusiastic *Can Such Things Be?* panels into a tribute to Amelia Earhart. In the center of the drawing, Araminta, a Brinkley girl from the 1800s, pokes her bonneted head through the page to stare in amazement at women riding, swimming, skating, running, playing tennis. At her left stands the great aviatrix herself, face turned upwards to the sky. Nell writes:

AMERICAN GIRL

-:-   -:-   -:-

Drawn by
NELL BRINKLEY

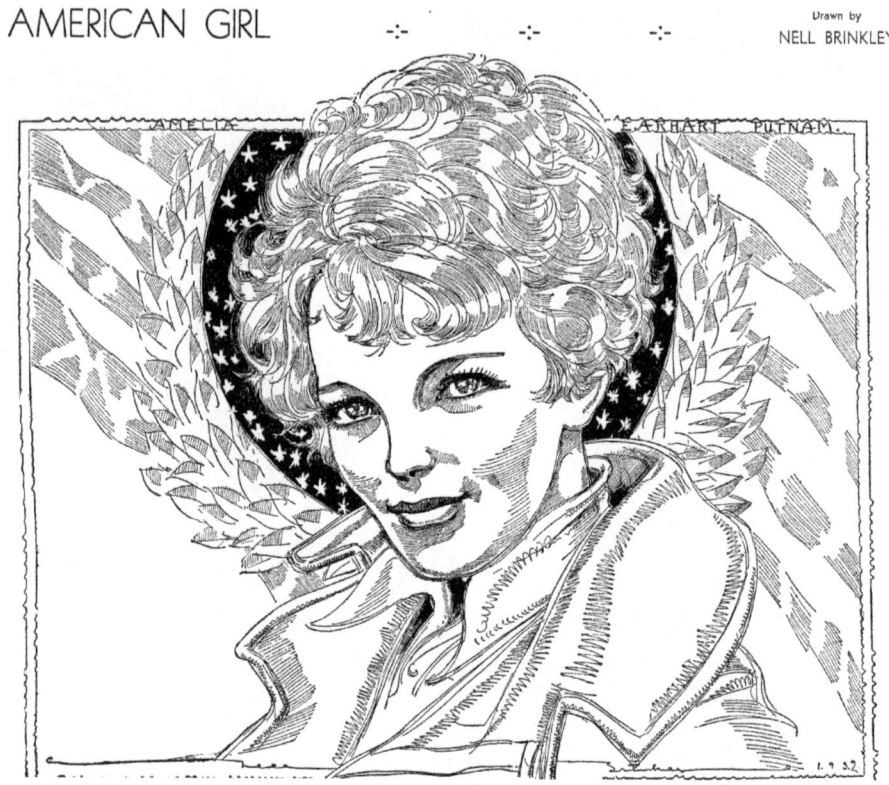

"American Girl," 1932.

THIS is better than what [Araminta] had—this body freedom, with the world her playground, even as the men, that the girl in this day's World has. This right to have the same fun her brother or her sweetheart have in the world of play and sport!... Poor Araminta skated in a skirt to her ankles and never won anything! And this ... a girl in a man's overall and leather coat, big shoes, a helmet in her hand. The air is free to her, too. She flew the Atlantic alone, in a ship of the air!

The Great Depression doesn't seem to have affected Nell financially; the family, along with an assortment of cats and dogs, lived quietly but well in the house on Pryor Terrace. They kept horses, and they had live-in servants and an Italian gardener. Nell's son, nicknamed Bobby,[4] took violin lessons and had a riding instructor. They dressed for dinner every night, a formality which Bobby hated so much that in later years he refused to eat anywhere but in the kitchen. One of the servants drove the little boy to school and there were times that he was privately tutored at home.

Seven. The Thirties

'CAN SUCH THINGS BE?'

Drawn By
NELL BRINKLEY

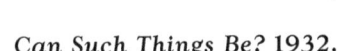

Can Such Things Be? 1932.

If Nell sometimes seemed overprotective of her only child, it was because she feared kidnapping—and she had reason. The baby son of her hero, Charles Lindbergh, had been kidnapped in 1932. In her daily commentary, Nell wrote this plea to the unknown kidnappers:

> Charles and Anne Lindbergh have had to do what it is a pity they must do—they have offered to bargain, at any place, in any way, through any one, with the kidnapers [sic] of their little son, giving their word for the safety of the kidnapers, giving them what they ask, if they will only give their child back to them. Wherever you are, whoever you are, clear your soul!

The Lindbergh baby was eventually found dead, and an unemployed German laborer, Bruno Hauptmann, was accused of his kidnapping and murder.[5] Nell covered the 1935 trial, yet another "Trial of the Century."

The delight Nell took in the son she had waited so long for shines

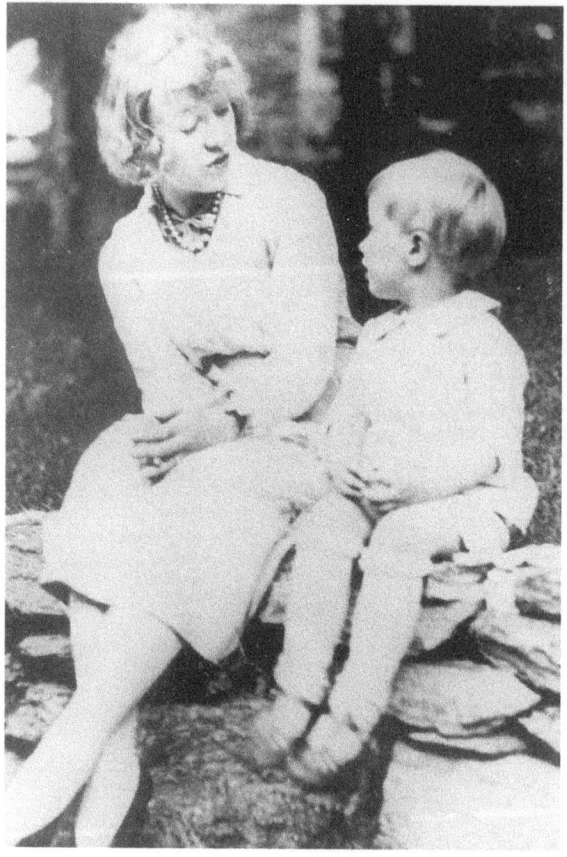

Nell and little Bobby, late 1920s.

from her work as she shares her daily life with the reader. In "The Family Affair," from April 1931, she draws herself, her husband and Bobby, a charmingly Brinkley-esque family pleasantly dickering over vacation destinations. Describing herself as a sun-wary vacationer with "thin, blond skin [that] burns in the sun like a piece of tissue under a burning-glass," her husband as "a boat boy," who dislikes Nell's beloved mountains, she declares Bobby is "the only one with a truly open, generous, anywhere-in-the-world-where-a-boy-can-play, princely mind that shouts with joy at every destination!"

In July 1932, Nell draws 9-year-old Bobby on summer vacation, grungy and cute and lazing in a hammock, and writes of her son and his friends,

> A little boy I know, and the little boys HE knows, and the little girl with the brown curls and the pink dress that he admires, and the little girls she knows ... are personages of leisure again.
>
> They sit up in the morning and say to their folks, "I can hardly believe that I don't have to go to school!" And the delighted mother who is so happy to have them home all day, she can hardly believe that the small man or woman does not have to set out to the temple of learning at "quarter to nine."

If Nell's joy at having her son home for vacation puzzles parents for whom summer vacation is a nightmare, it's important to remember that

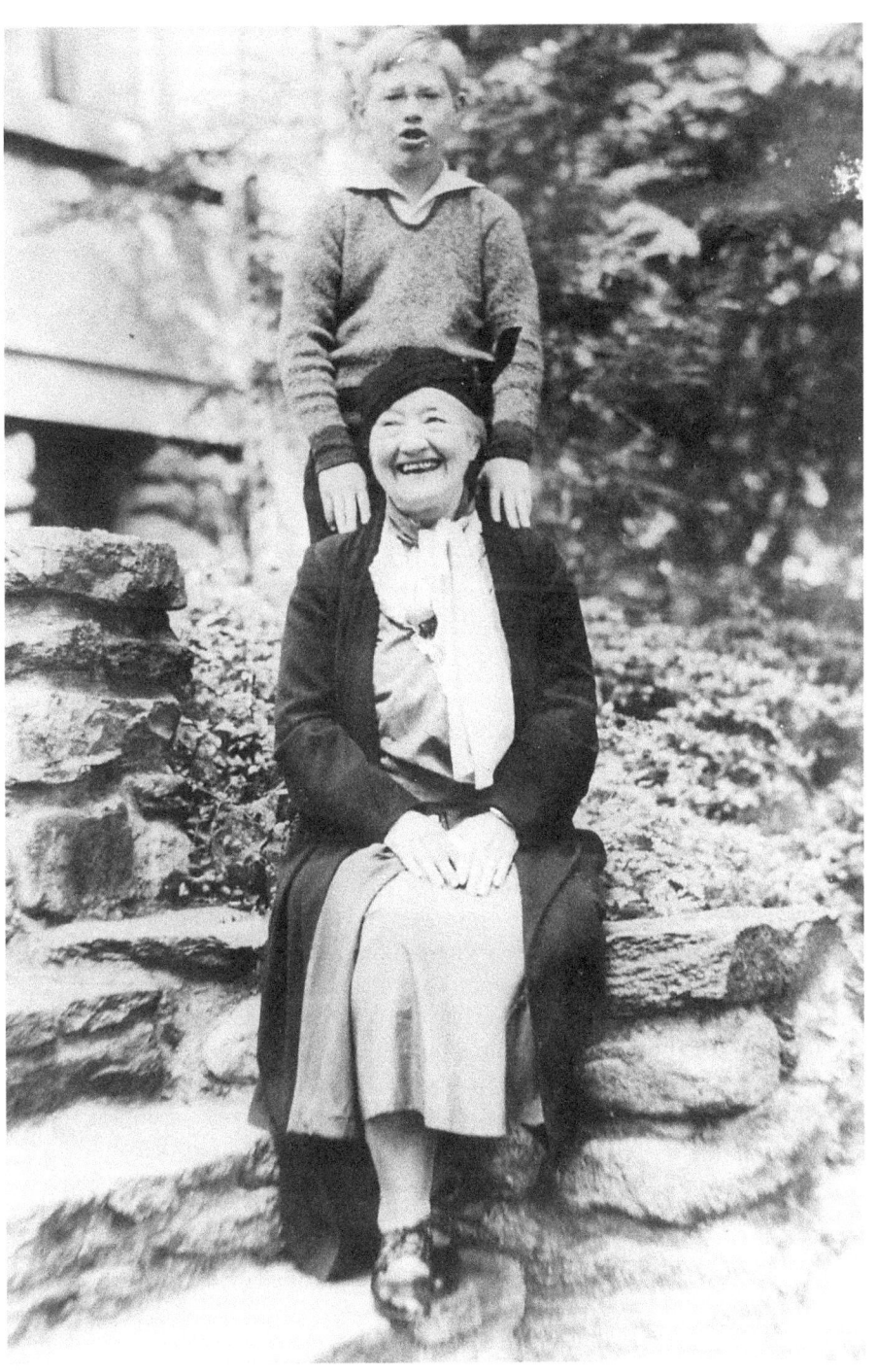

May and Bobby, circa 1930.

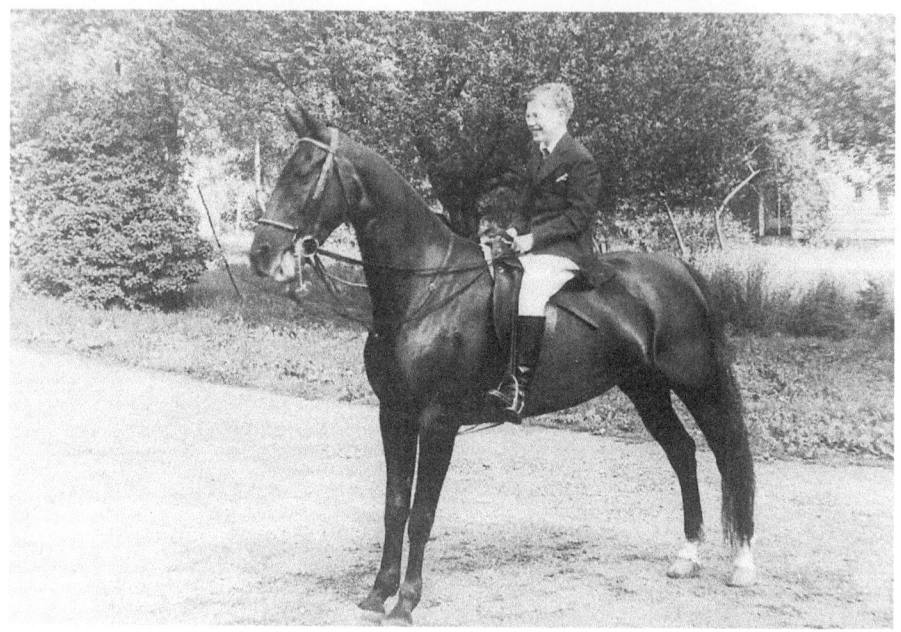

Bobby on horseback, circa 1935.

Nell had on hand a whole raft of servants, plus a willing grandmother to entertain and take care of the kid.

Vacation and travel continued to be grist for Nell's mill, and every vacation was a working vacation, with Nell recording her adventures for her daily panel. In an April 15 episode of her 1929 series *Westward Ho!*, subtitled "Back to Work," Nell draws herself on the left-hand side of the panel, shaking hands with an anthropomorphic bottle of waterproof ink, above the title "Good-bye work!" Then on the right-hand side, she's shown opening a box of thumb tacks, while a cartoon pencil and a bottle of Chinese White wait for her, above the words, "Hello work!" She writes, "There at the end of the line, three thousand miles long I find 'work' again waiting."

Nell often didn't wait to arrive at her destination, but worked en route. In 1932, she visited Québec, drawing as she traveled. For "Vacation Faces," she again put herself into the center of the panel, surrounding herself with charming sketches of the people she met during her trip. These are flesh and blood portraits, not Betties and Billies: a 75-year-old man with 17 children, an old woman, two very real little boys. On another of her numerous trips to Canada, with a deadline fast approaching, Nell tried to draw on the train with her suitcase propped up on her knees, but the train swayed so much she couldn't work. Finally she got her lucky break: the engine overheated,

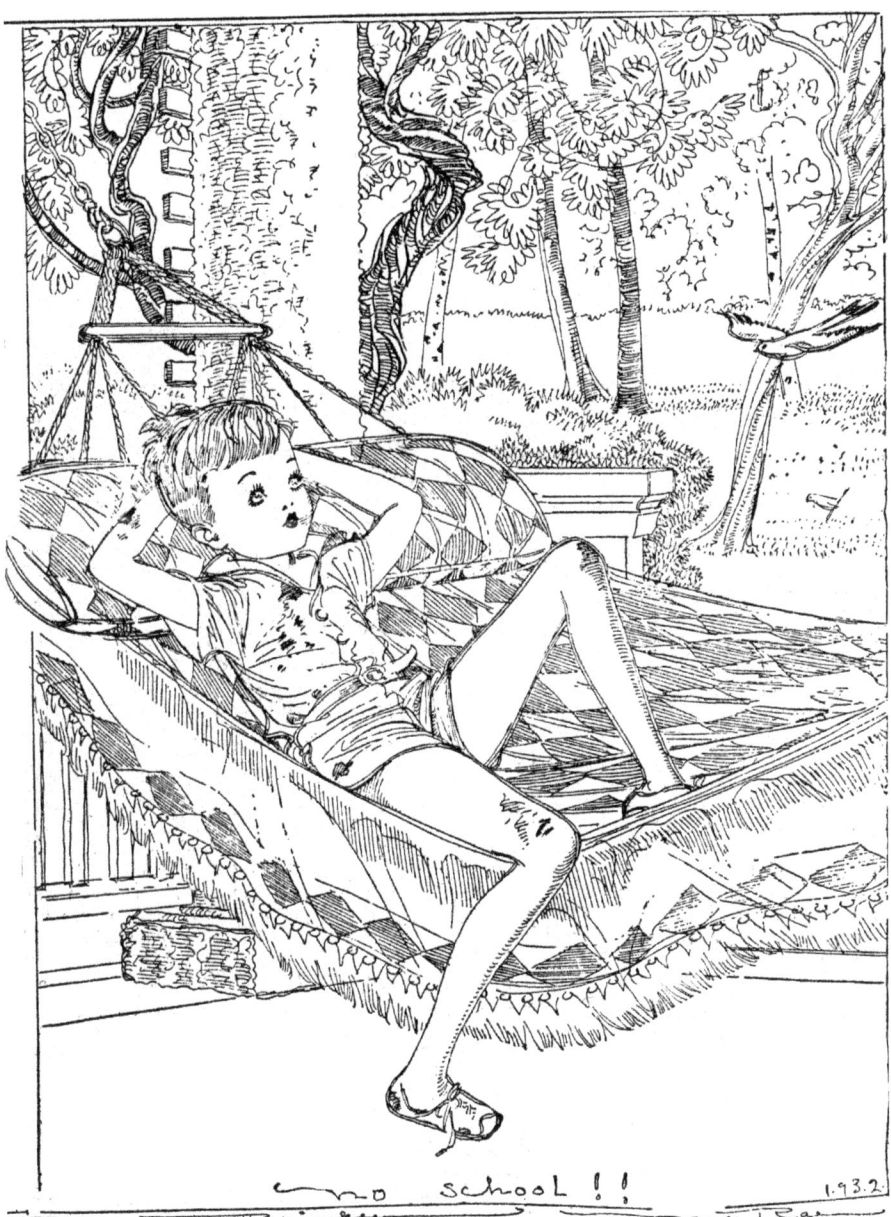

"Gentleman of Leisure," 1932.

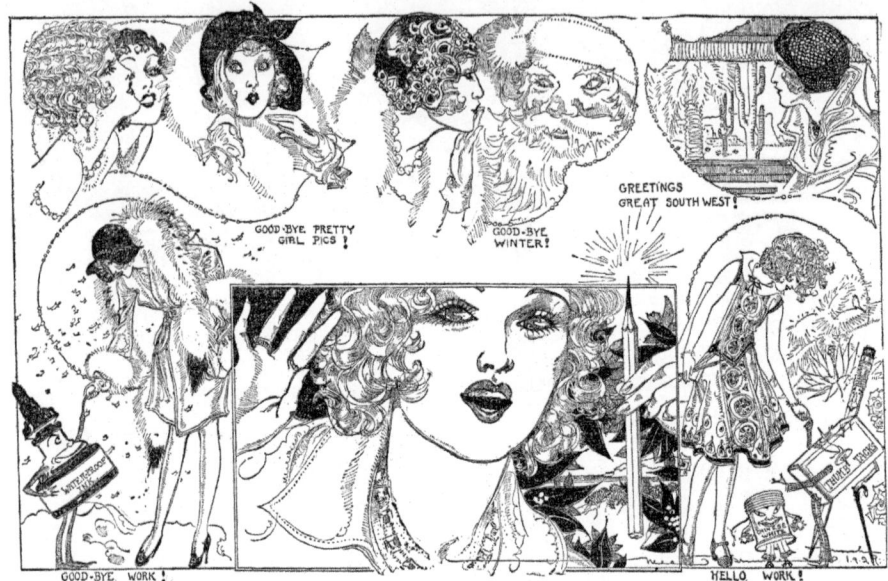

Westward Ho! "Back to Work," April 15, 1929.

and the train had to stand on the track for three hours, during which time Nell finished her art and met her deadline.

In September 1932, Nell got up close and personal with her fans, dedicating two panels to two real girls of the many who sent her fan letters, giving them drawing advice. Along with the sketches of heads in "Making Faces," dated October 3, she wrote, "A lesson for Janet, aged 11 yrs. of the pale-green letter." Beneath the panel, her commentary ran: "It's high time I answered, by way of a picture or two, some of the letters from kindly eleven-and-twelve-and-fifteen-year-olds, who first praise and then question." The panel above the commentary demonstrates, with ovals and guidelines, just how to draw a Brinkley girl's face. On September 27, Nell did the same thing with hands this time, dedicating a panel full of Brinkley-style hands to an 11-year-old girl named Mildred.

Throughout the thirties Nell continued to churn out art on the subjects her fans loved most: romance, pretty girls, and fashion. She put herself into some of the cutest of the latter. In her August 4, 1931, panel, "Down to the Sea," the artist has drawn herself, sitting at her drawing board in the middle of her picture. Surrounding her are Betties dressed in the scrumptious beach fashions of the early thirties. A week later, in "Hot

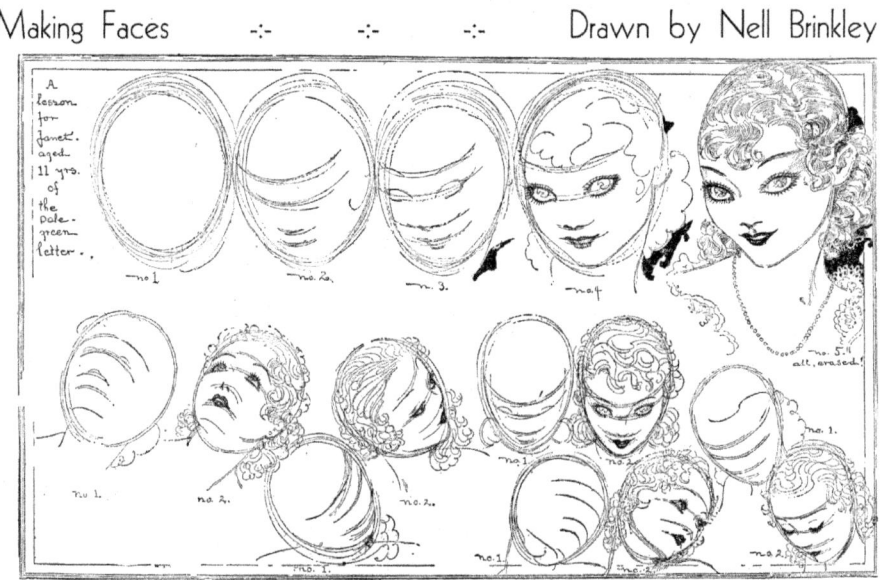

"Making Faces," 1932.

Weather Art," she contrasts her image of what she'd *like to* look like while drawing, with what she *really* looks like in the dog days of summer—this in a time before air conditioning.

On May 15, 1934, the *San Francisco Examiner* ran a brief article, headlined "Nell Brinkley Is White House Guest":

> Nell Brinkley, noted artist of the Hearst newspapers, was a guest today at the press conference of Mrs. Roosevelt in the White House. It proved to be a particularly interesting conference and during the exchange of questions and answers Miss Brinkley found opportunity to make sketches of the first lady.

That was the entire article. We will probably never know what was said, or whether Nell herself took part in that "exchange of questions and answers." What we do have, however, is the record of that meeting: her beautiful renderings of Eleanor Roosevelt, which Nell incorporated into a series called *Miss America Sees Washington, D.C.* The series started in April 1934 and told the story of Sue, Sally and Sylvia, who visit the capital and are invited to tea at the White House with the First Lady.[6]

For "Sally, Sue and Sylvia Report an Informal Tea,"[7] Nell produced a painstakingly accurate rendition of "The Sitting Room Where Informal

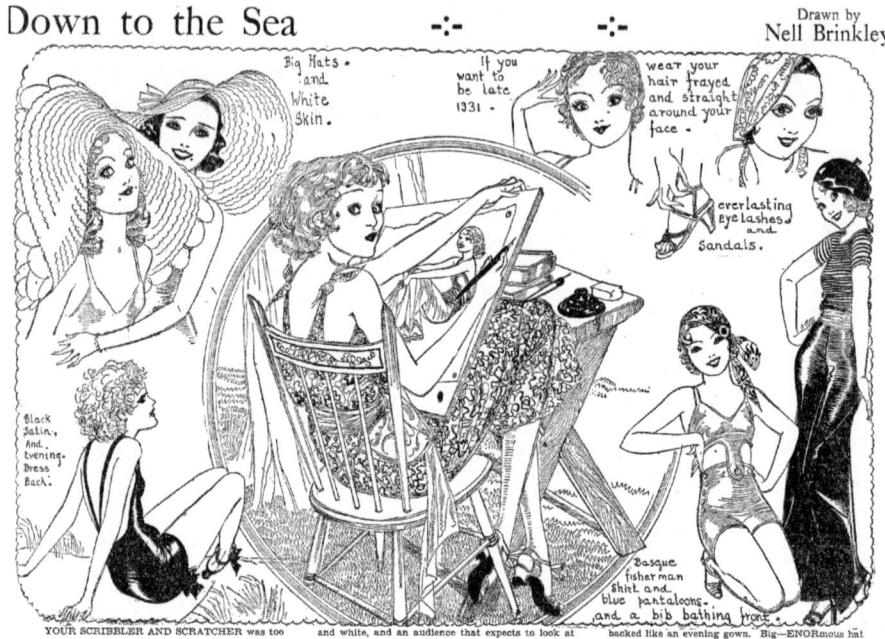

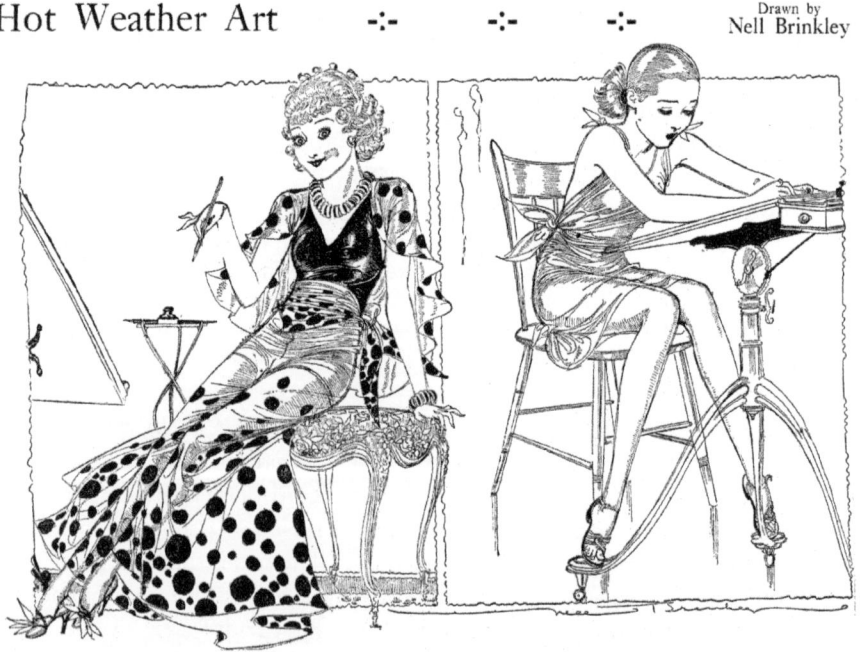

Top: "Down to the Sea," 1931. Bottom: "Hot Weather Art," 1931.

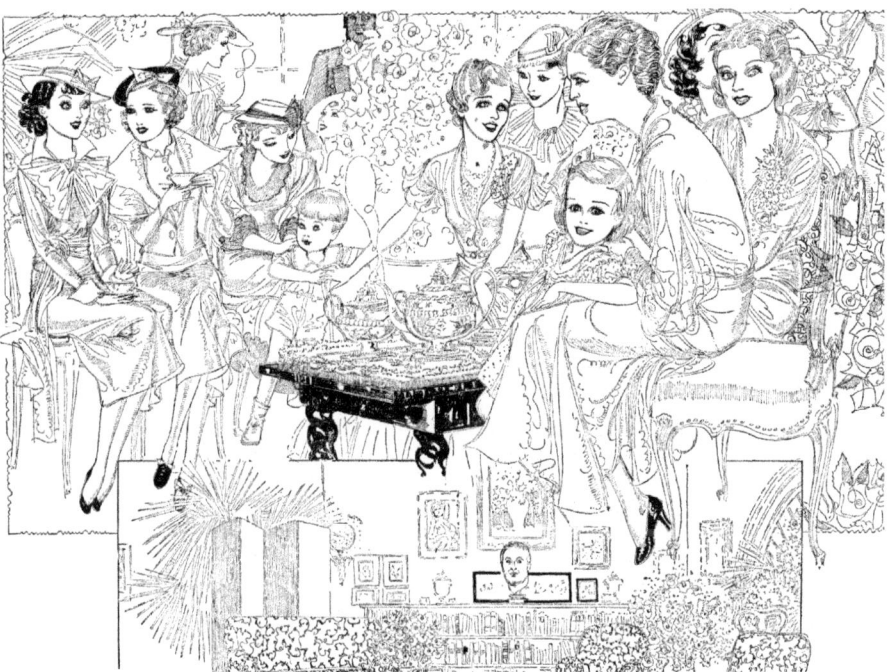

Miss America Sees Washington, D.C., "Sally, Sue and Sylvia Report an Informal Tea," 1934.

Teas Are Given," and managed to glamorize Eleanor Roosevelt, who was one of the most important women of the 20th century, but was never a beauty queen. The next week's panel, "The First Lady's Famous Monday Morning Press Conference," which was the conference which Nell had attended, shows a Brinkley-ized Eleanor surrounded by girl reporters, who are busily scribbling in their notebooks One of these is probably Nell. She writes:

> Now neither Sue nor Sally can draw a picture any more than they can walk a tight rope, so they got me to make the picture. But they went as newspaper women, so the story is theirs.... She tells some family episodes and personal views that it's a pity to leave unrecorded. But she holds up her hand, and her voice rises, and she says, "Off the record!" So the Monday Morning Press Conference regretfully buries some delightful stories that must go unwritten. Questions and answers fly—and so does the time. Everyone says goodbye to Mrs. Roosevelt. She is gracious, equally, to each one.[8]

Eleanor pops up one more time, still glamorized, at the end of the series, when the three heroines decide to fly home from Washington. The

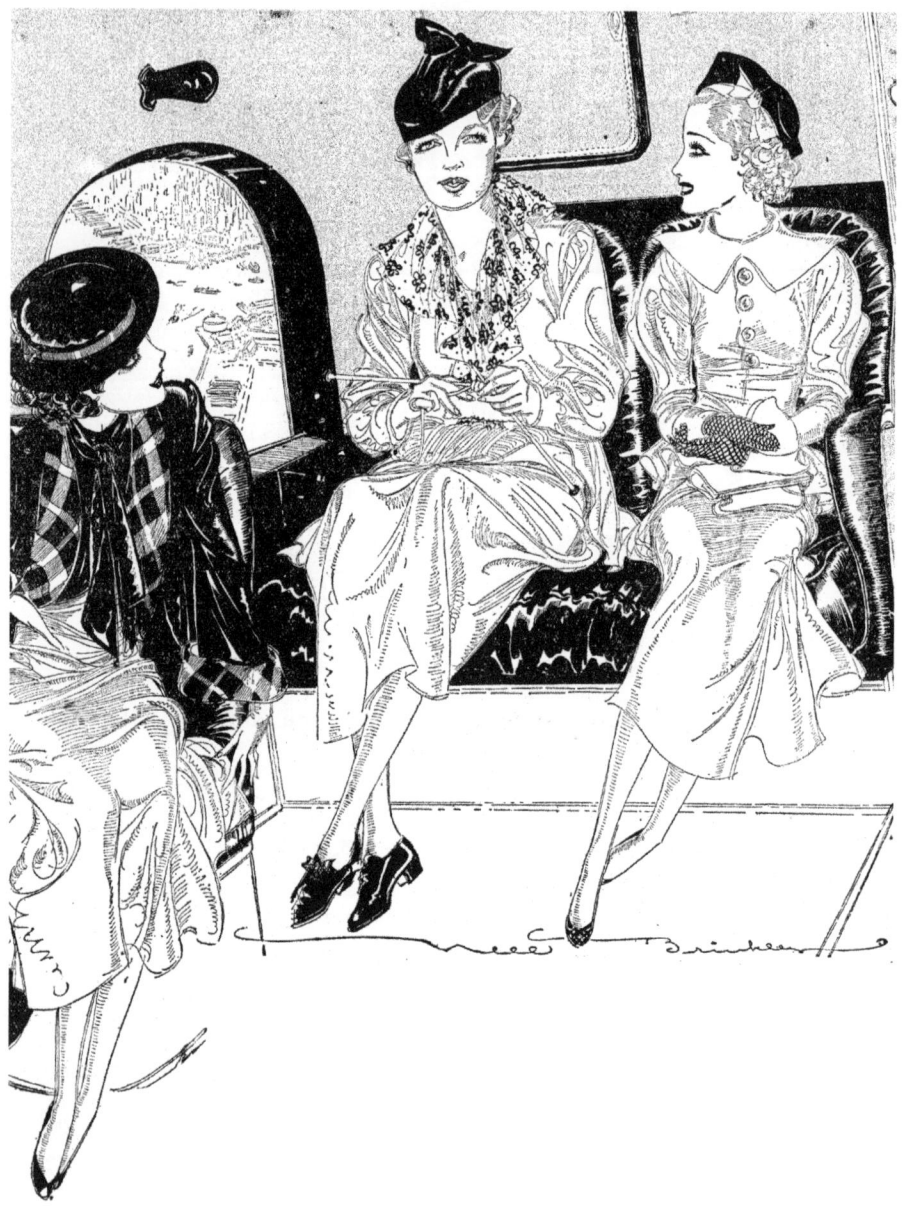

Miss America Sees Washington, D.C., "Her Visit Ended, She Flies Back with the First Lady," 1934.

First Lady catches the same flight and sits "earnestly threshing out some charitable project with her secretary, knitting some soft, white child's thing right through the business of smiles and talk."

Nell was 12 years older than her husband. Bruce was in his thirties and still handsome. Nell, who had once been a stunner, was in her forties and had not aged well. One day she went to the theater with a visiting childhood friend, Edna Bradley. There she found Bruce, whom in 1929 she had described as "a husband 'beyond compare' unless there be another such on another star," sitting in the audience with his on-the-sly girlfriend. Nell had already felt betrayed by a government she personified as a man, Uncle Sam; now another man betrayed her. She drew herself in a sad panel called "Time, the Old Humorist, Will Have His Sly Joke," wistfully remembering past friends, even her long-gone Scottish terrier, Grizzy. She wrote, "Time remembers a pair of lovers when all they cared about was to love each other. Now he finds them far apart, not caring in the least where the other is or what doing."[9]

They divorced in 1936, and that year Nell produced a series of gloomy panels called *What Went Wrong with Love?* "In her heart and a secret corner of her mind," she wrote, "she is able to go as into a closed and secret garden, and sit with romance. Poor as she may be. Disillusioned. Made perhaps to admit that a figure she built was never what she believed."

A betrayed Nell was an unforgiving Nell. She cut off all contact between her husband and their son. Bruce remarried, but died in 1941.[10] His obituary was headlined "Bruce McRae Dies in Florida, Ex-Husband of Nell Brinkley." Although Nell was by then in retirement, her name was still newsworthy.

But Nell's star was fading fast. Newspapers were dropping her panels, others were carrying it weekly instead of daily. In New York, Hearst's syndicate moved her from the upscale *Journal* to the much lower-class *Mirror*; in San Francisco she went from the *Examiner* to the trashier *Call-Bulletin*. The heyday for such artists as Nell Brinkley had, it seems, passed. But her last work was perhaps her most interesting, as Nell created a magnificent Sunday series in 1937, *Heroines of Today*, in which Nell gave real women the Brinkley treatment. In lively full-color pages resembling illustrations from the action pulp magazines of the day, Nell presented glamorized portraits of heroines and related their acts of courage: a forest-fire spotter, a soldier, a police detective, a woman who rescued four people from drowning, a "jungle queen" who, left alone in the jungles of British Guiana when her trader husband died, acted as nurse and magistrate to the tribes and kept her husband's company going.

For "Woman Warrior," Nell comments:

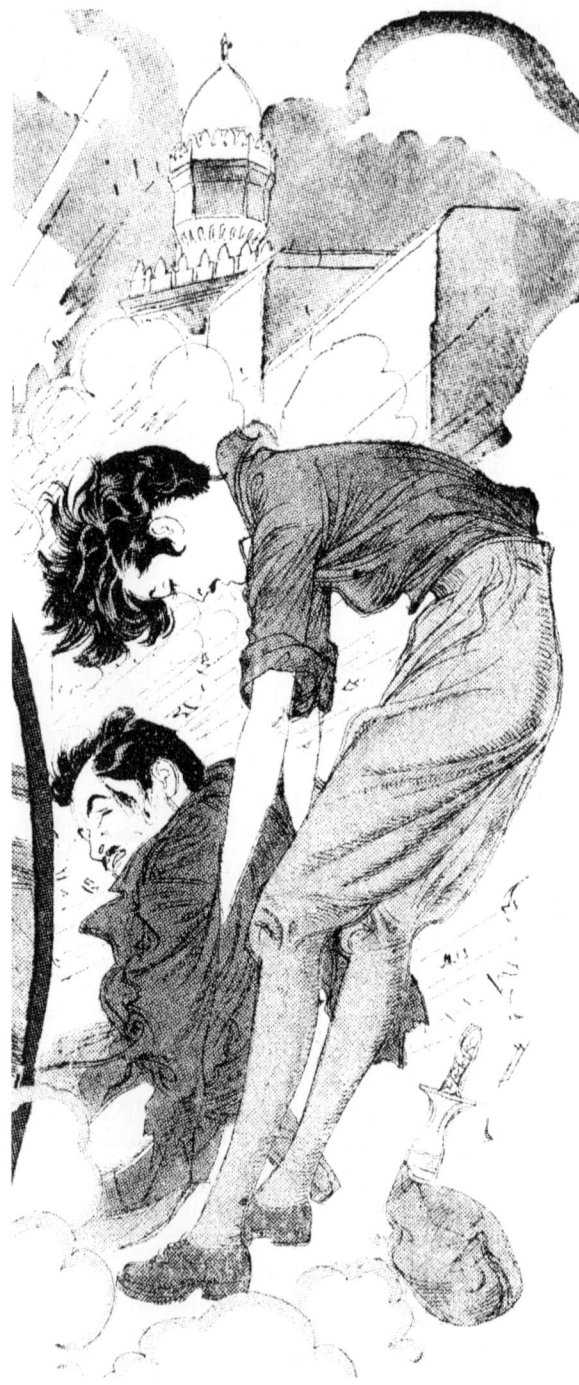

Today, Soviet Russia has women shouldering rifles, manning machine guns, operating tanks. Turkey, which now gives military training to school girls, pays homage to an aviatrix who single-handed, defeated a regiment of rebellious Kurds. And in presently war-torn Spain, uncounted numbers of women are in the fighting lines, emulating Russia's "Battalion of Death" of World War fame.

She shows us Austrian born Rosetta Millington, who, "after going to the war front as a Red Cross worker, served for 27 months as the only woman even to gain enlistment in the Spanish Foreign Legion." Millington had been dismissed when it was discovered that she was a woman.

Nell's dashing rendering of Rosetta Millington in uniform leaves the reader thinking that if her "immediate superiors" had

Heroines of Today, "Woman Warrior," 1937.

not realized she was a woman, they must have been blind. In the center of the page, Rosetta sits in a house dress, peeling potatoes and smiling wistfully as she recalls firing a rifle and a machine gun, dragging a wounded comrade to safety. "Back in civil life," explains Nell, "she married, came to America with her husband.... But—'My 15-year enlistment is not up until 1939,' says Rosetta with a gleam in her eye. 'I am now a housewife, but only a housewife second. First of all I am a soldier, and I long to go to war again.'"

For "Quick-Trigger Woman," Nell presents patrolewoman Mary A. Shanley, who "captured two notorious gunmen single-handed a few weeks ago" and was promoted to second-grade detective. Always feeling the need to show the femininity of her women, Nell manages to contrast Mary's purse with male detectives' shoulder holsters as she touts her heroine's quick-draw toughness.

The policewoman is drawn shooting her gun into the air to warn the crooks, who drop their weapons and surrender. Grinning proudly, she hauls them off. Her prisoners, embarrassed at being captured by a woman, hide their faces in shame. After work, Detective Shanley nibbles crackers in bed and reads a mystery novel *The Purple Passage*.

Heroines of Today was an unsurpassed last act. Nell retired, but she didn't stop drawing. She spent her retirement years illustrating children's books and painting. The brother and sister Nell drew for Virginia Pearson's 1940 children's music book, *Play a Tune*, are named—yes, Betty and Billy. Freed from deadline constraints, she even took the time to do the book's lettering herself. She also finally had time to fulfill her desire to work with color.[11]

In 1943, Bobby disappointed Nell by marrying Anne Toth, a young woman she didn't approve of. Perhaps Nell felt her son was simply too young, at 20,[12] to take this important step; perhaps, overprotective mother that she was, she simply believed that no one was good enough for her little boy. Feeling once again betrayed by a man, she disinherited him. She was left alone now, with her art and her ever-faithful mother.

In 1913, Nell had written about mothers, "Our grown up arms reach for her when we stagger and stumble. Always her arms are there to catch us lest we fall."[13] And May, who had always been there, was there for Nell when she fell ill with cancer. But there was only so much that even the most devoted mother could do. Cancer, in the early 1940s, was incurable. Nell grew too ill to work, and left her many paintings unfinished. She tried faith healers and religion. A few months before she died, she claimed to see Jesus at her bedside, calling to her.

The year 1944 brought with it only bad tiding for illustrators, and loss. Rose O'Neill, creator of the Kewpies, died in April of that year, and

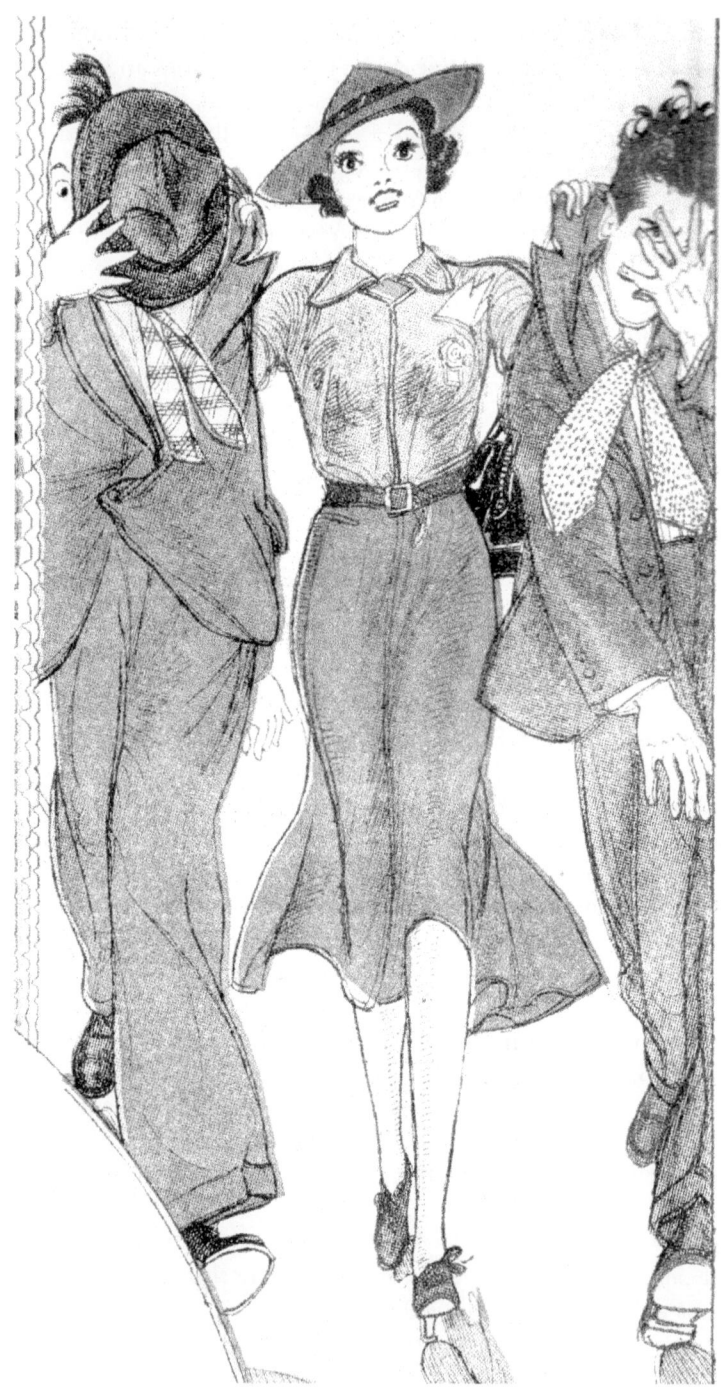

Seven. The Thirties   133

> When the pretty waltz ended, Betty sat down on the floor, hugging her rag doll closer still.
> When Billy asked, "May I play the music box just once more before I go downstairs? It plays such a pretty tune." Mrs. Barton answered, "Certainly dear, but then you must go right downstairs and do your practicing."
> "Oh Mother!" Billy protested, "Do I have to practice? I promised to meet some of the boys over at the brook. We're going fishing. Only I don't know where my fishing rod and net are."
> "They're there in the hall closet, Billy," Mrs. Barton said, "but you must do your practicing before you go."
> "Oh, all right," Billy replied, and he lifted the cover of the music box, which repeated the first little tinkling tune.

Illustration from Play a Tune, *1940. It looks like Nell has also hand-lettered the page.*

Charles Dana Gibson, who had drawn Evelyn Nesbitt before Nell did and whose Gibson girls had been supplanted by Nell's Brinkley girls, died in December. Nell died on October 21, 1944,[14] without ever having had the chance to reconcile herself with Bobby and his wife.

Nell's obituaries, which ran in newspapers around the nation, listed her age as 56, but she was really 58. The newspapers described her as having

Opposite: Heroines of Today, "Quick-Trigger Woman," *1937.*

died after "a long illness." This was a code for cancer, a disease that in those days was so terrifying that it was almost unmentionable.[15]

Nell left May, her sole beneficiary, an estate of $56,305. She was buried in Beechmont cemetery, in the family plot that she and Bruce had bought for her father. May hung on for four more years, long enough to see the birth of her grandchild, Anne, before dying on March 15, 1948, at the age of 82. Her obituary in the *New York Times* was headlined "Nell Brinkley's Mother Dies."

As recently as 1966, Nell was still remembered widely enough, at least in Colorado, for a feature in the July 29 *Denver Post*, her old newspaper. In the article, titled "Creator of 'Brinkley Girls' Was Precocious Child," Donna Logan interviewed Nell's childhood friend, 77-year-old Edna Bradley. "She was quite famous," Bradley said. "I remember the Ziegfeld Follies of 1919 or 1921 had a special 'Nell Brinkley' skit where all the girls were dressed in black and white and Mae Murray was the star dancer."[16]

This was the last mention of Nell in the American press. Today, except for a minuscule group of scholars, fans and collectors, she's completely forgotten, even though the name of Charles Dana Gibson, whom she supplanted, lives on. Traditionally, despite the fact that women make up 52 percent of the population, women's art has been considered trivial and unworthy of inclusion in history books. An uncredited writer of Nell's day snidely described her as drawing "suggestive and pleasing feminine hysterics." Perhaps it's because Nell's work has been regarded as beautiful but lightweight that her name hasn't survived as the names of Gibson or John Held, Jr., have. The *Random House Dictionary of the English Language* has an entry for *Gibson girl*. There is no corresponding entry for *Brinkley girl*. Gibson, while undeniably one of the great illustrators of the 20th century, was no heavyweight.

Of the women cartoonists contemporary to Nell, Rose O'Neill lives on through her Kewpies. More people have heard of her creations than of their creator. Kewpie fan club members all over America still attend an annual "Kewpiesta" held in the artist's home town of Branson, Missouri. And like O'Neill with her Kewpies, the average person recognizes the Campbell Kids but not the name Grace Drayton.

Held and Gibson also had the distinction of being published in books and magazines. While Nell did do some book and magazine illustration, the bulk of her work appeared in newspapers. During the 1940s, the greater part of then-existing pulp paper, including pulp magazines, comics, and newspapers, was sacrificed for the war effort in nationwide paper drives. Thus most of Nell's existing printed art disappeared, while art in the better-quality magazines and books survived.

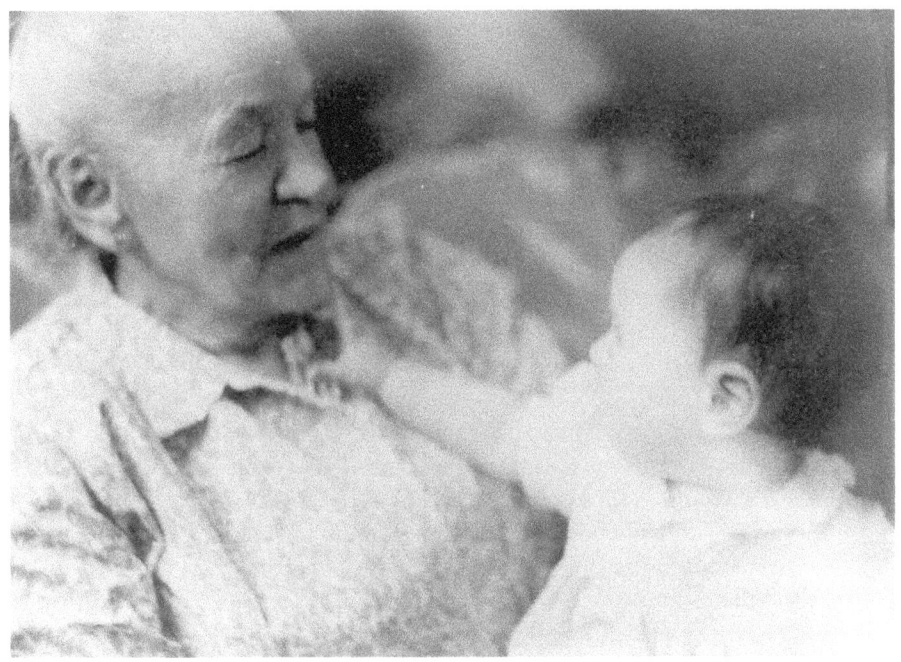

May and her granddaughter, Anne, 1945.

Yet Nell survived in another way: women cartoonists in the generations following her had read her work when they were young girls and had been influenced by it. Hilda Terry, creator of Teena, and Marty Links, creator of Bobby Sox, two comic strips which were nationally syndicated for over 20 years, remember their childhood fascination with Nell's panels. Although their style is much simpler and more cartoony and their genre is humor rather than romance, both artists display strong Nell Brinkley influence in their attention to fashion, particularly the loving detail they gave to their teenage heroines' fashionably ruffled party dresses. And though it's much harder to see in their style, Marie Severin and Ramona Fradon, two of the rare women who have drawn action superhero comics for Marvel Comics and DC Comics, were also Nell Brinkley fans as children.

The true inheritor of the Brinkley mystique, however, is undoubtedly Dale Messick, who created the newspaper strip Brenda Starr, Reporter, in 1941 and drew it until her retirement in 1980. As a schoolgirl after World War I, young Dale entertained her friends by drawing a comic inspired by Nell's weekly serials. Like Kathleen and Golden-Eyes, Messick's heroine went overseas as a Red Cross nurse and faced a "fate worse than death" from a German spy based on silent star Eric Von Stroheim before finally arriving home victorious in a panel in which the heroine watches the Statue of Liberty from the deck of her returning ship.

Debuting some 30 years later, the *Brenda Starr* strip still resembled an old-time serial: the valiant red-haired girl reporter is continually extricating herself from danger; she's kidnapped by gangsters, marooned on desert islands disguised as a juvenile delinquent in order to infiltrate a girl gang. Like Nell's flight-happy heroines, she flies in open-cockpit planes and parachutes to safety. Throughout all her perils, she manages, as the Brinkley girls had, to stay magnificently dressed, and is always in love with her handsome "mystery man." The strip's audience, like Nell's, was primarily female.[17] From the exquisite attention paid to fashion details to the ongoing theme of romance to her pulpy adventures, Dale Messick's plucky protagonist was in every way the daughter of the Brinkley girl.

Art criticism is as fickle as fashion; artists go in and out of style. Norman Rockwell and J.C. Leyendecker, Nell's New Rochelle neighbors, went from fame to ridicule before being recognized once again as great illustrators. Erte, who in the 1920s designed magnificent fantasy fashions for the same women's magazines that published Nell, lived long enough to reap the rewards of revival, which popularized his work within the form of books, prints and statuettes. The glamorous art deco society painter, Tamara deLempika, long consigned to the lot of the once-favored, also saw her place in art history restored. It's time for Nell.

Notes

1. Hoovervilles took their name, of course, from then-president Herbert Hoover, who opposed the bonus demand, insisting that "prosperity was just around the corner."

2. In its entry on Nell, *The National Cyclopedia of American Biography* (date unknown) relates, "In religion she was a Presbyterian and in politics a Republican." No other article mentions her politics, and the source of this statement is not given. After reading "The Man of the Hour," it is impossible to believe that Nell, at least after 1932, could have remained a Republican.

3. A month after this commentary appeared, troops, wearing gas masks and wielding bayonets, backed by cavalry and tanks, burned the Hoovervilles to the ground and gassed over one thousand people. In August of that year, Nell again referred to the war veteran, calling him the "patient ex-soldier of World War fame and of glory set apart so brutally by our government from the rest of the country...."

4. Everyone had a nickname: Nell also called her son Buie, and she referred to herself as Hansie. May was Dombo, and her father was Dampa.

5. Many today doubt that Hauptmann was the kidnapper, believing him merely a scapegoat handed over to a clamoring public.

6. Nell did another 1934 series with the same three Brinkley girls, *Miss America Goes to the Chicago World's Fair*. In that one, besides taking the reader on a tour of the fair, she supplied paper dolls of her three heroines, explaining that the paper dolls were "By request of Joy and Martha and Bianca, of Gretchen and Marie and Sheila, of Aurelita, Astrid, Mary and Ruth, and so on and on."

7. June 2, 1934.

8. To repeat: these are not the words of a Republican!

9. January 19, 1935.

10. Bruce died of heart disease, the McRae curse, which had carried off his father in 1927. Bruce III also died young of heart disease, in 1982.

11. She left behind scores of paintings in every media, most of them unfinished. Although she painted some landscapes and some children, the majority of her paintings were of women.

12. Anne Toth was also 20. The couple stayed married for the rest of their lives.

13. "Sayings of Mothers," 1913

14. In its January 1945 issue, *American Artist* magazine wrote, "The late Nell Brinkley, who died in October, attracted more amateur copyists than did Charles Dana Gibson. Like Rose Cecil O'Neill, who came before her, she was quite an eyeful herself and was past master as a cheesecake artist."

15. Cancer wasn't the last disease deemed unmentionable. In the 1980s and early 90s, people who succumbed to the complications of AIDS were described as having died after "a long illness."

16. This was the first newspaper article to name the cause of Nell's death as cancer.

17. When the Tucson *Daily Citizen* dropped the strip in 1973, the paper was bombarded with hundreds of angry letters and phone calls, most of them from women.

Afterword

> Footsteps may falter, weary grow the way, still we can hear it at the close of day.
> So till the end, when life's dim shadows fall.
> —"Love's Old Sweet Song," G. Clifton Bingham and James J. Molloy, 1884

A rainy mid–September day was perfect for visiting Beechmont cemetery, in New Rochelle. The well-kept lawns were still green, but the sky was dark and fitting for a graveside visit. I strolled past tall and ancient chestnut trees that dated back to 1854. Nell's family plot was past a man-made lake where Canada geese pecked at fallen chestnuts scattered on the grass.

The plot is modest and dwarfed by other, more flamboyant monuments. Robert's urn is by far the most outstanding of the memorials, and the first one you see. May's much smaller circular marker, of matching pink-veined grey marble, stands beside it, the separated parents reunited at last. There is a space next to it. For whose grave? Surely not Nell's husband; he and Nell were already divorced when she died.

Nell's marker, an exact duplicate of her mother's, stands a distance away from her parents', in the shade of a venerable chestnut tree. The marker reads,

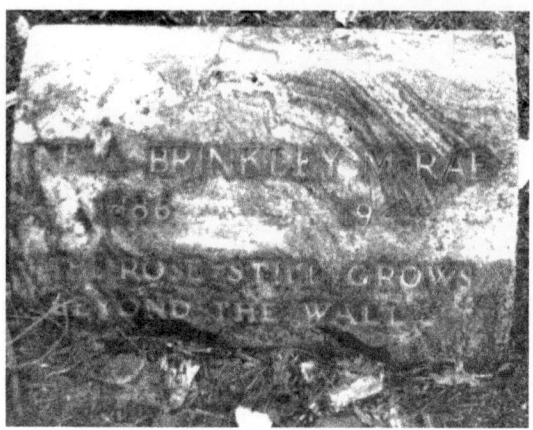

Nell's grave, Beechmont cemetery.

Nell Brinkley McRae
1886–1944
"The rose still grows beyond the wall."

The quotation is from a poem by A.L. Frink, "The Rose Beyond the Wall." I do not know who decided on it, Nell or her mother. But their graves, though kept clean, are bare. And no roses grow there.

Bibliography

American Illustrators Research Group 1980 Annual. Huntington Beach, Calif." American Illustrators Research Group, 1980.
America's Great Women Illustrators 1850–1950. New York City: The Society of Illustrators, 1985.
Armitage, Shelley. *John Held, Jr., Illustrator of the Jazz Age.* Syracuse: Syracuse University Press, 1987.
_____. *Kewpies and Beyond: The World of Rose O'Neill.* Jackson, Miss.: University Press of Mississippi, 1994.
Garrard, Mary D. *Artemesia Gentileschi.* Princeton, N.J.: Princeton University Press, 1989.
Horn, Maurice. *The World Encyclopedia of Comics.* New York City: Chelsea House, 1980.
Kessler-Harris, Alice. *Out to Work.* New York City: Oxford University Press, 1982.
Millstein, Beth, and Jean Bodin. *We, the American Women.* Chicago: Science Research Associates, 1977.
Reed, Walt, and Roger Reed. *The Illustrator in America, 1880–1980.* New York City: The Society of Illustrators, 1984.
Robbins, Trina. *A Century of Women Cartoonists.* Northampton, Mass.: Kitchen Sink Press, 1993.
_____, and Catherine Yronwode. *Women and the Comics.* Guerneville, Calif.: Eclipse Books, 1985.
Ross, Ishbel. *Ladies of the Press.* New York: Harper, 1936.
Rowbotham, Sheila. *A Century of Women.* New York City: Viking, 1997.
Scott, Anne Firor. *The American Woman, Who Was She?* Englewood Cliffs, N.J.: Prentice-Hall, 1971.
Thaw, Harry K. *The Traitor.* Philadelphia: Dorrance, 1926.
Women Artists in the Howard Pyle Tradition. Chadds Ford, Penn.: Brandywine River Museum, 1975.

Index

Abie the Agent 43–44, 111
The Adventures of Prudence Prim 101
advertising art 51, 53–54
Advice to the Lovelorn 11, 37
African women 42–43
Ahern, Gene 48
AIDS 137
Algonquin Round Table 111
Allman, W. R. 47, 48
American Artist 137
"American Girl" 118
American Illustrators Research Group 1
American Sunday Monthly 74
"Another Air Raid" 65–66
antiques 82
anti-suffrage 58
Araminta 117
Armitage, Shelley 1
art academies 32
Art Students League 32
"Art's Rival" 84
Astor, Mary 107
atomic power 96

Babette 68, 69
babies 79, 84–85, 104; as subject of women's art 33, 35–36
baby talk 10, 23, 71

Barney Google 111
Barrymore, Ethel 11–12
"Baseball Fannie" 20–21
bathing suits 38–39, 55
beauty 2, 10, 42–43, 57, 93, 108
Bell Telephone 32
Bernhardt, Sarah 114, 116
Betties 10, 20–23, 26, 47, 55, 63, 101, 104, 124
Betty and Billy series 1
Betty and Billy, and Their Love Through the Ages 99–101
Betty and Veronica 23
Betty Boop 23
Beverly of Graustark 108
Billies 10, 20–22, 43, 47, 63
birth of Nell Brinkley 26
Black, Winifred 9, 23
Blackbeard, Bill 1–2
blackface performance 41, 64
Blosser, Merrill 48
"Blue-Eyed Fay, Love Me or I Die..." 55, 58
bobbed hair 51, 54
bobby sox 135
Bogart, Humphrey 35
Bonheur, Rosa 114, 116
boom times 86

INDEX

Boucher 23
Bow, Clara 13
"A Boy You Can't Forget" 105
boyish women 86
Bradley, Edna 129, 134
Breakfast Club 110–111
Brenda Starr, Reporter 135–137
Briggs, Clare 44, 48
Bringing Up Father 111
Brinkley, May French 23, 26, 45, 51–52, 82, 85, 121, 131, 134–135, 139
Brinkley, Robert Serrett 26–29, 113–115, 139
"The Brinkley Bathing Girl" 39
"The Brinkley Coon" 41
Brinkley Girls 20–23
Brisbane, Arthur 10–11, 29, 111
Bryn Mawr 32
bump on nose 93–94
Bunk 14–15, 17, 21
Burk, Billie 107
business girls 57, 59

Cakewalks 41
Campbell Kids 35–36
Can Such Things Be? 52, 117, 119
Canada 122
cancer 131, 134, 137
career women 32, 56–57
careers 63
Carew, Kate 36
The Cartoonist 5
Cartoons Magazine 44
Cassatt, Mary 33
Castle, Irene and Vernon 7, 60
The Charleston 3
Chesterton, G. K. 114
Chicago Evening American 37
child labor 105
Chinese women 43
Christy, Howard Chandler 21
Cinderella 55
Circulation 47
Clarke, Anne Macrae 5, 134–135
Cleveland Press 47, 48
"Clothes Don't Always Make the Woman" 90, 92
Cobb, Irvin 23
Cody, Buffalo Bill 26
Cohan, George M. 41
college girls 3
Colliers 39
collies 75–78
color 12–13, 20, 74; printing 32
comic strips 10–11, 96, 101

"Coming and Going" 38, 55
Condo, A. D. 48
coon songs 41
copycat cartoonists 47, 49, 137
Corelli, Marie 114
Cory, Fanny Y. 36
cosmetics 51, 53
courtroom art 9, 18, 31
craft vs. art 33
crystal balls 72, 101
"Cupid in a Quandary" 57
cupids 21, 36, 43–44, 55, 60, 65–66, 90, 92

Davies, Marion 107–110, 112
Day of the Girl series 2, 88–89
death of Nell Brinkley 131, 133–134
De Beck, Billy 110–111
DeLempika, Tamara 136
Denver Post 9–10, 23, 25, 27, 29, 37, 79, 92, 134
Denver Times 27
Dimples' Day Dreams 101
divorce 18, 29, 129
Dix, Dorothy 9, 11, 17–18, 23
Dollie Dimples 36
Dolly Dingle 36
Dolly Drake 36
Dolly sisters 60–61
Dorgan, Thomas Aloysius (TAD) 13–15, 17, 19–21, 23, 48, 56
Dottie Darling 36
doughboys 77
"Down to the Sea" 124, 126
drawing advice 124–125
Drayton, Grace 35–36, 134
Drexel Institute 32
Duncan, Isadora 89
Duval, Alphonese 44

Earhart, Amelia 2, 116–118
Edgewater, Colorado 26–27
Edgewater Historical Society 3
editorial cartoons 27
Egypt 101, 103
Erte 136

Fairfax, Beatrix 11, 37
fame 93–94
"The Family Affair" 120
fathers 29, 113
feminism 2, 32, 57, 78, 101
Ferber, Edna 13
Ferguson, Don 5
Fisher, Harrison 21

Index

Flack, Dorothy 49
flappers 3, 43, 86–89
flight 49–51, 66, 103, 116, 128–129, 136
Floradora Sextette 17, 23
fluffiness 90
fluffy feminism 101
The Fluffy Ruffles Girl 21
The Fortunes of Flossie 101
fortunetellers 72
Fox, Connie 3
Fradon, Ramona 135

Garden, Mary 11
Gentileschi, Artemesia 32
"Gentleman of Leisure" 123
Geyer, Madge 49
Gibson, Charles Dana 2–3, 7, 20–21, 23, 37–38, 40, 133–134, 137
Gibson Girls 3, 7, 17, 20, 23, 26, 39, 134
Giles, Roy A. 25
Girls Who Work for Uncle Sam 5, 71, 73
Gish, Lillian 62, 107
Glyn, Elinor 13, 18
Golden-Eyes and Her Hero, Bill 5, 75–78, 96, 101, 135
Good Housekeeping 35
gravesites 139–140
Great Depression 114, 118
The Great White Way 110–111
Greek women 89–90
Greely-Smith, Nixola 9, 23
Green, Elizabeth Shippen 32
Grey, Henry Judd 106

Harper's Bazaar 51
Hauptmann, Bruno 119, 136
Hearst, William Randolph 3, 107, 109–110, 112
Hearst Castle 109
Hearst newspapers 21, 36, 51, 125
Heggelund, Gail 2–3
Held, John, Jr. 1–3, 101, 112, 134
Helen of Troy 89, 91
Heroines of Today 129–132
Hershfield, Harry 43, 110–111
"Hobnobbing with Egypt" 101, 103–104
Hoffer, Marian 71, 73
Hogan, Ernest 41
homeliness 93
Hoovervilles 115, 136
Hope, Eleanor 49
horsemen 33–34, 122
horsewomen 88, 111
"Hot Weather Art" 126
household duties 51

Humphrey, Maude 35, 40
Hunt, William Holman 85–86
Hunter, Frances Tipton 35
husbands 85

illustration 32–33, 36
imitators of Nell Brinkley 47, 49, 137
immigrants 80
impoverished European nobility 3, 39
Inuit: men 43; women 42–43
"The Invitation, or, a Modern Story Without Words" 96, 98
Ireland 105–106
The "It Girl" 13

Jazz Age 112
Jesus Christ 85–86, 131
Jewish women 43–44
jobless veterans 115
Joplin, Scott 41

Kathleen and the Great Secret 96, 98–99, 135
Kewpies 35–36, 134
kidnapping 119
King, Fay 36–37, 110
Korean men 43
Kurland, Michael 5

LaDor, John 17–18
Larned, W. L. 21
Lechtaler, Althea 2–3
Lehar, Franz 7–8
Leialoha, Steve 5
Leyendecker, J. C. 44, 136
Lhamon, W. T. 64
Liberty bonds 75–76
Life 39
The Light of the World 85–86
Lindbergh, Charles 9, 103–105, 117, 119
Links, Marty 135
"A Little Ghost and the Flapperettes" 87–88
Little Smearo 29
Logan, Donna 134
London, Jack 13
Los Angeles Examiner 21, 23, 57

McCay, Winsor 110
McCutcheon, John T. 48
McGill, W. K. 11
McManus, George 110–111
McMein, Neysa 111–112
McRae, Bruce 79–80
McRae, Bruce, Jr. 79, 81–85, 129, 137

INDEX

McRae, Bruce, III 79–80, 82–85, 118–121, 131, 133
maids 3, 55
"The Man of the Hour" 115, 117, 136
Maori men 43
marriage 79
married names 81
The Maude Humphrey Baby 35
The Merry Widow 7–9, 11
Messick, Dale 135
Michelangelo 19, 23
"Milady's Battle of 1925" 96–97
Millington, Rosetta 130–131
"Miss America Goes to the Chicago World's Fair" 137
"Miss America Sees Washington D.C." 125, 127–128
"Miss 1914" 58, 60
modern woman 92
Mohr, Jean 36
Mona Lisa 39
Morgan, Wallace 21
Morris, Mildred 71, 73
motherhood 63
mothers 104, 131; as subject of women's art 33, 36
Mount Holyoke 32
Murray, Mae 134
musicals 60
My How Funny series 52

Native American men 43
Nazimova, Ala 11
"The Nell Brinkley Girl" 21
"Nell Brinkley Studies" 21
Nesbitt, Evelyn 9–18, 23, 40, 133
Nethersole, Olga 21, 23, 112
New Rochelle, N.Y. 43–44, 79, 82, 113, 139–140
New Rochelle Public Library 2, 5
New Rochelle Standard Star 82, 112
New York Daily News 107
New York Evening Journal 9–17, 23, 29, 36, 129
New York Mirror 129
New York Times 134
nicknames 5, 29, 136
19th Amendment 86
No Man's Land 76–77
Nolan, Chris 5
Noland, James R. 23, 25–26, 29
nouveau riche 39
nurses 76

Oakley, Thornton 36
Oakley, Violet 32, 36
Oberlin College 32, 40
O'Neill, Rose 35–36, 131, 134, 137
operettas 7–9
The Other Woman 37
Oyl, Olive 37

Paddock, Mr. 27
Parker, Dorothy 111
parodies 86; of Brinkley 14–15, 17, 21
patriotism 65, 68, 78
Patsy Kildare, Outlaw 37
Patterson, Ada 9, 23
Pearson, Virginia 131
Pennsylvania Academy of the Fine Arts 32
Phidias 23
Philadelphia School of Design for Women 32
photoengraving 32
Play a Tune 131, 133
plays 60, 79
Point of View 52
portraits 94–95
Powers, T. E. 11, 19
prettiness 2, 10, 42–43, 57, 93, 108
Pretty Polly 101
Pryor Terrace 5, 82, 85, 95, 118
Pyle, Ellen Thompson 36
Pyle, Howard 32–33, 36

Québec 122

racism 41–42
Radcliffe 32
radio 110
Raphael 19, 23
rape 9, 23
Red Cross 76, 130, 135
"Rich Girl, Poor Girl" 80–81
rich women 3, 55, 63, 79–82
Riggs, Elayne 3
Rockefellers 7
Rockwell, Norman 43–44, 136
Rocky Mountain News 25
Rogers, Will 7, 60
Roland, Madame 114, 116
Romances of Gloriette 101
rooftop garden performances 3, 9
Roosevelt, Eleanor 2, 125, 127–128

St. Patrick's Day 105–106
"Sally, Sue and Sylvia Report an Informal Tea" 125, 127
San Francisco Call 44, 46
San Francisco Call-Bulletin 129

Index

San Francisco Examiner 49, 125, 129
"The San Francisco Girl" 47
Sapho 21, 23
Satterfield, Bob 48
scandal 9
Schorer, Eleanor 47
science 96
self portraits 93–94
Sequoia National Monument 114
servants 122
Severin, Marie 135
Sévigné, Madame de 114, 116
sewing 69
Shanley, Mary A. 131–132
"Shine On, Harvest Moon" 22
short skirts 87
silent films 13, 60, 107
Silk Hat Harry 14–15
The Sketch 44, 48
Simpson, O. J. 9
slang 10
Smith, Jessie Wilcox 32, 36
Smith, Sidney 48
Smith College 32
smoking 60, 87
Snyder, Ruth 106–107
"Sob-Sisters" 23
Society of Illustrators 5
songs about Nell Brinkley 39, 41
Sparta 88–90
sports 86
Staël, Madame de 114, 116
Sterrett, Cliff 48
Stop! Look! Listen! 107, 112
suffrage movement 57–58, 60, 64, 86, 90
Sunny Sue 101–102
Suratt, Valeska 11
surfing 38, 55
swimsuits 38–39, 55
Swinnerton, James 23
switchboard operators 32

TAD see Dorgan, Thomas Aloysius
Teena 135
Terry, Hilda 135
Thaw, Harry K. 9, 17–18, 23, 31
Thompson, Steve 5
Thorne, Stella 49
Three Weeks 13
Toth, Anne 131, 137
Townsend, Inez 36
The Traitor 18, 23
Trial of the Century 9, 119
trials 9, 106

"The Tug of War" 63–64
Tutankhamen 101, 103–104
typewriters 32, 62

Uncle Sam 71, 73–76, 129
"Uncle Sam's Girl-Shower" 71, 74
"Uncle Sam's Schoolgirls" 73, 75
uniforms 65, 130
United States Post Office 32
upper class women 31, 39

"Vacation Faces" 122
Van Arsdale, Walt 47
Vanderbilts 7
Vassar 32
veterans 115, 117
Victorian era 39
Von Stroheim, Eric 135
voting 60

war brides 68
Washington, D.C. 71, 73, 115–116, 125, 127–128
Wayne, Frances 25
Wellesley College 32
Wells, Carolyn 101
Wells, H. G. 114
Westward Ho! 94–95, 112, 124
"What Is Beautiful?" 42
"What Is Beauty?" 42
"What Went Wrong with Love?" 129
White, Stanford 9, 18, 23
White House 125
"Who Knocks in the Dead o' Night?" 86–87
Wilcox, Ella Wheeler 11
Witwer, H. C. 110
women artists 31
women's colleges 32
working class 3, 9, 115
working women 2–3, 55–60, 62–63, 71, 73, 86, 115–116
World Encyclopedia of Cartoons 1–2
World War I 49, 65–78
"Worry, the Dragon" 104
writing style 94, 101

Yeats, W. B. 105–106
yellow journalism 3
Yolanda 108, 110

Ziegfeld Follies 7, 9, 22, 39, 61, 107, 109, 134
Zulu women 42–43

www.ingramcontent.com/pod-product-compliance
Ingram Content Group UK Ltd.
Pitfield, Milton Keynes, MK11 3LW, UK
UKHW042017140426
5217IPUK00015B/1220